GREAT
BRITISH
JOURNEYS

NICHOLAS CRANE

PHOENIX

A PHOENIX PAPERBACK

First published in Great Britain in 2007
by Weidenfeld & Nicolson
This paperback edition published in 2008
by Phoenix,
an imprint of Orion Books Ltd,
Orion House, 5 Upper St Martin's Lane,
London WC2H 9EA

An Hachette Livre UK company

1 3 5 7 9 10 8 6 4 2

A CIP catalogue record for this book
is available from the British Library.

ISBN 978-0-7538-2430-6

Designed by Bryony Newhouse

Printed in Great Britain by
Clays Ltd, St Ives plc

The Orion Publishing Group's policy is to use papers that are natural, renewable
and recyclable products and made from wood grown in sustainable forests.
The logging and manufacturing processes are expected to conform to the
environmental regulations of the country of origin.

www.orionbooks.co.uk

➤ Contents ◂

⤞ *Introduction* ⤝

A few years ago, I walked the length of England in a straight line.
Actually, it wasn't quite a straight line. I did allow myself the luxury
of straying 1,000 metres each side of the line. I walked, slept, and
procured my provisions within an imaginary, 2,000-metre wide,
glass-walled corridor which ran up and down dale from the
Northumbrian coast to the English Channel. Naturally, there were
obstacles to overcome. I had to wade the Tyne, cross the production
lines of the Longbridge car factory, and ask the Army if they would
mind escorting me through the live firing ranges on Salisbury Plain.
By the time I caught sight of Poole Harbour (the Royal Marines
helped out with that one), I'd tramped Pennine moors, the Black
Country tarmac maze and the golden corn country of Wessex.
My accommodation had included a shepherd's barn, dripping
woods and cheerful inns, and along the line, I'd enjoyed unexpected
encounters with gamekeepers, war-veterans, poachers, retired
hippies, factory workers and farmers. The people I met, and the
places I saw, were an unfamiliar cross-section of life and landscapes.
I felt as if I was seeing my own country for the first time. Every hill
crested and corner turned revealed a new view to explore. On some
days, I barely managed five miles; once, I walked back up the line
to visit something I'd missed the day before. Fifty-three days of
rambling and chatting produced a two-inch brick of notes which I
tidied into a book called *Two Degrees West*. Reviews were mixed. The
Daily Mail called me 'a prat', while the *Daily Telegraph* generously
took the view that I was 'a genius'. I do concede that my longitudinal
hike was open to misunderstanding. The purpose had not been to
see whether it was possible to walk a straight line from one end of
the country to the other without being shot, arrested, drowned or
electrocuted (although all these possibilities certainly added a tang

of adrenaline to the unforgivable daily trespass). What interested me was breaking free from the conventions of travel writing, which generally rule that the route taken is dictated by the author's quest. Whether it's a circumnavigation by canoe, or a psychogeographical journey into the imagination, the material harvested is dictated by the author's choice of route. A journey which followed a straight line would be different; it would act like a cross-section through the nation, restricting the author to a random sample of people and places, and producing a more objective take on the human and physical landscape. That was the idea, anyway. And, as I said, the *Mail* thought it prattish. But it worked for me: I enjoyed two months of high-spirited, unpredictable yomping, I wrote my experimental travel narrative, and somewhere around the mid-section of my topographical transect, I began wondering who discovered Britain.

It's one of those questions which seems so ridiculously obvious, and yet I struggled to find the answer. We're familiar with stories of adventurers departing European shores to explore the blanks on the world map, but *who* put Britain on the map? I grew up with the conceit that Columbus 'discovered' America, and that Captain Cook 'discovered' New Zealand. And yet I don't recall being taught about the discovery of Britain. Who can it have been? The Romans? Brutus? Pytheas the Greek? Bill Bryson? Not the French, surely? The answer, of course, is that every landmass was revealed to its own population over millennia, by countless explorers – most of them indigenous; Britain was 'discovered' by Britons. Would it be possible, I wondered, to put together a shortlist of homegrown British explorers; a Pantheon of travellers who changed the way the archipelago was viewed?

Britain is an explorer's dream. Wrapped up in 11,000 miles of coastline is an extraordinarily diverse collection of landscapes. We have it all, from teetering peaks and gentle downs, to saltmarshes and beech woods. In Britain, you are never more than a mile from new scenery. Such an intensity of variety lends itself to travel stories. It's not difficult to imagine a Neolithic trader flopping exhaustedly into his timber home on the banks of the Thames and relating tales of sky-high peaks in the land where he'd sought his polished stone axes. Or of Bronze Age warriors returning from the west with stories of frightful capes and of rocks which can be melted into weapons. To my mind, the most amazing journeys ever undertaken on British soil must have been those of the post-glacial hunter-gatherers who began the great migration northward when the climate suddenly warmed 10,000 years ago. Then, Britain was a gigantic game park speckled with birch and pine, and these first explorers must have shadowed the herds of wild horse and deer upon which they preyed. They left a mound of hazelnut shells outside Edinburgh, and built boats to reach Ireland. At Mount Sandel in Antrim they camped in circular tent-houses dated to about 7000 BC. But none of these Stone Age explorers were carrying notebooks. In fact we have to wait a very long time indeed for intact accounts of complete journeys through Britain; 9,000 years of British travel passed unrecorded. Fully documented journeys begin in the Middle Ages, when government agents, emissaries, messengers, kings and archbishops were criss-crossing the kingdom on affairs of state or Church. It was horsemen with quills, riding on rutted, boggy ways which had been neglected since the Romans went home, who opened the book of British travel narratives.

So, who were the travellers who changed the way we viewed our islands? Who were Britain's great explorers? The list turned out to be very long, and it was a painful task to whittle it down. Each candidate had to have left a detailed account of their travels; and as a group, they had to represent a fairly complete geographical coverage of mainland Britain. Oh, and they had to cover a time-span of 800 years, from the Middle Ages to the twentieth century. And there had to be eight of them. Eight, because this book was originally conceived to appear alongside a series of eight one-hour films for BBC2. The selected octuplet are not a definitive list. The seventeenth-century Hebridean explorer Martin Martin is not here, and neither are Johnson and Boswell, or George Borrow, Arthur Young, William of Worcester or J. B. Priestley. All of them rekindled interest in British travel, but the eight in these pages seemed to work best as a team.

The finalists are an eclectic bunch who travelled between the 1180s and the 1930s. Meet them on a railway platform, and you'd be rubbing shoulders with a naturalist and a spy, a couple of Churchmen, a minor aristocrat, a journalist, a political activist and a librarian. A couple of them had seen the inside of prison, one would go mad, and the motorist privately believed that Britain might be better governed from Berlin. Their motives for travelling ranged from royal commission to newspaper commission, and from spiritual enlightenment to political conviction. One was a tourist. All of them felt that they belonged to a generation which had forgotten – or had never learned – the value of their native land. 'The modern itch after the knowledge of foreign parts,' wrote Martin Martin in 1703, 'is so prevalent that the generality of mankind bestow little thought or time upon their place of nativity.' Gaelic-speaking Martin presented a British readership with islands as extraordinary as anything then being discovered in the southern oceans. And neither was domestic travel without its quota of danger and discomfort. The trials which appear in these eight accounts include near-shipwrecks and highwaymen, blizzards, floods, quicksands and the inevitable rain. Variously, these travellers recorded their journeys as field notes, as travel journals and as published narratives. All eight shared a passion for Britain. As topographical audits, their journeys are invaluable records of lost landscapes, and as explorers, they invite us to view this remarkable archipelago with a renewed sense of wonder.

GERALD
OF WALES

1188

A crusader in Wales

Route taken by Gerald of Wales during his journey of 1188

- - - Route by land

Castle

Cathedral, Abbey, Religious House

N
W E
S

Anglesey

Bangor

Caernarfon

Yr Eifl

Snowdonia

Nefyn

Cardigan Bay

Cadair Idris

Towyn

Dovey Estuary

Aberystwyth

Rhuddlan

St Asaph

Chester

Whitchurch

Oswestry

Shrewsbury

Ludlow

Radnor

Leominster

Strata Florida

St Dogmael's Abbey

Cardigan

River Teifi

Lampeter

Cenarth

Nevern Castle

St David's

Newgale Beach

Whitland Abbey

Carmarthen

Haverfordwest

Kidwelly

Manorbier Castle

Swansea

Briton Ferry

Margam Abbey

Hay-on-Wye

Black Mountains

Llandew

Brecon

Llanthony Abbey

Hereford

Abergavenny

Usk

Newport

Gold Cliff

Cardiff

Bristol Channel

0   10   20   30 miles

0   10   20   30   40   50 kilometres

T he hunter-gatherers who explored Britain as the ice sheets melted left no record of their extraordinary treks, and so the earliest complete account of a genuinely great British journey survives from the twelfth century, when the garrulous son of a Norman knight undertook an epic circuit of Wales to recruit crusaders for a misguided adventure in the Middle East. Riding through a land before the age of maps. Giraldus Cambrensis — Gerald the Welshman — has been hailed as the first serious natural historian of Wales and one of the founders of British geography. Three manuscript copies of the first version of The Journey through Wales *have survived, although it is the third version (Gerald's final revision), translated by Lewis Thorpe in the 1970s, which endures today as the standard edition.*

★

Rain had been falling for days and the track had turned into a flooded cesspit of mud and dung. My socks were waterlogged and I was soaked to the skin. The wind was so strong that the rain smacking the hood of my jacket sounded like gravel hitting glass. Beyond a field-gate, the track divided. As I extracted the map from an inside pocket, a gust of wind caught the sodden folds and tore Powys in half. Crouching in the slime, I took a compass bearing on each of the diverging tracks then transferred the bearings to the pieces of the map. There was no doubt about it. We were lost. How on earth, I wondered, had England's leading cleric found his way through these hills eight hundred years ago?

The earliest great British journey to be fully recorded began at the city gates of Hereford one spring day in 1188. Heading west for a little-known land was the Archbishop of Canterbury, the King's Chief Justiciar, a Bishop, the Court Chaplain, and a retinue of episcopal attendants, servants and soldiers. The month of March was a few days old. Above the meandering Wye, vineyards slept behind sunny walls. In the fields, ploughmen turned the stiff, winter soil while women and children tugged at weeds. Wagons loaded with manure creaked through the ruts, and flocks of sheep could be seen gathering for the trek to upland grazing. On the steep valley sides, the forests were taking colour.

Hindsight recognises that these were good days for England. The seasons were predictable. Planting began in April, and the months of June, July and August were reliably warm and settled. Harvests were generally dependable and winters mild. A century after the Normans stormed ashore at Pevensey to annihilate Harold's Anglo-Saxon army, England had become the stable, northern colony of Europe's most powerful 'empire' – a vast federation of Angevin dominions which stretched all the way from the Pyrenees to the Grampians. For the man in the field, life could have been a lot worse. The English economy was growing faster than at any time in the medieval period and a new breed of merchant was adjusting pleasurably to the ethos of profit. To the tinkle of silver, shiploads of wool and corn were being exported to the cities of Flanders. England's population of around three million was reproducing as never before; between 1086 and 1300 it would double. Ports were growing in the east, and towns were being created in the west. Markets were appearing. Land itself was breaking free of its feudal yoke and beginning to change hands for money. In England's richest, most populous region, East Anglia, Bishop Herbert de Losinga built a titanic cathedral. After thirty years of energetic rule under Henry II, England was secure and prosperous.

It was against this backdrop of domestic well-being that England's ruling classes decided to join the forces of the 'Holy Empire' in a crazed adventure in the Middle East. Their demon had been born in Tikrit, close to Baghdad, and he had risen to launch an Islamic jihad against the Christian presence in Palestine. When Saladin took Jerusalem in October 1187, Henry II responded to the call for an immediate crusade. A swingeing 'Saladin tithe' was ordained, and the Archbishop of Canterbury was despatched to Wales to recruit crusaders.

As he rode westward along the Wye, Archbishop Baldwin knew that he was embarking upon a journey of some risk. His own king regarded the Welsh as 'a wild people who cannot be tamed', while an earlier Archbishop of Canterbury had complained that the Welsh were 'Christians in name only ... barbarians'. Baldwin was out of his depth. A humble monk from Devon, he had become Abbot of the Cistercian house of Forde in the tranquil Axe valley before being appointed Bishop of Worcester and then – in 1184 – Archbishop of Canterbury. A gentle, sincere man, softened by the southern shires of England, he did not speak Welsh, and was not familiar with the wilder parts of Britain. He would be the first Archbishop of Canterbury ever to set foot in Wales.

Riding with Baldwin – in a role which ranged from diplomat to local 'fixer' and recruitment officer – was the Court Chaplain to Henry II. Gerald de Barri was uniquely suited to easing the Archbishop's passage through Wales. An Anglo-Norman-Welsh hybrid, his father was a Norman knight, William de Barri, and his mother was the daughter of the Welsh princess, Nest, who'd been a mistress of Henry I. Gerald had been educated in Latin and the classics at the Benedictine Abbey of St Peter in Gloucester, and after visits to Paris, he had been awarded benefices in both England and Wales, where he'd been instrumental in purging the diocese of St David's of corrupt churchmen. After being appointed Archdeacon of Brecon, he moved closer to the Angevin orbit in 1184, when he was made Court Chaplain to Henry II, who used him as a go-between when dealing with Welsh princes. But Gerald had another, more discreet, role on the Archbishop's mission. Three years earlier, he had accompanied Prince John to Ireland on a mission which had yielded material for two books, *The Topography of Ireland* and *The Conquest of Ireland*. Now he had ambitions to write about Wales.

Towards the end of that first day on the road, the Archbishop's entourage emerged from the shadow of Hergest Ridge onto a level, triangular vale framed by rounded mountains. At the western apex of this triangle rose the great earth mound and timber battlements of Radnor, the frontier outpost built and held by the Braiose family. Climb the mound today and it's hard not to think of Radnor as a

Norman Alamo. From the grassy crown, you can look down on the roofs of the village, and the rectangular grid of Norman streets. It seems impregnable, but only eight years after Henry II's crusaders called by, the castle was destroyed by the Welsh. Radnor lay at the limit of Anglo-Norman control; the mountains which lifted the western horizon were part of the interior of 'Welsh Wales' – a vast no-go region for the likes of English Archbishops.

Some of the most powerful men in the British Isles were gathered at Radnor that evening. Waiting at the castle for the travellers was the Prince of South Wales, Rhys ap Gruffydd ap Rhys – first-cousin-once-removed of Gerald. For over thirty years 'The Lord Rhys' had played a game of defiance and submission with Henry II. He had won and lost land, but by 1188 he controlled the old kingdom of Deheubarth, a vast territory which stretched north to the Dovey and west to the coast of Pembrokeshire. To keep the peace, Henry had appointed Rhys his deputy in Wales. Having ridden with the Archbishop from Hereford, Chief Justiciar Ranulf de Glanville, was there too. An East Anglian baron, de Glanville was Henry II's right-hand man in England. Others from Wales included the Bishop of St David's, Peter de Leia, and the son of the Prince of Elfael.

To this motley group of mixed interests, the Archbishop delivered the mission's inaugural sermon and recruiting call. For the benefit of Welsh speakers, an interpreter stood beside Baldwin. No sooner had Baldwin finished, than the first man sprang forward. It was the Court Chaplain, Gerald de Barri. 'I myself,' he claimed, 'was the first to stand up ... I threw myself at the holy man's feet and devoutly took the sign of the Cross.'

This seems to have been a prepared double-act, concocted in advance by Gerald and the Archbishop: 'It was the urgent admonition given some time before by the King,' admitted Gerald later, 'which inspired me to give this example to the others, and the persuasion and oft-repeated promises of the Archbishop and the Chief Justiciar, who never tired of repeating the King's words.' Lest readers doubt his sincerity, Gerald added: 'I acted of my own free will, after anxiously talking the matter over time and time again, in view of the insult and injury being done at this moment to the Cross of Christ.'

The Court Chaplain's theatrics worked, and as soon as Gerald had taken his vow, the Bishop of St David's, Peter de Leia, followed his example. Then Einion ab Einion Clud, the son of the Prince of Elfael, stepped forward to take the Cross, 'and many others too'. Conspicuously failing to take the Cross was the Lord Rhys, although Gerald diplomatically allows that the prince 'went home quite determined to make the holy journey'. This less-than-unanimous endorsement of a counter-jihad should have warned the Archbishop that his mission would be challenging.

*

Ahead of the mission lay a daunting circumnavigation of Wales. Gerald himself had estimated that Wales was about eight days travel in length and four days in its breadth. A complete circuit should therefore take twenty-four days. In fact, the mission would spend thirty-four days on the road and a further seventeen days resting and preaching. The total distance they would ride through the mud and stones of Wales would be around a thousand miles – equivalent to riding from London to Milan. Anyone attempting a feat like this today would find the day-to-day logistics a formidable adventure. Route-finding, difficult terrain, weather and procuring food for horse and rider, would be a constant preoccupation. But Gerald seldom mentions the trials of the road. To the medieval long-haul traveller, the discomforts were no more remarkable (and just as tedious) as the trials of modern air travel. Gerald is far more concerned with the nature of the land he is passing through. He refers to himself as 'a careful investigator of natural history', a universal discipline which allowed him to explore everything created by God, from archaeology, hydrology and zoology, to anthropology, geography and climatology. Gerald's was a young, dynamic world, rich with wonder. Wherever he looked, he saw evidence of God's ingenuity and wisdom. His catch-all curiosity skipped from killer-toads and the occult to Welsh history, sea-level change and divine retribution. Travelling was an opportunity to harvest the fruits of Creation.

From Radnor, the mission rode over the hills towards the valley of the River Wye, which they forded – probably in the shallows near Clyro – to reach Hay-on-Wye. The castle stood on a strategically sited mound above the river-cliff of the Wye, with a ravine cut by a tributary running along one side of the mound. The mound is still there, with the tarmac road on one side, and the old cattle market on the other. Today, Hay is a bibliophiles' paradise, its narrow streets lined with so many second-hand bookshops that it's impossible not to tread its pavements without falling into a reflective trance. The sudden appearance on Hay's streets of the Archbishop of Canterbury 800 years ago did not have quite the same effect: 'After the sermon,' reports Gerald, 'we saw a great number of men who wanted to take the Cross come running towards the castle ... leaving their cloaks behind in the hands of the wives and friends who had tried to hold them back.'

Few of Hay's recruits had any idea of the perils involved in making a 3,000-mile journey by land and sea, or knew what it was like to face a blizzard of arrows from Turkish horsemen, although they may well have been familiar with the fate of forebears who had taken the Cross. The medieval 'Brut' recorded that, forty years earlier, some pilgrims from Wales 'were drowned on the sea of Greece, in going with the Cross to Jerusalem'. At around the same time, the Brut of Gwent noted that so many Welsh pilgrims left for the Holy Land, that 'their absence was severely felt'. Once the Cross and the vow were taken, the pilgrimage was enforced by a penalty of excommunication. Only in exceptional circumstances could absolution be granted. In the flailing limbs and the screams and the shouts of loved ones, a distant Holy War erupted in communities who knew little of the world beyond their own valley walls. Every husband who vowed to free the Holy Land – or die in the attempt – was breaking his marriage vow. Families splintered as men fell for the spell of the Cross ... or took advantage of a marital exit strategy. Under canon law, wives could prevent their husbands participating in the crusade on the grounds that a prolonged absence abrogated their marriage vows. All knew that there was little chance of returning from the Holy Land.

From Hay, the mission probed deeper into the Welsh heartland.

While the Wye curled to Baldwin's right, the dark face of the Black Mountains reared up on his left. There were streams to ford, and beyond the castle at Bronllys, gentle, wooded hills which opened presently to reveal Llanddew: Gerald's archdeaconery.

Today, Llanddew is little more than a hamlet. The remains of Gerald's home stand in the garden of the old vicarage. The corner of his hall can be seen, and his doorway, and the well. Over the waving trees, one can glimpse the distant tilt of the Brecon Beacons. It is a quiet place, and still feels remote. The Ordnance Survey map carries a hint of Llanddew's former eminence, labelling its south-facing slope 'Bishop's Meadow'. When Henry VIII's topographer, John Leland, rode by in the 1530s, Gerald's archdeaconery had 'fallen douen for the more part', while the Bishop's Palace had become 'no thing but an onsemeli ruine'. Two hundred years earlier, this had been Gerald's home; the place where he pared his quill, meditated and prayed. 'I occupy a tiny dwelling-place,' he writes of Llanddew, 'convenient enough for my studies and my work, and here I pass my time in a sort of happy-go-lucky mediocrity.' To a modern suburb-anite, Gerald's home wouldn't seem so tiny; the ruined gable suggests that he had room to swing more than a few cats. Gerald gives the impression that he is content with his modest seclusion at Llanddew: 'The house gives me pleasure and it is conducive to thoughts of the next world,' he muses. 'I would not change it for all the riches of Croesus.'

Not riches, maybe, but Gerald would have traded Llanddew for St David's. For over a decade, he had been manoeuvring to free Wales from domination by the Archbishopric of Canterbury, and key to this aim was the raising of St David's to an archbishopric. But first Gerald had to become the Bishop of St David's, and in this, he had been thwarted by his travelling companion, Peter de Leia, who had beaten Gerald in the election twelve years earlier. Gerald now found himself shackled by this journey to the two men – the Archbishop of Canterbury and the Bishop of St David's – who stood between him and ecclesiastical freedom for Wales.

Gerald was a dreamer, and at Llandew, he drifts off on one of his periodic digressions to a nearby mountain valley so that he can share his favourite religious house. Established in the early 1100s, the abbey of Llanddewi Nant Honddu ('The English have corrupted the name to Llanthony') had been in the spiritual vanguard of religious reform in Britain. Gerald knew Llanthony intimately, possibly even trained there. Snuggled into a valley 'no more than three arrow-shots in width', it is, sighs Gerald, better located than 'any of the other monasteries in the whole Island of Britain'. Its church, he writes, is built with squared stones and roofed with sheets of lead, which the architect in Gerald praises for being 'admirably suited to the nature of the place'. And that nature was one of contemplation. Setting up the abbey's daughter house in Gloucester as an emblem of the modern, vice-ridden, acquisitive world, he asks that the sanctuary on the Honddu be reserved for those whose minds are tuned to spirituality. Let those, he asks, who prefer books and prayers, and helping the needy, come to the Honddu, with its promise of eternal bliss and 'the concourse of angels'. Those who strive for earthly possessions, for entertainment and for the company of mortal men, can go to Gloucester and 'clamour about the affairs and the pretences of the world'. It is Gloucester's lust for greater wealth, Gerald reminds us, which causes vice 'and all of the cares which follow in its train'. Here, in Llanthony, 'let the golden mean continue to flourish'. And then he is away, strewing the page with elegant phrases plucked from Ovid and Horace, Lucan and Petronius. 'Mortal appetite for success is insatiable!' 'Why can we not learn to temper our desires and be satisfied with what we have?' Last time I visited Llanthony the snow was slanting hard against the old red sandstone of its ruined walls.

*

Separating the wilder reaches of inner Wales from the fertile, colonised, Anglo-Norman valleys of the south, were the Black Mountains. Gerald is unclear whether the mission cut through the heart of the mountains to reach the Usk valley, or skirted their western flank. 'From Llanddew,' he writes, 'we made our way along the rugged pass of Coed Grwyne or Grwyne Wood, by a narrow trackway overgrown with trees.' At least two authorities have identified the pass of 'Coed Grwyne' as the saddle at the head of the valley of Grwyne Fawr, in the Black Mountains, but it would have made far more sense to have avoided the 1,800-foot climb and simply followed the old Roman road down the Usk from Brecon to Abergavenny. Perhaps the 'Coed' Gerald refers to was a lost place-name at Blwch (Welsh for 'pass'), where the modern A40 still climbs to a tight notch in an outlying ridge of the Black Mountains. Shutting out the grunting coaches and streams of cars, it isn't difficult to imagine this as a rugged, overgrown mountain track.

Baldwin was no mountaineer, and Gerald writes that the Archbishop was 'in a hurry to reach Usk Castle'. Down here, as they closed on the Anglo-Norman coastal belt, the Archbishop could expect a more positive response to his recruiting mission. And the Usk valley proved fruitful: after the sermon at Abergavenny, 'many took the Cross'; by the stone keep at Usk Castle, 'a large group of men was signed with the Cross'; at Newport, where the Usk runs into the sea, 'many people were persuaded to take the Cross'. But Gerald is coy with his numbers, and it is not until the end of his book that he finally reveals how many Welshmen responded to the invitation to fight Saladin. 'About three thousand men were signed,' he claims as they end their journey, 'all of them highly skilled in the use of the spear and the arrow, most experienced in military affairs and only too keen to attack the enemies of our faith at the first opportunity.' If we are to assume that Gerald's final figure is a modest exaggeration, and that they actually recruited around 2,500, then the mission was conscripting an average of around fifty a day. At the same time in Mainz, it is said that no fewer than 13,000 took the Cross in a single day. Admittedly, the gathering at Mainz was a grander affair (among others, the German Emperor was there) than one of Baldwin's back-country sermons, but it would be unsurprising if the Archbishop were not impatient to increase his tally.

*

The mouth of the Usk was a turning point marked by a natural signpost Gerald calls the 'Golden Rock'. It is still there, jutting into the Bristol Channel like a stranded hulk: 'High above the water,' writes Gerald, 'not far from Caerleon, there stands a rocky eminence which dominates the River Severn. When the sun's rays strike it, the stone shines very bright and takes on a golden sheen.'

Up on the brow of the cliff where the grass has been eroded around the modern navigation beacon, you can see stratified layers of bronze-coloured alluvium – Gerald's golden rock. In medieval times this was the most important landmark on this stretch of coast, both for shipping and for land travellers; it has survived on the Ordnance Survey as 'Gold Cliff'. Here, the Archbishop's mission joined the well-travelled 'coast road' to St David's, still ten days or so to the west. But in leaving behind the less-trodden tracks and ominous forests of inner Wales, the mission was now confronted by dangerous river crossings.

The problem was not just the width of the rivers at their outlets. The tides of the Severn Estuary have the largest range in the British Isles, and the estuaries which the coast road crossed were notorious for their quicksands, shifting bars, strong currents and sudden floods. Gerald sets the scene for this litany of aquatic trials by telling a story about a notorious ford just beyond Newport. Almost facing Gold Cliff was a 'small stream known as the Nant Pencarn', which 'winds through the district called Wentloog'. The river can probably be identified as the Ebbw, on Wentlooge Level (a farmhouse close to the river is still called Pen-carn). Today, the Ebbw – or 'wild horse river' – has been broken by suburbs, factories and a motorway, but in the days before the Level was drained for farmland, the river was 'passable only at certain places and by certain fords'. It wasn't the *depth* of Nant Pencarn which posed difficulties, but 'the way in which it has hollowed out its bed and ... the muddiness of the marsh-land which surrounds it'. Gerald goes on to relate that in earlier times the public road had crossed the river at a place named Rhyd Pencarn – which he translates as 'the ford beneath the overhanging rock'. Fords, like forests and passes, had many associations with calamity, and here Gerald repeats one that he got from the Scottish seer, Merlin Silvester, who prophesied that, should 'a strong man with a freckled face cross over Rhyd Pencarn on his way to lead an invasion of South Wales', the Welsh could expect to get beaten. Gerald had cause to believe this, since his own, strong, freckled King Henry II had indeed galloped through this ford en route to defeat The Lord Rhys in 1163. Eight hundred years on, the river can be found beyond some scrubland. Canalised between concrete, and speckled with refuse, the 'Nant Pencarn' has lost a little of its romance.

Of the various river-mouths the mission was forced to ford on its journey west, the worst by far lay just beyond the Cistercian monastery of Margam. Any fears coursing through the Archbishop's entourage were put on hold for the evening, for Margam was one of the most charitable Cistercian house in Wales. Walls, arches and the shell of the chapter house still stand beside Junction 38 of the M4, mute on mown lawns. In 1188, the monastery was thriving in its secluded cleft below the tumuli-dotted heights of Mynydd Margam. Here, the travellers received 'the most open-handed hospitality'. But as soon as they rode from the gates, they were faced by an alarming change of scenery. Outside Margam, the broad coastal plain they'd followed from the mouth of the Usk was pinched out of existence by a forested wall which reached to the tide line.

Anticipating difficulties, the mission was to be guided that day by the local prince, Morgan ap Caradog ap Iestyn. Following the road along the sands below the hills, first they had to cross the Afan. Here, the riders were 'delayed for some time' as the ebbing tide combined with the flow of the river to make the Afan unfordable. Today, the river is shuttered between suburban terraces and concrete highway walls. Try to wade it (I did, and it was fast and surprisingly deep) and you realise how, and why, the crusaders ran into trouble. The Afan's unnerving turbulence is due to it falling 1,600 feet during its thirteen-mile course.

Far worse was to follow. Anxious not to be caught by the tide, the mission hurried along the coast road towards the next obstacle: the River Neath, notorious, writes Gerald, for being 'the most dangerous and difficult of access of all the rivers of South Wales, on account of its quicksands'.

Set off in Gerald's hoof-prints today, and you find the six miles of sands from Margam to Neath buried beneath the derelict site of

the Margam steelworks, a housing estate (appropriately named
Sandfields), and a decomposing wasteland of metal tubing, pylons
and tanks which used to be one of the largest petrochemical works
in Europe. Where Gerald and his companions splashed across tidal
sands, two thousand workers mass-produced Styrene, Ethanol,
Vinyl Acetate and Isoproponal, a colourless solvent used for automotive windscreen wash.

As the riders approached the mouth of the Neath, they split into
two groups. Several of the packhorses took a lower route, and – for
fear of quicksand – appear to have been trotting. Gerald's packhorse
was caught and began sinking. Nervous servants ran across the
quicksand to the stricken animal and hauled at the harnesses and
ropes. Gerald records that the animal was 'almost sucked down into
the abyss'. Tragedy was averted, recalls Gerald, though 'not without
some damage done to my books and baggage'.

The danger was far from over. Their guide, Morgan, entreated
them all to move slowly and carefully but, writes Gerald, 'against the
advice of our leader, our fear of the unusual surface made us hurry
across the quicksands'. Still, they had not reached the River Neath,
and this was no place to be caught by an incoming tide. Quoting
Virgil, Gerald notes that 'Terror gave us wings.' The travellers
appear to have suffered further problems with the sands, for Gerald
adds that they endured 'considerable danger and quite a few upsets'
before the river eventually came in sight. It was only as they realise
that they have 'won through' that they heed Morgan's advice and
accept that 'it is better to advance more slowly and with great
circumspection over such dangerous terrain'.

The Neath itself proved far too difficult to ford, 'for the passages
through the river change with every monthly tide and they cannot
be located at all after a heavy fall of rain, when the waters are swollen
with floods and inundations'. They crossed by boat, probably at
the spot now known as Briton Ferry, where the river squeezes
between a pair of low foothills. The Neath pilot who ferried me
across the river here, told me that local boatmen still speak of the
days when poorer travellers had to wade across a submerged,
wooden causeway. In sight of the old ford, the giddy stalks of the

M4 lean skyward bearing a modern road which can whisk motorists all the way to London in less time than it took Gerald to ride ten miles of seashore.

Exhausted, the mission spent the night in the castle at Swansea, where Gerald overheard two monks talking about the episode in the quicksand. 'It's hard country, this,' said one. 'Not at all,' quipped the other. 'Yesterday we found it far too soft.'

*

For Gerald, the Neath was a personal deliverance; this river marked the boundary between the diocese of Llandaff and that of St David's. Ahead of him lay his own birthplace and the city of his dreams. Here, he was on home turf, and as the mission made its way towards St David's, he prepared to spring back onto his pages bathed in a virtuous aura. His first chance came at Haverfordwest.

Beyond the Neath, the mountains backed away from the shore-line and the travellers were able to follow a safer route through the populous countryside of Dyfed. This should have been perfect recruiting country, and yet Gerald suggests that the mission was struggling. Apparently, plotters in Cardigan and St David's were attempting to disrupt Baldwin's tour, and – by failing to record large-scale responses to the Archbishop's sermons since Swansea – Gerald implies that the recruitment drive was flagging. Then, at Haverfordwest, Gerald reappears for another of his dramatic turns. Taking over from Baldwin, he addresses the crowd, first in Latin and then in French. Admitting that few among his audience understood a word, he claims that many of them were 'moved to tears … rushing forward in equal numbers to receive the sign of the Cross'. Modesty was not one of Gerald's handicaps.

Having set the mission on its feet again, Gerald launches into a promotional digression on the kingdom of Dyfed. A patchwork of woods and fields surrounded on three sides by a ragged coast, Dyfed was blessed with the riches of land and sea. 'Of all the different parts of Wales,' enthuses Gerald, 'Dyved, with its seven cantrefs, is at once the most beautiful and the most productive.'

In that warm, stable twelfth-century climate, there is food in abundance: 'This is a region rich in wheat,' he continues, 'with fish from the sea and plenty of wine for sale.' Gerald had been born here over forty years earlier, and his narrative takes a sentimental ramble through his childhood home at Manorbier, down by the sea. Then, as now, the turrets and crenellations of his father's seat rise above a sandy beach and rocky headland. Gerald refers to his home as a 'fortified mansion', but later accretions have turned the de Barri 'mansion' into an enormous castle. Among the more recent walls and turrets lurk places which Gerald knew as a boy. The most impressive is the hall-block built at around the time of Gerald's birth. William de Barri broke with Norman convention and integrated his keep with the curtain wall, creating an extended domestic complex which fed an enormous hall. To the sides were the buttery, pantry and kitchen. Above the buttery are the ruins of William's withdrawing room. Some have speculated that Gerald was born up here, in one of the first rooms to catch the morning sun.

Outside the walls is Gerald's boyhood playground. The little valley between the castle and church still carries its stream between ponds where Gerald used to fish. The ruins of the mill that he mentions can also be seen, although his 'attractive orchard' has now disappeared beneath the car-park and public lavatories. And the storms of intervening centuries have piled sand against Manorbier's walls, separating Gerald's home from the open sea. He writes of the view from the rocky headland beyond the castle, and if you walk the footpath there today, you can choose the spot where Gerald sat and gazed: 'Boats on their way to Ireland from almost any part of Britain scud by before the east wind, and from this vantage point you can see them brave the ever-changing violence of the winds and the blind fury of the waters.' Enchanted Manorbier is one of those rare places that carries a living memory.

*

The tip of Pembrokeshire is the Welsh Land's End. 'St David's,' reminds Gerald, 'is in a remote corner of the country,' chosen for its location by men who 'wanted to live as far removed as possible from worldly upsets'. Here, he says, there are no woods, no rivers and no pastures. The soil is 'rocky and barren' and the peninsula is 'exposed to the winds and to extremely inclement weather'. This is the most western point in mainland Wales, further west even than Scotland's Cape Wrath. As you approach St David's along the Pembrokeshire Coast Path, successive headlands reveal long views of fearsomely ragged reefs and the ever-beating sea. At Solva, a miniature Norwegian fjord curls inland, offering a deep-draught anchorage to sea-going vessels. At sheltered havens like this, bedraggled pilgrims tottered ashore for the final walk to the shrine of St David.

The cathedral crouches in a hollow, hunching its shoulders against Irish gales and the memories of Viking raiders. Close to the iron-bound casket containing the Saint's relics is a carved stone effigy, hands pressed in prayer, face smashed off. The tomb is said to be that of Gerald. Nearby is an undamaged, armoured figure with a lined face and long moustache, reputed to be the Lord Rhys. Keeping the prince and author company are a worthy crew of knights, priests and the odd Bishop.

On the mission's arrival, Peter de Leia, the Bishop of St David's, made sure that his fellow-travellers were well accommodated. Modern pilgrims lurching off buses at Britain's smallest cathedral city are greeted by the familiar range of urban services, from espresso bar to delicatessen. Gerald gives the impression of an English Archbishop who didn't want to hang about in a Welsh bishopric. Baldwin spent a night at St David's, celebrated early-morning Mass in the Cathedral, then 'hurried off through Cemais to meet Prince Rhys in Cardigan'. One of the things on the Archbishop's mind must have been the need to secure support for the crusade from the Prince of South Wales and his two sons, Gruffydd and Maelgwn.

Gerald stayed behind, apparently ordered by the Archbishop to 'preach to the people'. The tactic which worked so well in Haverfordwest – of preaching in French or Latin to a Welsh-speaking audience – did indeed persuade a large number of men to take the Cross. But his success was short lived, for an interpreter then translated Gerald's sermon into Welsh, and his new recruits abruptly changed their minds. The benefits of a trip to the Holy Land had clearly been lost in translation.

Gerald's stake in the journey changed at St David's. Since Hereford, the itinerary had been curiously autobiographical, allowing him to weave a narrative which linked his archdeaconery in Llanddew, his beloved Llanthony, his birthplace in Manorbier, and St David's, the object of his sublunary dreams. But from here, the journey would take Gerald off the edge of his mental map, into lands beyond the control of the Anglo-Normans and their temperamental ally, the Lord Rhys.

*

Gerald left St David's with his rival, Peter de Leia, who had been charged with accompanying the mission to the borders of Deheubarth. Riding against the flow of in-bound pilgrims, they took the uneven track into the badlands of west Wales. Their route led them through the heart of the cantref of Cemais, a particular hotspot for its Angevin lords. Cemais was notionally ruled by the FitzMartin family, who had always struggled to keep the Welsh under control (an earlier FitzMartin, Robert, had been routed in battle at Crug Mawr near Cardigan). Cemais was now under the lordship of William FitzMartin, who had taken the precaution of marrying the daughter of the Lord Rhys, but this had failed to settle the troubled district. Three years after Gerald passed this way, young William would find himself besieged in his castle by his Welsh father-in-law.

Gerald and de Leia probably spent their first night out of St David's at Nevern Castle, the FitzMartin seat. For the second night, they made it to St Dogmael's Abbey, just outside Cardigan, where Gerald was reunited with Archbishop Baldwin. In the morning, they rode to Cardigan, and the great castle of the Lord Rhys. It must have been here that Baldwin and Gerald learned that the most powerful prince in Wales would not be joining the crusade after all. According to Gerald, the Lord Rhys had arrived home from greeting the Archbishop at Radnor, and thrown himself into many days of preparation for the journey to the Holy Land. He'd collected pack-animals and saddles, raised funds and persuaded others to take the Cross too. But his wife Gwenllian had 'put a sudden stop to his noble intentions by playing upon his weakness and exercising her womanly charms'. This was a great blow to the Archbishop, for the absence of Rhys would hardly encourage other Welshmen to take the Cross. Among those who did not were the two sons of the Lord Rhys, Maelgwn and Gruffydd.

Escorted by the Lord Rhys and his sons, the mission now left the coast for a detour into the interior. Way inland, by the rising of the River Teifi was a monastery that had recently been endowed by Rhys. Their guide was the river itself, and Gerald opens this riparian diversion at a delightful place he calls 'Cenarth Mawr'. He writes of a church, a mill, a bridge over the river with a fishing station, and a 'most attractive garden'. Salmon can be seen leaping up the falls here, 'about as far as the height of the tallest spear'. Cenarth has grown, and now has a couple of pubs and a coracle museum. Above the waterfalls, a footpath cuts through the woods beside deep, clear water. It was a lovely spot until a carpark was built on the rocks beside the bridge.

The Teifi seems to have released the natural historian in Gerald. So fullsome are the pages about the river and its creatures that it's as if he's describing the Garden of Eden. There is no river like it: the Teifi is 'better stocked with the finest salmon than any other stream in Wales'; it is the only river in Wales and England south of the Humber 'where you can find beavers'. He writes in detail of the salmon, and the astonishing contortions they have to perform in leaping up waterfalls, 'just as birds fly into the wind'. Sometimes, he says, 'in order to give more power to the leap, they go so far as to put their tails right in their mouths.' He describes how the beavers build their dams, and their 'castle-like lodges' in the river, their methods of 'carting timber' from the woods to the water, the nature of their teeth and the means by which they survive underwater. Hunted for their body parts, Gerald repeats an observation made in 'Eastern countries', that cornered beavers save themselves from death by cutting off their own testicles and throwing them down before the hunter's eyes.

Repeatedly, Gerald conjures up landscapes of unimaginable beauty and natural diversity. Earlier in the journey, he describes Llangorse Lake, near Brecon, with its plentiful supply of pike and perch, trout, tench and 'mud-loving eels'. He writes of plagues of poisonous toads, tame jackdaws, of pastures full of cattle, and woodland 'teeming with wild animals'. Often, he mixes hearsay with his own, more factual reports. He includes in his description of Llangorse, stories of the lake's 'miraculous' ability to change colour from bright green to scarlet, and reports that the water had been seen 'completely covered with buildings or rich pasture-lands'. Elsewhere, he writes of immigrant Flemings who can foretell the future by reading the right shoulder-blade of rams, and of a rich man who got bitten by a viper after dreaming that he would find a gold torque if he put his hand in a hole by a waterfall. 'It seems to me,' rationalises Gerald, 'that dreams are like rumours; you must use your common sense, and then accept some but refuse to believe others.'

He has a strong sense too of natural forces. In the Black Mountains, Gerald strives to explain the local weather system, arguing that the high rainfall is 'due to the mountains'. The further east one travels, he observes, 'the more the sky above seems to be pure and limpid ... because the wind which blows it clear is harsher and more piercing'. Conversely, the further west you go, the 'more cloudy and more thick' becomes the air. It's a fairly neat resumé of the principal air currents which strike the British isles. He also stumbles across evidence of sea-level rise. Forced to cross the sands of Newgale Bay on the way to St David's, Gerald comes across a 'curious phenomenon' which had been first observed in the aftermath of a great storm twenty years earlier: 'Tree trunks ... standing in the sea, with their tops lopped off, and with the cuts made by the axes as clear as if they had been felled only yesterday.' To Gerald, this had been a 'forest grove, cut down at the time of the Flood, or perhaps a little later', which had then succumbed 'by slow degrees' to the waves 'which encroach relentlessly upon the land and never cease to wash it away'. By the late 1100s, sea-levels had been rising for nearly three hundred years, as the 'Medieval Warm Period' heated the oceans and increased their volume. Generations of Gerald's countrymen had grown up with tales of retreating coasts, inundations by water and drifting sand.

*

Thirty-five days after crossing the border into Wales, the travellers came to a dark gulf. Three times wider than any estuary they'd crossed so far, the Dovey was not just a dramatic natural feature, but a formidable border. This was the limit of the diocese of St David's, and the edge of Lord Rhys' domain. The Dovey, wrote Gerald, 'divides North Wales from South Wales'.

It must have been an uneasy moment for those in the party whose fate it was to cross the water. They had reached the point of no return. It would be less difficult to continue with their circumnavigation of Wales than to return the way they had come, and in any case, the Archbishop had undertaken to celebrate Mass in each of the Welsh cathedrals – which meant pressing on to Bangor and to St Asaph. But the Lord Rhys and Peter de Leia had no such obligations; they took their leave of the Archbishop and turned for their homes in the south.

Beyond the water rose ominously gloomy, forested hills. Over there was 'the territory of the sons of Cynan' – the brothers Gruffydd and Maredudd ap Cynan. Maredudd ruled Eifionydd, and Gruffydd held Merionydd and Ardudwy. In Gerald's eyes, the far shore of the Dovey, symbolised the untouchable interior of Wales. It was 'wilder and less accessible' than other regions and the 'rudest and roughest of all the Welsh districts'. Culturally, this was a foreign country, inhabited by Welsh men and women who had never been subjugated by the Normans, and who therefore spoke no French or Latin. Even their weaponry was different. In the north, noted Gerald, the weapon of choice was not the bow, but the long spear. Hurled like a javelin, at close quarters, it would pierce a cuirass of chain mail. Opportunities to recruit crusaders would be rare. The Dovey was Gerald's Rubicon. Sinister to many, the Dovey took its name from the Welsh word 'duf', for 'dark' or 'black'. Depleted in numbers, the mission embarked upon boats and was rowed into the current.

*

As soon as they stepped ashore, the travellers knew that they had arrived in another land. Immense mountains crowded the coast, leaving little space for the road. Ominously, the ruler of Merionydd, Gruffydd ap Cynan, failed to greet them on the northern shore, though he would show up the next day, apologising 'humbly and devoutly'. They spent the night at Towyn, then continued north, confined between the sea and the lower slopes of Cadair Idris, the chair of Idris – a mythical Welsh warrior. Never had the terrain looked so intimidating: 'The mountains are very high,' remembers Gerald, 'with narrow ridges and a great number of very sharp peaks all jumbled together in confusion. If the shepherds who shout to each other and exchange comments from these lofty summits should ever decide to meet, it would take them almost the whole day to climb down and up again.'

They reached another estuary, the Mawddach. No doubt recalling the quicksand incident on the Neath, the Archbishop and Gerald embarked upon a twenty-mile detour which allowed them to cross the much narrower waters of the Wnion and the Mawddach, far inland. Meanwhile, the prince's impetuous son, Maelgwyn ap Rhys, found a ford near the sea and rode across the mouth of the estuary. That night, the mission made it to Llanfair, but was confronted the next morning by yet another huge gulf of water, Traeth Bach, the last of the Cardigan Bay estuaries. Gerald's note-taking appears to have become patchy by this stage of the journey, and he fails to mention whether they rode across the sands at low tide, or enlisted the help of rowing boats at high tide. There are signs too that the author was confused by the unfamiliar terrain. Beyond the Dovey, geographical errors creep into his account. A couple of rivers are misplaced, and he appears to have moved a mountain pass from the Lleyn peninsula to the foothills of Snowdonia. After five hundred miles in the saddle, he was unquestionably tired.

Beyond Traeth Bach, the mission rode obliquely across the Lleyn peninsula to Nefyn on the southern shore of Caernarfon Bay. Nefyn was a long way off the mission's shortest route to Bangor, and a visit to this modest village today provides few clues to its medieval attraction. The forlorn churchyard is padlocked and has sheep grazing among the graves. What might be the motte of the medieval castle rises as a grassy pimple in the nearby children's playground. Why did the mission come here? A clue can be found on the Ordnance Survey maps. While most of the north is solidly mountainous, two areas are low lying. Eight hundred years ago, the Lleyn peninsula and Anglesey were fertile and populous, and one of the oldest Welsh settlements hereabouts was Nefyn. The main town for the region, it was also the princely court – a tradition that was said to reach back to the presence here of King Arthur's court. One hundred years after Gerald came this way, Edward II humiliated the defeated Welsh by staging at Nefyn an Arthurian Round Table of such extravagance that the floor collapsed. Over three centuries after Gerald rode this way, John Leland left detailed descriptions of the Lleyn in his *Itinerary*, recording the abundance of corn and the practice among locals of living from both land and sea. Many of the peninsula's small stone-walled fields survive to this day. Leland's entry for Nefyn is particularly fascinating, for he records that the 'townelet' has 'faires every yere'. The surrounding countryside, he warns, 'is mountainyus'. Here at Nefyn, for the first time since he had crossed the Dovey, Baldwin preached. It was Palm Sunday, and the result appears to have been gratifying, for 'many people took the Cross'.

For Gerald, Nefyn produced an unexpected reward. The monasteries and churches that had been their way stations since Hereford were also the medieval equivalent of public libraries, and for Gerald these had provided moments of succour on a gruelling journey through a literary wilderness. Now, at Nefyn, Gerald found books, and in particular, an extremely rare manuscript; a work, he says, which he 'had long been looking for'. Written in the 'ancient British language', the book was regarded with such awe by its custodians that it had been kept hidden at Nefyn for as long as anyone could remember. 'There,' recalls Gerald, 'I myself, Archdeacon of St David's, discovered the works of Merlin Silvester...' Not to be confused with the Welsh Merlin (Ambrosius), who was born of a Carmarthen incubus, Merlin Silvester (or Celidonius or 'Merlin the Wild' as he becomes in Gerald's *Conquest of Ireland*) came from Scotland and had dispensed prophecies from the great Caledonian

Forest. It was Silvester who provided Gerald with the prophecy about fording the Ebbw on the south coast of Wales. In an age before the printed word, the discovery of a manuscript could be a moment of extraordinary excitement; a rare insight into the unlit past.

The route Gerald followed from Nefyn is unclear in the narrative, but obvious on the ground. A straight line from Nefyn to Caernarfon and Bangor takes the traveller through a notch in the crest of the only cluster of peaks on the Lleyn peninsula – the mountains of Yr Eifl. It's also the course taken by the Roman road which once ran from Nefyn to the fort at Segontium, the Imperial stronghold which has since been swallowed by the eastern suburbs of Caernarvon. Further corroboration that the Yr Eifl route was once well known is provided by John Leland, who mentions this forgotten pass no fewer than three times. To Leland, Bwlch yr Eifl was not just the border between two 'hundreds' or administrative districts, but it also overlooked a remarkable cleft which Henry VIII's topographer calls 'Vortigern's Valley'. This precipitous gulch is identifiable as Nant Gwrtheyrn, and was of particular fascination for Leland, both because it was the supposed landing place in the sixth century of Saint Bennow (believed at the time to have been a grand-nephew of King Arthur), and because there had been a dramatic landslide here: 'A peace of this roke is fallen,' he noted, 'and vailleith after a strange fascion.' Blwch yr Eifl was clearly a familiar landmark for Tudor travellers.

From Nefyn, the climb towards Bwlch yr Eifl drags out for nearly seven miles, skirting a mountain flank high above the sea, then twisting through a valley, crossing a broad saddle and scaling a long ridge before tackling the pass itself. On their left was Vortigera's abyss, plunging to a sliver of valley floor and the sea. This was the longest, steepest climb on the entire circumnavigation, and it became the scene for the most amusing exchange Gerald records. 'Our road led us to a valley,' he writes, 'where the going was hard, with many steep climbs up and down.' As the Archbishop and Court Chaplain rode towards the pass, they must have been talking about their impending departure for the Holy Land, and the difficulties they would soon face. Climbing down from their horses, they began walking up the long, winding trail 'in intention at least rehearsing what we thought we would experience when we went on our pilgrimage to Jerusalem'.

As they were unused to walking, the exercise took its toll: 'We walked the whole length of the valley,' continues Gerald, 'and we were very tired by the time we reached the farther end. The -Archbishop sat himself down on a convenient oak-tree, which had been completely uprooted and overturned by the force of the winds, for he needed to rest and recover his breath.' Looking up, the Archbishop asked his exhausted retinue: 'Which of you, now, in all my company, can soothe my tired ears by whistling a tune?' Just then, a bird in a nearby coppice began to sing. Some of the travellers thought that it was a green woodpecker, others that it was an oriole. When one remarked that it couldn't be a nightingale, because such a bird wasn't seen in north Wales, the Archbishop quipped: 'If it never comes to Wales, the nightingale is a very sensible bird.' Then he added: 'We are not quite so wise, for not only have we come here, but we have traversed the whole country!'

When the weary travellers eventually reached the summit of Bwlch yr Eifl, they would have seen – if it was a clear morning – an astonishing view. So steep is the northern side of the pass that it appears to fall vertically to the fields one thousand feet below. Beyond the greensward, the long curve of Caernarfon Bay leads the eye to the flat pan of Anglesey, and, roaming to the right, a mass of seething peaks. This spectacular stage was to be the setting for Baldwin's final effort to persuade the Welsh to accompany him to the Holy Land.

Next morning in Bangor, the metropolitan see of Gwynedd, Baldwin took to the high altar and exerted the full weight of episcopal leverage. The Welsh Bishop of Bangor found himself 'hard pressed ... rather than persuaded' by Baldwin, but took the Cross, as did 'a number of other people'. It clearly wasn't a stampede. Then the crusaders embarked in boats and crossed the Menai Straits to Anglesey, where they held a series of open-air sermons 'near the seashore where the surrounding rocks form a sort of circular theatre'. This seems to have been a bluff called Cerrig y Borth, where an amphitheatre of rock can still be found among the trees. Evidently an enormous crowd had assembled, for Gerald claims the presence of 'all the inhabitants of the island and quite a few from the adjacent mainland'. The crowd included the Prince of North Wales, Rhodri ab Owain Gwynedd, and a contingent from his household. Confession was heard and then – with a local archdeacon translating into Welsh – Baldwin preached, followed by the Abbot of Strata Florida, Seisyll. The difficulties in Bangor were repeated. A 'band of youths' from Rhodri's household sat unmoved on a rock, despite the Archbishop and the other preachers 'exhorting them again and again'. Not one of them, remonstrates Gerald, could be persuaded to pick up their spears and march to Jerusalem. It was 'as if trying to extract blood from a stone'. Three days later, the young men were variously wounded or killed whilst pursuing a local band of robbers. And soon after that, Rhodri was dispossessed of his lands by his own nephews. It was, remarks Gerald, 'divine vengeance'.

For Baldwin, the episodes in Bangor and on Anglesey had been a cruel confirmation of Welsh indifference to a Holy War. After a night in Bangor, the mission turned towards the English border, 'the sea on one side and a steep cliff on the other'. Gwynedd had exposed the flawed core of both men's aspirations. Baldwin could no more persuade thousands of Welsh to fight a Holy War in a faraway desert than he could whistle up a nightingale in Lleyn. And Gerald knew that a hollowness lay within the heart of his literary masterpiece. For days, the mission had been edging around a geographical feature whose physical scale was matched by its role in Welsh mythology; a feature so embedded in the British imagination that it appeared on maps drawn on the far side of England. On Matthew Paris's map of the late 1250s, Snowdonia is the only mountain range shown in Britain. The Mappa Mundi now hanging in Hereford was drawn thirty or so years later, and on this, Snowdonia is shown as a thirteen-headed massif occupying the whole of North Wales (curiously, there are fourteen peaks in Snowdonia higher than three thousand feet, so the mapmaker's symbol might not be quite as arbitrary as it first appears). Snowdonia shows up again (as a giant cogwheel) on the most important medieval map of Britain, the 'Gough map' of 1360. Among the Welsh, Snowdonia was a symbol of national redoubtability: the resting place of Gruffudd ap Llywelyn, the only man ever to have ruled the whole of Wales; while Gerald was a young man, Wales had fallen under the compass of its own king for seven extraordinary years.

To the Welsh, these mountains are, explains Gerald, called 'Eryi', the haunt of the eagles; to the English they are the 'Snow Mountains'. When looked at from Anglesey, 'they seem to rear their lofty summits right up to the clouds'. And these crowded peaks are far from barren: 'They are thought to be so enormous and to extend so far that, as the old saying goes: 'Just as Anglesey can supply all the inhabitants of Wales with corn, so, if all the herds were gathered together, Snowdon could afford sufficient pasture.' Borrowing from Virgil, Gerald adds:

And what they crop by day the shorter night renews,
Thus feeding all the flocks thanks to its cooling dews.

By the time the mission sights Snowdonia, it is apparent that this is not – as our author claims – a journey *through* Wales, but a journey around its periphery. Through sleight of the quill, Gerald has been playing a clever game of deception. As we ride with him around the Anglo-Norman edge of the country, he's been regaling us with tales of the Welsh interior. Hearsay and prodigious research allow him to penetrate the fastness that is out of bounds to those of Marcher blood. Gerald knows every river that reaches the sea, but has no first-hand knowledge of Snowdonia's scale or nature. 'At the very top of the mountains,' he writes, 'two lakes are to be found... One has a floating island, which moves about and is often driven to the opposite side by the force of the winds.' Shepherds, he adds, 'are amazed to see the flocks which are feeding there carried off to distant parts of the lake.' The second lake is even weirder. It abounds in eels, trout and perch, all of which have only one eye (the right one). And of course, Gerald has been told the tale of Snowdonia's eagle, which assumes that war will break out 'every fifth feast-day' and so perches on a particular stone 'hoping to satiate its hunger with the bodies of dead men'. The stone has been pierced by the eagle cleaning and sharpening its beak.

In the medieval imagination, Snowdonia was the most spectacular, impenetrable geographical feature in Britain. Treading wearily along the cliff-shelf towards Conway, Gerald knew all too well that the real Wales was beyond his reach.

The ride back to Hereford was executed at a punishing pace. At the start of the journey over a month earlier, they had been dawdling along at an average of around twenty miles a day, but the hundred or so miles from Bangor to Chester were covered in just three days. Baldwin preached at St Asaph Cathedral, then the mission decided to carry on riding rather than stay the night. The travellers reached Chester the night before Good Friday and spent three fruitful days through Easter convincing the town's finest menfolk to fight for Christ. For the final leg of the journey, the daily average soared to an astonishing forty-five miles, although they were so tired by the time they reached Shrewsbury that Gerald writes of the need 'to rest and recover our breath'. By then, they had been on the road for over six weeks. One final day in the saddle took them back to Hereford: 'We thus described a full circle,' concludes Gerald, 'and returned once more to the place from which we had begun this rather exhausting journey through Wales.'

*

By the time Gerald returned from his great journey, his mental map of Wales was astonishly comprehensive. He knew the basic shape of the coastline, the location of the major mountain ranges and the courses of the principal rivers. He carried a score of castles in his head, and knew where to find every monastery and most of the churches. Had he committed his Welsh geography to vellum, he'd be hailed as the best mapmaker of his age. Late in life, Gerald did direct the drawing of at least one map. More of a picture than an exercise in cartography, it is a stylised depiction of Europe, with Rome at the top and Ireland at the bottom. The whole 'map' is intended to draw the viewer's eye from Britain to Rome by way of a central corridor which connects the English Channel with Flanders,

Paris, Lausanne, the Great St Bernard Pass, Pavia and Tuscany. In the British Isles, eight sees are elegantly depicted and labelled in red ink. Missing are the sees of Canterbury and St David's. It is impossible to imagine a more graphic insight into Gerald's state of mind.

The Third Crusade was a fiasco. Gerald got as far as Chinon before being sent back to England – with Peter de Leia – by the King. Baldwin and de Glanville were less lucky; both died in the Holy Land. Gerald wrote his own epitaph in the preface to *The Journey Through Wales*: 'This little work is like a clear mirror, reflecting the wild and trackless places we passed through. It likewise names each spring and rushing river, and records our witty sayings, the hazards of the road, and the various accidents that befell us. It describes the landscape, and the notable things that have happened there both recently and a long time ago, with occasional digressions about natural wonders: and it portrays the country itself, as well as the origins, customs and ways of the inhabitants.' Time has been the judge of Gerald. He once wrote that his purpose had been to 'rescue from oblivion, the secrets of his native land'. In that, his crusading mission was a triumph.

JOHN
LELAND

1536–45

The madness of maps

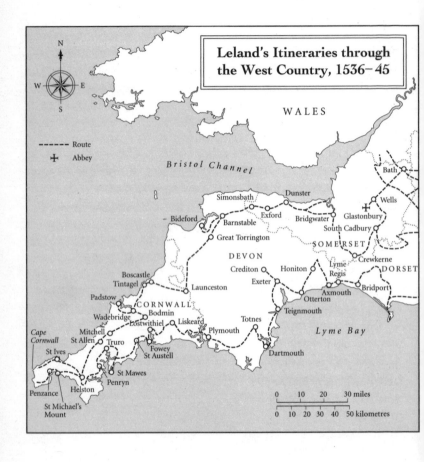

Leland's Itineraries through the West Country, 1536–45

- - - - - Route
✛ Abbey

WALES

Bristol Channel

WELLS
Bath
Glastonbury ✛
Simonsbath
Dunster
Exford
Bridgwater
South Cadbury
Bideford
Barnstable
Great Torrington
SOMERSET
Crewkerne
DEVON
Crediton
Honiton
Lyme
Regis
DORSET
Boscastle
Tintagel
Launceston
Exeter
Axmouth
Bridport
Padstow
CORNWALL
Bodmin
Wadebridge
Lostwithiel
Liskeard
Plymouth
Otterton
Teignmouth
Totnes
Lyme Bay
Mitchell
St Allen
Truro
Fowey
St Austell
Cape Cornwall
St Ives
St Mawes
Penryn
Dartmouth
Penzance
Helston
St Michael's
Mount

| 0 | 10 | 20 | | 30 miles |
| 0 | 10 | 20 | 30 | 40 | 50 kilometres |

F or the best part of ten years, Henry VIII's antiquarian, John Leland, travelled the length and breadth of the kingdom in an attempt to record the treasures of its threatened monasteries, and to reinvigorate England's identity by restoring its Arthurian past. But Leland's fascination with the worked landscape turned his 'laboryeuse Journey and Serche' into a topographical audit on an unimaginable scale. Eventually he went mad, but his manuscripts have been a Tudor touch-stone for the last five hundred years. One of those who turned to Leland's journeys was William Camden, whose county-by-county description of the British Isles, Britannia, *became the standard geographical reference for nearly two hundred years.*

*

The month was January. For weeks, the west coast of Britain had been battered by gales. Roofs had been ripped off, trees toppled. One of the gales had taken only two days to cross the Atlantic. But in the lull between storms, the skies momentarily cleared, and it was on one of these days, in the harbour of St Mawes in Cornwall. that I hoisted the rust-coloured sails of a gaff-rigger and turned the bow towards open water. Beyond Carricknath Point, white horses flickered across the open sea. But in the other direction, inland, a vast expanse of uncluttered water glittered between sheltering hills. Some five miles long and stretching to two miles in width, the combined area of Carrick Roads and Falmouth Harbour is claimed locally to be the third largest natural harbour in the world. John Leland had no doubts about its significance. To Henry VIII's peripatetic topographer, this was the most important harbour in the land; 'very notable and famose, and yn a maner the most principale of al Britayne'.

Leland took particular trouble to describe the harbour's complex geography. He devotes more space to it than any other harbour in his *Itinerary*, noting the creeks and anchorages, the depth of the water in fathoms, the locations of noblemen's houses, churches, piers, bridges and woodland. This was, he concluded, a safe refuge for the 'greatest shyppes that travayle be the ocean'. Two years earlier, Henry VIII had begun constructing a pair of revolutionary artillery forts to protect the anchorage. Tacking to and fro through the swell, alternately I came in range of the gun-ports of Pendennis Castle and St Mawes Castle, the 'fortelet lately buylded by the contery for the defense of the haven'. Beside it, basking in unseasonable sun, were the pastel cottages and hotels of St Mawes, 'a poor fischar village'. Between the two castles, I passed the 'blynd roke', sited, says Leland, 'nerer the west syde of the haven then the east'. Today, it is marked by a tapered warning beacon, for the rock is submerged at high tide – or, as Leland puts it – 'covered at ful see'. Here, at a glance, was Leland's Tudor harbour, immediately recognisable despite the passage of half a millennium.

*

As the pale cliffs of Calais receded, John Leland may well have reflected upon the future he had seen. The year was 1529, and he had just boarded a ship on the coast of northern France. Three years earlier, he had arrived in Paris, the largest and most exciting city in northern Europe. Twenties Paris seethed with poets and printers, bibliophiles and mathematicians, and above all, with dangerous ideas. Here, a young man could immerse himself in what historians would come to know as the 'mighty surging of a new age', the Renaissance. Less a movement than a series of intoxicating tides which had been washing northward across Europe for over a century, the new age was changing the landscape of state, religion and culture, at an unprecedented pace. Continental cities teemed with self-aware Europeans whose quest for knowledge was encompassing the globe with voyages of discovery. The figurehead of early sixteenth-century humanism was Erasmus of Rotterdam. 'Immortal God,' Erasmus had exclaimed twelve years earlier, 'what a world I see dawning! Why can I not grow young again?'

Leland's ship bore him back to an island kingdom whose peripheral location had left it far behind the various revolutions which were sweeping the continent. Across the spectrum, from art and architecture to mathematics and printing, England was half-a-century behind the times. But revolution of a home-grown kind was being unleashed. For a thousand years, virtually everyone on Europe's largest island had lived as Catholic Christians. Now, Henry VIII was about to prise his kingdom away from the papacy and trigger a process of national self-discovery. Stepping ashore in Kent, John Leland knew that he would play a role in England's rebirth.

From the coast, all roads led to London, a city whose population at the time was barely half the size of modern Cambridge. But in terms of status, it overwhelmed every settlement in the land: 'London is not said to be in England,' mused a visiting Swiss student at the time, 'but rather England to be in London.' Leland knew the city well. He had been born here in around 1503, and then been sent to St Paul's School, which had recently reopened under the Dean of the Cathedral, John Colet. Colet had made St Paul's the first school in the kingdom to teach Greek; its first High Master, William Lily, had compiled a work which would become Henry VIII's authorised grammar book. Versed in the classics, Leland had graduated from Cambridge University in 1521 or 1522, then been appointed tutor to Thomas Howard, the Duke of Norfolk's son. After the Duke's death in 1524, a couple of unsatisfactory years at Oxford (where Leland had been unimpressed by the old-fashioned teaching) had been followed by the scholarship to study in Paris.

At the time, Paris was four times the size of London, a vast, bustling metropolis of 200,000, with a university which was equalled in northern Europe only by Louvain. Unlike London, Paris was awash with books. Print, the medium by which Europeans were dispersing new ideas, discoveries, doctrines and forms of expression, had barely crossed the Channel. Between 1520 and 1529, England produced 550 books, most of them typeset, bound and sold by foreigners working in a small number of London presses. Meanwhile, Paris was printing 300 titles every year. Some of the most popular were chivalrous thrillers recycled from medieval legends. Along with *Quatre fils Aymon*, *Fierabras* and *Pierre de Provence*, each of which had appeared in nearly twenty editions by 1536, Leland may have dipped into romantic editions of *King Arthur* – although Arthur himself was seldom at the centre of the action. The only French romance which cast him as the hero was *The Knight of the Parrot*, a work which failed to take off on the English side of the Channel.

Where the French could marvel at the latest printed maps and globes, not a single map of any sort had been printed in England. Here in Paris, Leland may have run into some of the giants of the northern Renaissance, the Lutheran-leaning scholar Guillaume Budé and perhaps even Erasmus himself. Also in Paris at this time was one of Europe's leading mathematicians and topographers, Oronce Finé. A man of many disciplines (he was a leading cartographer, book illustrator, wood engraver and educationalist), Finé had been recently released from a long spell of imprisonment for charges related to the occult. His cartographic works included a heart-shaped map of the world, and an enormous map of France based on co-ordinates of latitude and longitude that Finé had determined for 124 cities, towns and villages. While Leland was in Paris, Finé was working on mathematical instruments, an astronomical treatise and dabbling in verse; the year after Leland left the city, Finé wrote a poem praising mathematics. Finé had – quite literally – put France on the map; his six-sheet masterwork was the first map of France to be compiled and printed in that country.

In coming back to London, Leland was not only returning to the city which had set him on the path of humanist learning. He was also returning to the court of King Henry VIII. Ultimately, destiny would link Leland to his monarch in the most pitiful manner, but in 1529, both were in the ascendant. Henry had succeeded to the throne while Leland was still a small boy, and the first twenty years of his reign were building to a climax. With Wolsey's prosecution in the year that Leland sailed home, Henry had cleared the way for his marriage to Thomas Howard's niece, Anne Boleyn, and begun hacking at the thousand-year bond between England and the papacy. The King's hatchet-man was the son of a Putney blacksmith,

Thomas Cromwell. Manipulative, ruthless, with a background in money-lending and law, Cromwell was perfectly cut as a Henrican courtier. Already, he had assisted Wolsey in dissolving some of the smaller monasteries, the proceeds of which had been used to endow new colleges at Oxford and Ipswich.

With no apparent funds, nor an immediate family, Leland had to make the most of his court contacts, his fashionable education and his experience in Paris. He was familiar to Cromwell, and appears to have sought patronage from Anthony Denny, and the 'Master of the Posts', Sir Brian Tuke. Both were recipients of Leland's poems. Leland was soon appointed royal chaplain and awarded an absentee living in the Marches of Calais. He also gained a post in one of the Royal libraries. In 1533, his poetry was recited at Anne Boleyn's coronation.

It was in Leland's capacity as a humanist and as a librarian that he was granted the royal commission that would lead him towards the first great work of English topography. And towards madness. Specifically, he was (in the words of the great seventeenth-century Leland scholar, Anthony Wood) 'to make a search after England's Antiquities, and peruse the Libraries of all Cathedrals, Abbies, Priories, Colleges, etc. as also all places wherein Records, Writings and secrets of Antiquity were reposed'. To facilitate his quest, Leland was equipped with an official pass which was guaranteed to gain him access to all libraries.

*

Leland began his bibliographic mission immediately. Riding from library to library, he picked through the shelves, compiling lists of books and manuscripts, and on occasion removing volumes for the King's own collection. Given that there were nearly 600 monasteries in the country, he had undertaken an enormous – and urgent – task. Many religious houses had already been dissolved, and under the new vicar-general, Thomas Cromwell, reformation of the English church was accelerating. The act of 1536, suppressing all monasteries with an annual income of less than £200, was the beginning of the end for England's monastic tradition.

The passing of time has removed from the record all but fleeting glimpses of Leland during these years, but there are sightings of him in Somerset in 1533, and at St Albans in 1535. He must have felt that he was cantering through a nightmare. A patriot and a passionate upholder of the Tudor realm, he knew that the libraries he was frantically cataloguing would be thrown to the four winds, and he feared that England's bibliographic heritage would be plundered by foreigners. On 16 July 1536, Leland wrote to Cromwell, imploring the vicar-general to help him rescue books for the King's Library, where they 'would be a great profit to students, and honour to this realm; whereas now the Germans, perceiving our desidiousness and negligence, do send daily young scholars hither, that spoileth them, and cutteth them out of libraries, returning home and putting them abroad as monuments of their own country'. Leland's friend John Bale wrote to him from Ipswich, offering support and encouragement in their mission to preserve the glory of 'our England'.

The year 1536 transformed Leland into a reactionary. Not only were the monasteries being dismantled and their libraries stripped, but the very roots of Tudor legitimacy suddenly came under assault from an Italian historian. Published in Basle in 1534, Polydore Vergil's *Anglica Historia* re-wrote British history from a modern, humanist perspective. Out went the medieval legends which had allowed the Tudor kings to claim direct descent from King Arthur; in came revisionist vistas based – as Vergil put it – on 'a full rehersall and declaration of things don, not a gesse, or divination'. To Vergil, Geoffrey of Monmouth was a laughable fabulist who had embellished his 'histories' with 'most impudent lyeing', and who had 'concocted the great fable of King Arthur'. With a precise, humanist uppercut, Vergil floored Arthur, the Tudors – and Britain. Caught between his humanist reasoning and his nationalist pride, Leland was in an impossible position. In 1536, he responded to the *Anglica Historia* with an irate pamphlet which characterised Vergil as conceited and ignorant.

The nature of Leland's bibliographic quest shifted in emphasis. As he hastened between the disintegrating monasteries, he began taking notes on the fabric of the country: the roads and towns, and the nature of each county. Initially, this may have been little more than the excited observations of a loyal subject, 'totally enflammid', as he would write to his king, 'with a love to see thoroughly al those partes of this your opulente and ample reaulme'. But in Leland's mind, at least, it soon became a formalised survey.

He outlined his plan several years later, in a report to Henry VIII called *The New Year's Gift*. His exhaustive travel notes, he explained, would form the raw material for a map. Thinking perhaps of Oronce Finé, and the incredibly detailed printed maps then being pulled from presses in Paris and Antwerp, Leland understood that the best medium for geographical descriptions was the map rather than the printed word:

> And because that it may be more permanent, and farther knowne, then to have it engraved in sylver or brasse. I entend by the leave of God, within the space of xii moneths follwying, such a descripcion to make of your realme in wryttinge, that it shall be no mastery after, for the graver or painter to make the lyke by a perfect example.

It is a passage strewn with the seeds of failure. Leland was proposing to create a written, topographical description of the entire kingdom. Every river and bridge, hill and vale would be described, and its location identified using words alone. He would then present this extraordinary document to an engraver, who would try to visualise this textual landscape, and convert it into a map, or rather, an enormous number of maps.

Leland understood the pressing need for a detailed topography of England. He knew that monarchs and military leaders, the clergy and scholars, would all benefit from an accurate, comprehensive description of the kingdom. But words were the wrong medium. Unfortunately, he was fifty years too early. While geographers on the continent such as Van Deventer, Apian and Mercator were creating detailed, accurate maps using the latest methods of triangulation, in England such forms of surveying were barely known. Leland had set himself an impossible task. From 1538 or 1539, he resumed his travels with expeditionary zeal, taking to the road each summer, and compiling his notes through the winter. Later, he would claim to have travelled comprehensively throughout the entire kingdom of England and Wales.

Exploring the two countries with Leland's *Itinerary*, it's impossible not to cross his tracks, but there is one region which illustrates better than any other the scope of his passions and the nature of his journeys. In May 1542, Leland left London heading west for Somerset, Devon and Cornwall, three counties uniquely placed to shed light on our shadowy topographer. Not only are Cornwall and Somerset the most thoroughly described counties in the surviving *Itinerary*, but they have the most potent Arthurian connections. In the West Country, Leland revealed the essence of his age.

*

For modern travellers, the gateway to the West Country is the M4/M5 interchange, beyond the northern suburbs of Bristol. But there is another, far older, and rather more evocative spot due south of here. Right in the centre of the West Country, where the Dorset uplands plummet to the Somerset Levels, is a prominent hill of well-drained limestone. It is crowned by an enormous fort. Archaeologists reckon that the site was occupied for nearly four thousand years, right through to Saxon times. Running by the foot of the hill was the ancient highway between eastern England and the West Country, a route whose tendrils reached across Salisbury Plain to the Thames estuary, to the North Downs, and to the chalk cliffs facing the continent.

The horizon was ablaze with a fiery sunrise when I squelched up the steep, deeply incised trackway between Cadbury's ramparts. Around the dark island of the deserted site were constellations of light: the torrent of silver and red streaming like tracer fire through a cutting on the A303; the linear dots of the runway lights at the Yeovilton airfield; solitary sparkles from isolated farms on the Somerset Levels. Pottering about among the grazing sheep, Leland found all the evidence he needed: the site itself was on a prominent hill, 'wunderfully enstrengtheid of nature', and around its crest were '4. diches or trenches, and a balky waulle of yerth betwixt every one of them', which was breached by '2. enteringes up by very stepe way'. The size of the site was staggering; he estimated it to be twenty acres (it's actually eighteen). Poking through the turf, he found 'the fundations and *rudera* of walles', and noted that 'much dusky blew stone' had been 'caryid away' by 'people of the villages'. A large number of Roman coins had been found, and 'within living memory', a silver horseshoe had been discovered. To Leland, it was clear that the extensive ruins were 'sumtyme a famose toun or castelle'. Further evidence that this was indeed Arthur's seat of power was provided by the names of surrounding villages associated with the word 'Camelot', and information from local people that King Arthur had 'much resortid' to the hilltop castle.

The procedures Leland followed here were a triumph of pioneering fieldwork; he was the first recorded person to link Cadbury Castle with Camelot. Medieval writers had settled on Caerleon and Carlisle for Arthur's court, but a West Country Camelot made more sense to Leland. The evidence he'd found on the ground established Arthur's power base as a real geographical location; the centre of British civilisation; the point of departure for chivalrous adventures.

Close to Camelot were three Somerset towns admired by Henry's topographer, yet ravaged by Cromwell. The categorist in Leland was always quick to identify towns by type; industrial centres would have their products listed; county towns would have their walls described; market towns their wares and so on. Here in Somerset, he had a trio of religious centres. Arriving in Bruton over Leland's 'est bridge' (with '3. archys of stone' still intact), I called at the home of the painter Richard Pomeroy. From an upstairs window in his house, he can look across the Brue to a solitary tower on a rounded hilltop. In Richard's painting of the dovecote, it appears to float like a memory. The dovecote belonged to Bruton's abbey, dissolved in 1539 after one of Cromwell's emissaries – a priest named Richard Layton – discovered Catholic relics in the buildings. The abbey was sold to the Berkeley family, who converted it into their mansion. Leland was impressed by Bruton's ecclesiastical fabric, noting that the abbots had spent a small fortune on a splendid new market cross, and on 'almoste reedifiying' the abbey. He must have been in

Bruton on his first trip to the West Country, a few years before the abbey was dissolved.

Wells too suffered at the hands of Cromwell. Behind the moat of the Bishop's Palace, the Great Hall now stands as a gaunt ruin surrounded by impeccable lawns. A latter-day Leland, Nikolaus Pevsner, regarded Wells as the 'most memorable of all Bishops' Palaces in England'. Even as a shell, it is overwhelming. The medieval ranges beside the gatehouse are imposing enough, but they are dwarfed by the eyeless wall of the Great Hall. Decorated with local sandstone, the hall's enormous windows were glazed, and it was floored with encaustic tiles. Gigantic timbers supported a roof of lead (the Bishops of Bath and Wells had a monopoly on the Mendip lead mines). A banquet held in the Great Hall in 1337 was attended by 286 guests, and had an industrial shopping list of 672 loaves, 349 pipes of ale, 86 pipes of wine, and a variety of fish: pike, eel, hake, salmon, plaice, bream, pollock and pickerell. A butcher produced a sheep, half a cow, ducks and chicken. Such was the power and wealth of a medieval bishop, and the riches of an abbey's estates. After Henry VIII died, one of his son's regents – Sir John Gates – stripped the Hall of its timber and lead, and the weather did its worst.

Leland passed through Wells on the eve of oblivion. He records that the Great Hall is 'exceding fayre', and that the present bishop, William Knight, is busy building 'a crosse in the market place, a right sumptuus peace of worke'. Along the northern side of the market place, one of Knight's predecessors, Bishop Beckington, had built twelve 'right exceding fair houses al uniforme of stone high and fair windoid'. Only his death, laments Leland, prevented him from building a corresponding row along the south side of the market square. Had he accomplished it, Wells would have 'bene a spectacle to al market places in the west...'

It was in the chained library that I felt for the first time the tickle of Leland's cloak. It is a long room of creaking boards and ghostly browsers. Pools of daylight fall across the spines of books. This was the 'great librarie ... having windowes on eche side of it', that had been built – so Leland tells us – by Thomas Bubwith, the Archdeacon of Wells. Strange it was to pause in one of those bays of leathery tomes, and look, just as Leland did, at wonder upon the wealth of accumulated literature: here was Livy and Homer and Tacitus ... Thomas Aquinas, Sleidan's *History of the Reformation* ... Downames' *Guide to Godliness*. But the spine which made the hairs on my neck tingle was the one which provoked Leland's fury in 1536. There, in the library in Wells, was the Basle edition, published by Simon Grynaeus, of Polydore Vergil's *Anglica Historia*. A very long time ago, someone had been through the volume page by page, carefully highlighting passages with a pencil.

To Leland, Wells was all that a town should be, 'al for the most part buildid of stone'; large, wealthy, beautiful and built to endure. Leland had to look no further than Wells to be frightened by the future. The town that he celebrated had been built by bishops of the old Church. He must have wondered who would build the England of the future.

It was in the third of these Somerset towns that Cromwell's programme of 'visitations' wreaked a truly terrible outcome. 'From Welles to Glessenbyri about a 5. miles from north to south west,' noted Leland, as he rode between the two towns, logging every stone bridge and stream. On his first visit to Glastonbury, Leland appears to have been shown around the Abbey by the Abbot, Richard Whiting. Among other details, the *Itinerary* records that an earlier abbot, Richard Beere, had 'made a rich altare of sylver and gilt', and had founded an almshouse for ten or so 'poore wymen'. In 1539, three years before Leland returned to Glastonbury during his tour of 1542, Whiting was tied to a hurdle at the Abbey gates, then dragged through the town and up the slopes of the Tor, where he was hanged. His head was hacked off and his body cut into quarters, one to be displayed at Wells, one at Bath, one at Ilchester and one at Bridgwater. The head was placed over the gateway of Glastonbury Abbey. In his notes of 1542, Leland fails to make any mention of the Abbey.

Until Cromwell's avaricious eye fell upon the West Country, Glastonbury was the wealthiest Abbey in the land. The source of that wealth was not the Abbey itself, but its vast land holdings.

Glastonbury owned a huge swathe of property across the eastern part of Somerset, with outlying estates in Dorset and Wiltshire. Spaced across the estates were magnificent stone barns which acted as collecting centres for produce. Glastonbury's heartland estates were known as the Twelve Hides, and occupied fertile land less than a day's walk from the Abbey. Leland crossed the Twelve Hides more than once, and describes a mysterious lake which has disappeared from modern maps. According to Leland it was '4. miles in cumpace' during winter when water levels were highest, shrinking to two-and-a-half miles during drier spells. Apparently it was 'a good mile yn lenght'.

So what happened to Meare Pool? And where precisely was it? Look at a modern OS map and there are clues in the alignment of field patterns and drainage ditches, as if the landscape has had to 'heal' around a feature which has been surgically removed. There is also a hint of altered landscapes in the course of the minor road which links the hamlets of Upper and Lower Godney; at the western end of Lower Godney, the road just stops, as if it's collided with an invisible barrier. Using the field and dyke alignments, the Godney road and the absence of contours, it's possible to sketch out an approximate location for the Pool, which is corroborated on the map by a couple of features marked in the Gothic script which denotes 'Non-Roman Antiquities'. On what must have been the southern shore of the Pool are the 'Abbot's fish ho', and 'Lake Villages'.

Deeply curious, I headed off onto the Levels. Long, straight drainage ditches – locally called 'rhynes' – ran to the horizon, the exposed soil as dark as chocolate. At various times in my life, I've walked the East Anglian Fens, and the interminable flood plains of the Rhone and the Danube, but generally found them sinister places, stripped of humanity by industrial agriculture. Their flat, cloying muddiness makes the miles crawl and the mind wander into frightening precincts. But the Somerset Levels are different: this is pasture land, speckled with cattle, and the comforting hills are always in sight.

At Lower Godney, a public footpath passed through a back-garden and onto the grassland of the Levels. After a mile or so, the footpath met a wide rhyne. A couple of hundred yards beyond it, the land began to rise, very slightly. This must have marked the southern limit of the Pool. A bridge crossed the dyke, and there was a tall stone building standing alone in a gently sloping field. Leland makes no mention of the building, but a source from around 1540 describes it as having a hall, a parlour and chamber, and being 'pretty'. The upper rooms contained living quarters, and were reached by exterior steps. This was the centre of operations for fishing in the Pool. The Abbey's fish were salted and stored here.

Standing in the dusk, I watched the mist rising as if gauze was being drawn imperceptibly across the grassland. From the upper floor, the mere would have shone in the moonlight; a black inland sea rimmed by ribs of upland. In a single year back in the 1200s, the Meare fishery caught 224 sticks of eels, 30 great eels, 55 pike, 200 bream and around 120 white fish. The Fish House was first recorded in 1344, so by the time Leland came by, it had been standing for a couple of centuries. With the Dissolution of the Monasteries, Glastonbury's lands were sold off, and the Meare was drained and turned into pasture.

*

The counties Leland recorded so meticulously have been re-invented many times over during the last five centuries. Of the tens of thousands of places he described, the survivors are the structures and shapes on the landscape that escaped the wreckers' ball and the plough. Their rarity means that it's hard not to alight upon the most humble of ruins, or recognisable descriptions, with a faintly ridiculous exuberance. Equally frustrating is Leland's virtual absence from his own narrative. We know he is there, for he scatters the *Itinerary* with his presence. Here he is, for example, on the road from Glastonbury, heading towards the heights of Exmoor:

> ...I went over Thone by a wood bridge... The way or I cam ynto Bridgwater was causid with stone more then half a myle... I passid over 2. notable brokes bytwixt Stowe and S.Audres that ran from the montaynes to the se.

We can sense him, peering over hedges, pausing at road junctions, asking the way of passers-by. But we never meet him. We never find out what he is feeling, and we search his notes in vain for anything resembling a practical aside. Throughout the *Itinerary*, we learn nothing of the weather he endured, or the state of roadside hostelries. Where sixteenth-century humanists like Erasmus and Dürer left us with wonderfully detailed accounts of everyday travel, Leland feeds us not a tidbit on over-charging ferrymen or inconvenient plagues. Neither do we know much about his own circumstances as a traveller, although he does allude in *The New Year's Gift* to the human and financial burden of the enterprise, when he refers to the journeys 'sparynge neyther labour nor costes'.

So we have to fill in the gaps ourselves. Very likely, he travelled with a small entourage which probably included a servant, a scribe and a horseman. Like Gerald of Wales, he would have employed the services of local guides when negotiating difficult rivers and estuaries, and perhaps stretches of mountain and moorland. On one occasion, in south Lancashire, he refers to a guide who helped him cross the dangerous swamps west of Manchester. On another occasion, in Nottinghamshire, he mentions that he crossed the Trent by boat, while his horse was ridden through the ford. Possibly the river had been in spate at the time, and the water too deep for Leland to risk fording the Trent himself. Frequently, it is all but impossible to divine which routes he took. His traverse of the 'montaynes' of Exmoor is tantalisingly abbreviated. He notes that the first part of the route to Exford was 'al hylly and rokky, ful of brokes in every hilles botom and meatly woddid' and that the second part 'was partely on a moore and sumwhat baren of corne, and partely hylly'. The least difficult route between Dunster and Exford would have been the direct line that takes you over the roof of the moor, by way of Dunkery Beacon. Since there are no outcrops or crags in the district, the 'rokky' nature of the route must refer to Exmoor's stony tracks.

Finding features Leland describes in the countryside is far harder than locating urban remnants of his *Itinerary*. Often, it's unclear exactly what he is describing, such as these 'hillokkes' on Exmoor:

The boundes of Somersetshire go beyond this streame [the River Exe] one way by north west a 2. miles or more to a place caullid the Spanne, and the Tourres, for ther be hillokkes of yerth cast up of auncient tyme for markes and limites betwixt Somersetshir and Devonshire; and here about is the limes and boundes of Exmore forest.

So where are these 'hillokkes of yerth'? Well, Leland's dishevelled notes contain a second sighting of what appear to be the same 'hillokkes', in one of his descriptions of Devonshire:

The partition of the shire a mile and more by northe west from Simon's Bath at the towres. The toures be round hillockkes of yerth sette for limites.

Leland leaves a trail of clues which leads – eventually – to his hillocks. In Simonsbath, he mentions that 'ther is a bridge of woodde over this water'. Walk through Simonsbath today and you find that the bridge (no longer of timber) leads out of the village on the road which climbs to the moors. Over three miles (roughly equivalent to Leland's two Tudor miles), the road climbs to a cross-roads on a ridge at 1,500 feet above sea level. Turn right here, peer over the hedge, and there, silhouetted against the western skyline are some distinct hummocks. Cross the tussocks of Western Common, and Leland's 'hillokkes of yerth cast up in auncient tyme' turn into a series of Bronze Age burial mounds. On top of the highest mound, long-gone surveyors have left a concrete triangulation pillar. With binoculars and a 1:25,000 OS map, it's possible to spot other mounds, aligned roughly north-west / south-east along the crest of the ridge. Just as Leland said, they follow the county boundary of Somerset and Devon. In one direction are the billowing grasslands of Exmoor, and down below in the other, the fields and farms of Devon. It's a very ancient boundary; a boundary between two types of landscape which evolved to separate two counties. Walking guides to Exmoor still refer to the ridge Leland called 'Spanne' and 'the Tourres', as 'Span Head' and 'The Towers'.

*

The scale – and hopelessness – of Leland's ambition becomes most apparent when you tread his laborious steps. The notes he amassed in his *Itinerary* were a topographical databank of unparalleled volume. When he eventually completed his travels, he was able to report to Henry VIII that:

> In so muche that all my other occupacyons intermytted, I have so traveled in your domynions both by the see coastes and the myddle partes ... by the space of these vi. yeares past, that there is almost neyther cape nor baye, haven, creke or pere, ryver or confluence of ryvers, breches, washes, lakes, meres, fenny waters, mountaynes, valleys, mores, hethes, forestes, woodes, cyties, burges, castels, pryncypall manor places, monasteryes, and colleges, but I have seane them, and noted in so doynge a whole worlde of thynges verye memorable.

And he wasn't exaggerating. The man left no stone untrodden; no significant feature unrecorded. But with every page turned, the reader of his notes cries out for a map; he left us thousands of places in search of a location.

Leland was incapacitated by the absence of a measured survey. The geographical information in his notebooks carried no co-ordinates. They had been scribbled as words onto plain paper, not plotted onto a mathematical grid. The Bodleian Library in Oxford holds a rare and fascinating sketch map prepared by Leland. He'd probably drawn it following his tour of the north-east in 1544. It's a painful illustration of the impossibility of his task. The map is an attempt to make sense of the drainage basin of the Humber and the Witham. Annotated tributaries squiggle across the sketch, which includes a rough representation of the coast running north from the Wash, past the Humber estuary to Hornsey. Stare at the sketch for long enough, and it becomes apparent that one of the twenty or so waterways is drawn as a straight line. Leland appears to be trying to work out the role played by Britain's oldest canal, the Fossdyke. The sketch neatly shows how the Fossdyke – which was built by the Romans – links the Trent with the Witham, thus allowing ships to sail inland to Lincoln. In his *Itinerary*, Leland describes Bishop William Atwater's attempt to 'clense', or dredge, the dyke in order to reopen Lincoln to shipping. Atwater started at a place called Torksey, where the canal joined the Trent, and his dredging operation reached halfway to Lincoln before he died in around 1520, and the work was abandoned. On his sketch, Leland makes two attempts to place Torksey accurately.

The Bodleian sketch reveals the mind of a man who knew that he was ahead of his time. In 1533 – three years before Leland set off for the West Country – a scholar in Louvain had published the first printed description of the use of triangulation for surveying. While mathematical surveying took off in the Low Countries, it would be decades before the practice reached England. Leland was a poet, a librarian, an auditor. He was not a mathematician. Insomuch as they are arranged at all, the notes he left are organised around routes he travelled. A modern traveller could spend a lifetime trying to trace John Leland's footprints to and fro across England and Wales. But it would be a journey into madness, for Leland's quest had no end. His itinerary crosses and recrosses itself. He returns to places he has already visited, and describes them over again, slightly differently. With each visit, the *Itinerary* accumulates more layers but less form.

The *Itinerary* is clearest when its author is depicting a town or city, or a specific location; and at its most murky when he attempts to describe the form of a coastline, or drainage basin, or the distribution of a district's settlement. Notes of mileages and place-names are no substitute for a map, but Leland's bibliographic instinct was to compile lists rather than to make a sketch. As a result, his mental map is frequently awry. Dropping down from the heights of Exmoor, you might expect – if you trusted Leland's geography – to follow the river Taw from its rising on the moor, all the way to Barnstaple on the coast. Leland had, after all, written that the Taw 'risith in Exmore south est from Berstaple'. But the Taw rises on Dartmoor, on the far side of Devon. In his maplesss world, Leland had been unable to place the rivers and moors of the deep interior. On the coast, it was a different matter. Here, his description of the Taw was far more accurate.

In Barnstaple, the rush-hour still streams across the 'bridge of xvj. arches' Leland mentions. He was obsessed with bridges. To a Tudor traveller, a bridge was a measure of a district's viability. Fords and ferries were inconvenient, hazardous, and a hindrance to trade. As emphatically as the printed page and brass astrolabes, stone bridges were emblems of the future.

With all the care of a government inspector, Leland recorded each bridge that he came across, noting the number of its arches, whether they were of stone or timber, and any associated tales. In Barnstaple, he learns that the causeway across the salt marsh at the northern end of the bridge had been financed by a London merchant called Stawford, who had watched a woman from the nearby village of Pilton drown after she had been caught on the marsh by the rising tide. Although she had cried out for help, no-one had been courageous enough to brave the waters. Appalled by her fate, Stawford had given the prior of Barnstaple funds to construct a causeway and a pair of bridges to span the river Yeo, which ran across the marsh into the Taw. The bridge at Bideford, seven miles to the south-west, has a tale, too. Here, Leland is told that its construction ('xxiiij. arches and a chapelle of our Lady at the farther ende') had been inspired by a priest's vision. He also learned that a local guild provided a roster of men to keep the bridge clean of dung and refuse.

Both Barnstaple and Bideford lie on the huge, bifurcated estuary of the Taw and Torridge, at the innermost point of an enormous bay terminated by the frightful capes of Morte Point and Hartland Point. In Leland's day, the Taw / Torridge estuary was the largest and most important haven between Bristol and Land's End, and he devotes considerable effort into creating a word-map of its features. Beside their notable bridges, Barnstaple and Bideford were admired by Leland for their stone-built houses. Bideford had a fine parish church and a pleasant street lined with blacksmiths, chandleries and shipbuilders; 'a praty quik streat of smithes and other occupiers for ship crafte'.

A stone's throw from the spot where the woman from Pilton drowned, I launched a canoe into the ebbing tide of the Taw, and set off to explore the estuary. Leland's summary of the Taw's geography is brief: 'From Berstaple to the very haven mouth a v. miles: and the very mouth of it is no large thing, and a litle without is a barre.' In a different part of the *Itinerary*, he adds: 'The haven entery is barrid with sande, and the enterie into it is daungerus.' Reassuringly, he notes that the tide at Barnstaple is relatively placid – 'no very mayne streame at the ebbe'. He didn't warn me about the wind, though. Snatched like a leaf by a gust, the canoe spun around and scooted away from the quayside so violently that the swell on the river nearly turned the thing upside down.

Tracing an old itinerary gives a unique sense of purpose to a modern journey. Led by an invisible, talkative guide, you find yourself gazing at landforms and places you'd normally miss. Leaving Barnstaple more-or-less upright, the canoe yawed and bobbed past the mouth of the Yeo and beneath the scaffolded towers of a new bridge being built to carry Barnstaple's long-awaited western bypass over the Taw. Leland would not have believed his eyes. Two hundred feet above the water, tiny figures in hard hats and high-vis coats performed indecipherable tasks above the abyss. Beyond an industrial estate, a spit of salt marsh ran out to Penhill Point. In Leland's day this stretch of water would have been busy with trading ships, barges and fishing vessels. On this wintry morning, mine was the only boat in sight. The Taw has become another of Britain's secret wetlands: a discreet backwater for the Royal Marines; a serene interlude for hikers on the South West Coast path and cyclists on the Tarka Trail; a sanctuary for naturists and the rare Amber Sandbowl Snail. Travel by road from Bideford to Barnstaple and Braunton and your views of the estuary are limited to blurred glimpses of flat water; take to a boat and the Taw becomes a singular inland sea, rippling with enchantment.

Leland reckoned it was five 'Tudor' miles from Barnstaple to the bar at the 'very haven mouth'. After six (modern) miles I reached the widest part of the estuary, where the Torridge empties into the Taw. Out in the stream, I felt very small indeed. From here to the mouth of the estuary, the north shore is fringed with the largest sand-dune system in the UK; ochre waves running towards the horizon.

Ramming the canoe onto the sand at Crow Point, I refuelled with a quick sandwich taken beneath a windbreak of whispering marram grass, and then began the long tramp north-westwards, towards Leland's 'barre'.

Leland was as obsessive about sand bars as he was about bridges. Shoved across estuary mouths by enormous tidal forces, sand bars were the terror of Tudor shipping. At low tide, they would often be exposed, but at high water, when a ship had to break into – or out of – an estuary, they lurked beneath the surface, waiting to snag unwary keels. Wedged onto the sand, a sailing ship would quickly broach, then break her back. In recording the presence of estuarine bars, Leland had identified one of the most feared impediments to coastal trade. Not only had sand bars a habit of moving, but most were uncharted. The navigational charts circulating in Tudor Britain were one-off manuscripts based on hearsay and observation; measured surveys were still two centuries away. A mile or so along the sand, I came to Airy Point, and a range of enormous dunes. With binoculars, I could clearly see Leland's sand bar: a ferocious wall of tossing waves blocking the entrance to the estuary.

*

From Barnstaple, Leland continued south-westwards, towards the River Tamar. Few counties can boast such an emphatic geographical boundary, for the Tamar – as Leland points out – 'almost from the hed of it to the mouth devideth Devonshir and Cornewaule'. Extend the Tamar another three miles, and Cornwall would become an island.

In crossing the Tamar, Leland was straying into a foreign country. Cornwall was the least accessible county in the realm, and – as Richard Carew pointed out in 1602 – regarded by many of its inhabitants as 'a demi-island in an island'. In the early 1500s, the language of Cornish was still spoken in western Cornwall, and the county had long enjoyed its own form of self-government, through the 'Stanneries'. Agriculturally, Cornwall was regarded by outsiders as 'sterile and without fecunditee', but its mineral resources and ports were known the length and breadth of Europe.

For centuries, Cornwall had been the continent's chief supplier of tin, and since the Bronze Age, its havens had been bolt-holes for coastal traders.

To make matters even more daunting for a man with a King's commission, the Cornish were notorious rebels. Back in 1497, they had marched on London, where 15,000 of them were routed at Blackheath. Opposed to rule from London, and reluctant to adopt Protestantism, the Cornish were a rock in the Royal slipper. A few years after Leland's visit, their views on the new Book of Common Prayer were put to the King: 'We,' they had written in a letter to the monarch, 'the Cornyshe men, whereof certain of us understande no Englyshe, utterly refuse thys newe Service.' Leland seems to have been briefed to pay particular attention to Cornwall, for his description of the county is one of the most comprehensive in the entire *Itinerary*.

The gateway to the county lay a ten-minute ride beyond the Tamar. Today, the town of Launceston is so out of favour with modern travellers that it doesn't even merit a mention in the Lonely Planet guide to England. The *Blue Guide* is slightly more forthcoming, conceding that this one-time capital of Cornwall is 'a pleasant town once known as Dunheved' ('hill-head'). There are actually two hills, one of which is crowned by the cylindrical keep of the castle. Gazing at its formidable battlements, Leland concluded that it was 'the strongest, but not the biggist, that ever I saw in any auncient worke in Englande'.

Recalcitrant Cornwall is hidden from readers of Leland's notes. Methodically, he records the size of the bridges, the agriculture, the location of tin mines, ports and markets. The Cornish gentry are logged in their various granite piles, but the Cornish themselves are invisible. Asides about the landscape allude to the difficulties of eking a living from such a barren, windswept landscape. Beyond Launceston, Leland rides across miles of 'morisch and hilly ground' where the 'great scarsite of wod' forces the inhabitants to use gorse and heather as fuel. Places treasured today for their quintessential Cornish beauty are revolting and dilapidated. Leland's Padstow is an 'onclenly kept' Hideous-on-Sea, and Boscastle – another modern

Cornish showpiece – is 'a very filthy toun and il kept'. Repeatedly, Leland comes across reminders of faded glory. Bossiney has slipped from being 'a bygge thing for a fischar toun', blessed with 'great privileges' to a sad relic where 'a man may se there the ruines of a gret numbre of houses'. Tintagel – like Launceston – amazes Leland for its 'mervelus strong and notable forteres' and its 'inexpugnable' location on a 'high terrible cragge environid with the se'. But, like Launceston, most of Tintagel's structures 'be sore wether beten and yn ruine'. In this land of tottering masonry, Leland stumbled across the site of King Arthur's final stand. On the banks of the River Camel, he claims to have found Arthur's 'last feld', and by way of proof, he recounts that locals have ploughed up bones and horse harnesses. This is the end of the Arthurian trail which had begun for Leland at South Cadbury. Leland's discoveries neatly bracketed the West Country between Camelot and the site of the last battle. Here was Henry VIII's evidence that Cornwall was integral to his kingdom.

The Cornwall of John Leland is a place of physical decay, worn by the ravages of weather and time, and visited by inexplicable natural forces. By the time Leland travelled this way, the 'Little Ice Age' had gripped Britain for the best part of 200 years. Professor Brian Fagan has characterised the era as a 'climatic seesaw that swung constantly backwards and forwards, in volatile and sometimes disastrous shifts', which could bring 'arctic winters, blazing summers, serious droughts, torrential rain years, often bountiful harvests, and long periods of mild winters and warm summers'. These cycles of extreme cold or excessive rainfall could last from one year to a decade. British weather was utterly unreliable: 'The pendulum of climate change,' observes Fagan, 'rarely paused for more than a generation.'

It was during one or more of these violently erratic spells, that much of Tudor Cornwall got wrecked. Repeatedly, Leland comes across scenes of environmental havoc – usually caused by sand. Sand seems to have been strangling Cornwall's livelihood. Over twenty miles of the north coast, all the way from St Ives to Crantock, had been 'sore plagued ... with sandes' to the extent that 'no notable thing on the shore for so farre' could be found. At the mouth of the Hayle river on St Ives Bay, an entire castle has been 'drounid with sand'. In St Ives itself, most of the houses were 'sore oppressid or overcoverid with sandes that the stormy windes and rages castith up there'. The pier at St Ives had become 'sore chokid with sande'. Apparently, this 'calamitie' had been a problem in the area for over twenty years.

On Cornwall's other, southern coast, the trading town of Helston was also a hostage to shifting sands. South-easterly storms had a habit of pushing sand across the mouth of the estuary, creating a dam, behind which a huge inland lake would develop. Each time this happened, Helston's water-mills ceased to function and towns-people would have to dig through the sand bar to release the water and restore power to the mills.

The tin workings also contributed substantially to the difficulties of Cornwall's coastal communities. St Erth, a mile up the Hayle, had been throttled of trade after sand washed down from tin workings blocked the harbour, preventing 'good talle shippes' from berthing. A similar problem had occurred at Lostwithiel, where sand from tin workings had flowed down the Fowey from Bodmin Moor, and choked the bridge. Up at the headwaters of the Fowey, it's still possible to see the scars of tin 'streaming': parallel dykes over a hundred metres long, pooled with floodwater and flanked by marsh grass. In Leland's day this shallow valley would have been a teeming open-cast mine.

Intriguingly, Leland includes in his observations of landscape upheaval, a couple of references to major changes in sea level. Between Penzance and Mousehole, he finds that 'much land' has been 'devourid of the sea'. And in Mount's Bay, he records that 'betwyxt the Mont and Pensants be fownd neere the lowe water marke rootes of trees yn dyvers places, as a token of the grownde wasted'.

By 'wasted', Leland meant eroded. Somewhere in Mount's Bay was what appeared to be a submerged forest. This was not the only time he stumbled across ancient forests. Near Manchester, the guide he hired to lead him across Chat Moss told him that the roots of fir trees could be found in the peat. And in Suffolk he was told of a large forest which had been engulfed by the sea at Dunwich.

Frustratingly, the passage describing the Mount's Bay forest is followed by a marginal note, which is partly torn: 'Ther be found from the inward part of the … yvers … re stones … wes and … ois v. miles … the se.'

Ask around Penzance, however, and people do speak of tree roots being seen out in the Bay. With four divers, I spent a day aboard the 40-foot dive-catamaran *Pamela P*. Several dives failed to produce any sightings of ancient timber, although one of the divers did report that he had seen cavities in the sand filled with fine, peaty silt – evidence perhaps that we were searching in the right area. That evening, as I was walking away from *Pamela P*, along the harbour wall on St Michael's Mount, I was met by one of the island's staff. He was carrying a plastic carrier bag containing something angular and bulky. 'Thought you might be interested in seeing this…' he said, smiling. It was a large, twisted tree root. He had found it several years earlier, while walking on the beach near Penzance. 'They get washed clear in the storms,' he explained. 'Then another storm comes along and covers them with sand again. I haven't seen them for ages.'

*

Leland appears to have extended his travels to the very end of England, for he provides a detailed description of Penwith, the 'toe' of Cornwall which protrudes westwards from Penzance. The coast down here, he writes, is 'withowt havyn or creke, savyng yn dyver places ther remayne capstaynes lyke engins as shyppes doth way ther ancres by, wherwith they draw ther bootes up to dry land, and fisch but yn fayr wether'. So I went looking for winches in the form of ships' capstans.

The coast path west from Mousehole runs like a rocky belvedere for mile after mile above the broken edge of the Atlantic. Every rock and chasm seems to bear a tale that has been encoded on the Ordnance Survey map: Merlyn Rock, Point Spaniard, Zawn Organ, Little Heaver … Coffin Rock. About halfway to Land's End, the path ducks into the little cove of Penberth, where a concrete slip has been laid across the boulders so that boats can be launched. And there, beyond the slip, I came across a gigantic capstan. Mounted in a walled enclosure of huge rocks, it had once hauled fishing boats out of the water, exactly as Leland described. Close by, two men were chatting beside a pair of beached fishing boats. Teddy and Matt had just returned from an abortive expedition to catch bass off Land's End. The swell had been too dangerous, and they'd been forced back to Penberth with empty boats. They specialised in 'handlining', a slow, difficult, unpredictable method of fishing which harks back to an age before trawling. Here were the very fishermen Leland had talked about, men who fished 'but yn fayr wether'.

Pressing on along the coast path towards Land's End, I wondered whether the scholar from St Paul's had taken the same path during his never-ending tour. His was a journey with no destination. Beyond the major bridges, there were smaller bridges to list, and innumerable fords; after the big rivers, there were streams, and then streamlets. His notes are scattered with reminders to himself to go back and investigate the blanks on the map he could never complete.

I'd been heading in a general kind of way for Cape Cornwall, the promontory Leland mistakenly identified as being the westernmost point of Cornwall. It is one of only two places in Britain which merits the prefix 'Cape', and it's worthy of its name: a granite spear thrust into the shipping lane between the Scillies and Cornwall. But when I reached the Cape, and leant into the gale tasting salt on my lips, I knew that I'd been following a rarely glimpsed wraith. He left his mark just once, in the artillery fort he'd seen being built at St Mawes. Chiselled into the stonework are a number of short Latin poems written by Leland for his King. One of them reads:

SEMPER VIVET ANIMA REGIS
HENRICI OCTAVI QUI ANNO 34 SUI
REGNI HOC FECIT FIERI

May the spirit of King Henry VIII,
who had this castle built in the 34th year
of his reign, live forever

The fort was completed in 1543, the year after Leland left the West Country. He travelled on until 1545, by which time he had probably visited most – if not all – of the counties in England and Wales. By now the kingdom – and the King – were in awful shape. Famine had hit the population in 1545, and war with the French was crippling the country's fragile economy. Henry himself was crippled with leg ulcers, hugely overweight and ailing disgustingly. At the end of that year, Leland penned his *New Year's Gift* to the King, in which he set out his plans to produce a masterwork of improbable scale: a written topography of Britain which could be converted into the great map, a biographical dictionary of British writers, a history of England and Wales, books about the offshore islands, and more books on the British nobility. It was all a fantasy, quite beyond Leland's ability to complete, and too late for his King to see.

Henry VIII died on 28 January 1547. Some time during the following weeks, John Leland was struck by a severe mental breakdown. Although he lived for a further five years, he failed to resume work on his promised books and map. He left behind his list of every significant place in England and Wales; a list thousands of miles long, and spatially indecipherable. Had he been born fifty years later, he'd have realised that he needed to travel in the company of a surveyor, who would measure the distances between places and plot them onto a map. But surveying and mathematical mapmaking had yet to cross the Channel to England. It would not be until 1579 that the first detailed county survey of England and Wales would be published by an obscure surveyor from Yorkshire called Christopher Saxton. But the fieldwork Leland had promised his King remains one of the greatest treasures of the sixteenth century.

CELIA
FIENNES
1698

On horseback through England

Celia Fiennes' 'Great Journey to Newcastle and to Cornwall', 1698

*E*ngland's most remarkable woman traveller took to the road *at the end of the 1600s, a bare eighty years after the death of Queen Elizabeth I. At the time, Britain was being chilled by what is now known as the 'Little Ice Age'. Winters were longer and more savage than they are now, and the travelling season was correspondingly shorter and more temperamental.*

Eclectic, and crackling with brusque asides, the highly personalised travel journal of Celia Fiennes is regarded as the first comprehensive overview of England to follow the late sixteenth-century Britannia *of William Camden. It now appears that she was also the first recorded person to have travelled through every English county. The purpose of this epic undertaking was to excite her audience with England; to 'cure the evil itch of over-valueing foreign parts'.*

*

Crossing the River Esk on horseback finally convinced me that I was out of my depth. Celia Fiennes had ridden this way in 1698, fording the estuary with the assistance of a local guide. The estuary feeds into the Solway Firth, the enormous gulf which separates England from Scotland on the east coast. The crossing, she noted, 'is very broad and hazardous', with patches of quicksand exposed at low tide. Fortunately, I had an experienced guide in Penelope Mounsey-Heysham, whose home borders the estuary. Astride one of Penelope's race horses, I rode with her across the salt marshes, learning of the bones she had broken in riding accidents, and of the chances of being caught by quicksand, or swept out to sea if the tide misbehaved. 'Just follow me,' she repeated. 'The dogs will go in front, and if there are holes in the river, they'll find them first.' On our second attempt, we did find a safe crossing point. Mid-stream, with the tide lapping the horses' bellies and my riding boots filling with water, I was struck with two revelations: firstly, that I was probably going to reach the far bank alive, and secondly, that I could not have completed Fiennes' journey of 1698 on a horse.

Celia Fiennes was born in June 1662 at Newton Toney, on the eastern edge of Salisbury Plain, near the rising of the River Bourne. Few places in southern England were quite as remote as this. Each side of the Bourne billowed gentle waves of empty downland. It was perfect horse-riding country. In this generous seclusion, Celia grew up in the fading aura of a once-powerful aristocratic family. Her grandfather, William Fiennes, the 8th Baron and 1st Viscount Saye and Sele, had been one of the English peers who had helped to undermine Charles I, while her father, Nathaniel, had fought against the Royalists during the recent Civil War. With the monarchy restored to power, Colonel Nathaniel Fiennes and his wife Frances had settled on the edge of the Plain and raised a family. Their first three daughters all died in infancy, but Cecilia (later to become Celia) survived, and so did Mary, born a year later. Of her relationship with her father, Celia Fiennes provides just one memory; a story he told her of a pre-war journey across the Alps, 'where the clouds drive all about and as it were below them, which descends lower into mists then into raines, and soe tho' on the top it hold snow and haile falling on the passengers which at length the lower they go comes into raine and so into sun-shine at the foote of those valleys fruitful the sunshine and singing of birds'. To the genetically foot-loose, there are few images more alluring than sudden transitions between differing worlds.

The Colonel died when Celia was seven, and from that point on, her immediate company was largely female. Frances Fiennes steeped her girls in Protestant dissent, appointing a Nonconformist as her private chaplain, and holding illicit conventicles in her house. She was eventually fined for this in 1671. No record of Celia's education has survived, but it was normal at the time for well-bred daughters to have been taught to read and write at home, often with the aid of private tutors. Her familiarity with the homes of various relations strewn about England also suggests that she may have been sent away – like many of her kind – to accumulate knowledge in suitable households. Later, Fiennes opened the window on the limitations of country-house life. While men could hold (or bore witless, as Fiennes implies) an audience with tales from their latest continental Grand Tour, women had less exotic material to occupy their minds. If women could travel too, muses Fiennes, it 'would spare them the uneasye thoughts how to pass away tedious dayes, and tyme would not be a burthen when not at a card or dice table, and the fashions and manners or foreign parts less minded or desired'. We catch a momentary glimpse of Celia, perhaps as a teenager, when she writes of the downs around Newton Toney being 'a fine Champion Country pleasant for all sports – Rideing, Hunting, Courseing, Setting and Shooteing'. It is still lovely country, studded with ancient tumuli and carpeted in shivering grass.

In winter, Salisbury Plain could turn into Siberia. It's difficult to imagine, in these days of an overheating earth, just how bitter the winters would have been. As a girl, Celia would have been used to snow lying on the ground for twenty to thirty days each winter, an unthinkable hardship in the days of Gerald of Wales. Since then, the growing season had shrunk by around a month. Surrounded by high ground, Newton Toney would have been cut off from the outside world for considerable spells. The English climate had begun its latest phase of misbehaviour in the 1590s, and with various short-term fluctuations, the weather of the seventeenth century had been the coldest that Europe had experienced for 700 years. And the very coldest period of that chilly century began to bite in the 1680s, as Celia Fiennes approached eighteen. The Fiennes family were used to winters being snowy, restrictive, and potentially dangerous.

There was also a risk from highwaymen. In the aftermath of the Civil War, highway robbery had become an alternative source of income for those who had derived a livelihood from unsettled times. A century earlier, Camden had warned his readers that the Plain was 'but thinly inhabited, and infamous heretofore for frequent robberies'. While Celia Fiennes was growing up at Newton Toney, the Plain was being stalked by at least two notorious highwaymen:

William Davis, the 'Golden' farmer, who once had the nerve to rob the wife of General George Monck, and a mysterious, well-born gentleman, who was thought by some to be the son of Sir Walter Biss of Bishopstrow, a village over on the west side of the Plain. Biss was Wiltshire's own Robin Hood, popularised for robbing the rich to favour the poor. Davis was eventually hanged at Tyburn in 1689, while Biss was hanged at Salisbury in 1695.

Isolated on her Wessex prairie, Celia Fiennes grew up with far horizons. Visiting a city, her relations or a medicinal spa was an adventurous expedition. Travel excited her, and so did England. A horse's saddle was a slow-moving, extra-sensory viewpoint. She glided through the sounds and smells of town and country, over-hearing conversation, peering over hedgerows. Intuition was her only navigational aid. There was nothing dull about seventeenth-century travel. Roads varied from belly-deep sloughs to ringing pitch. Villages were rural business centres, with cobblers, tanners, brewers, bakers, mills and inns. England had been enjoying a commercial boom since Celia's childhood. Market towns were stuffed with produce, and innovative industries were springing up across the land. The landscape was racing through one of its periodic step-changes, and Fiennes was mesmerised.

Her first recorded ride was undertaken no later than 1682, and over the next thirty years she covered thousands of miles on journeys which ranged in duration from a few days to many weeks. Jotting notes as she travelled, she eventually compiled a fair copy of the experiences and observations that she had amassed on her seventeen most notable journeys. Of these, the longest, and most remarkable, was her last major ride, in 1698. But to understand the significance of that journey, we have to join her at around the age of twenty, still living at Newton Toney with her mother and sister. 'The Account,' she begins, 'off severall Journeys into severall parts of England with many Remarkes…'

*

She began at the spiritual centre of the Plain. It was a frequent gripe at the time that England's most spectacular cathedral should rise from such squalid streets. Water ran down the centre of Salisbury's thoroughfares, and this – according to Daniel Defoe – kept the streets 'dirty, full of wet and filth, and weeds'. Fiennes also found the streets 'not so clean or so easy to pass in', but, like Defoe, she was spellbound by the slender pinnacle which rose to touch the sky above the town's decrepit timber gables. Salisbury's spire had been raised in the early 1300s, and was the only one of its kind. Durham, Lincoln and Old St Paul's had all been built in timber and lead. Salisbury's spire was stone; 6,300 tons of it, quarried from the village of Chilmark, twelve miles to the west on the edge of the Plain. To Fiennes, the cathedral stood in spite of Man. Bishop Richard Poore's 449-foot long building 'lyes low in a watry meadow', she observes, balanced on 'foundations … in the water made of faggots and timber'. Above the swamp rises a miracle in creamy, fine-grained, oolitic limestone. Craning her head back, Fiennes searches for words as she describes the spire as being 'so high it appeares to us below as sharpe as a Dagger yet is in the compass on the top as bigg as a carte wheele … all stone and carved finely with spires and arches'. Stone was the future; timber the past. The soaring, octagonal Chapter House is miraculously supported, notes Fiennes, 'by one small stone Pillar in the middle'. Chiselled for eternity, the cathedral's stonework is a masterclass in materials and craftsmanship. Before she leaves, Fiennes lists the cathedral's effigies, monuments and paintings, in a roll-call of lords and ladies, a duke, a doctor and a judge. By the time she rides out of this emblematic Christian city, we are left in no doubt that the future of England will be wrought by every class, from nobleman to gentleman, merchant to artisan.

To Fiennes, Salisbury's spire is the centre of a compass, the hub of a wheel, from which all roads radiate. Her first three journeys, through her 'home' counties of Wiltshire, Dorset and Somerset, are packed with the thrills of discovery. She writes with an intimate, first-hand intensity, as if she has travelled halfway around the globe to explore a new and exotic land. On the edge of the Plain, Devizes is 'a very rich tradeing place for the clothing trade', and Warminster has 'Coale which is allmost as good as the sea-coale from New-Castle'. At Wilton, she discovers an earthly paradise:

The Gardens are very fine, with many gravel walkes with grass squaires set with fine brass and stone statues, with fish ponds and basons with figures in the middle spouting out water, dwarfe trees of all sorts and a fine flower garden, much wall fruite: the river runns through the garden that easeily conveys by pipes water to all parts. Grottoe is at the end of the garden just the middle off the house, its garnished with many fine figures of the Goddesses, and about 2 yards off the doore is severall pipes in a line that with a sluce spoutts water up to wett the Strangers; in the middle roome is a round table, a large pipe in the midst, on which they put a crown or gun or a branch, and so it spouts the water through the carvings and poynts all round the roome at the Artists pleasure to wet the Company; there are figures at each corner of the roome that can weep water on the beholders, and by a straight pipe on the table they force up the water into the hollow carving of the rooff like a crown or coronet to appearance, but is hollow within to retaine the water forced into it in great quantetyes, that disperses in the hollow cavity over the roome and descends in a shower of raine all about the roome; on each side is two little roomes which by the turning their wires the water runnes in the rockes you see and hear it, and also it is so contrived in one room that it makes the melody of Nightingerlls and all sorts of birds which engaged the curiosity of the Strangers to go in to see, but at the entrance off each room, is a line of pipes that appear not till by a sluce moved it washes the spectators, designed for diversion.

Fiennes' lines giggle with delight. Water at its most lucid and amusing would always lift her spirits. Wilton House was new. A triumph of Renaissance proportion and style, it had been rebuilt thirty years earlier by the fourth Earl of Pembroke to designs overseen by John Webb, a brilliant protégé of Inigo Jones.

On the south coast, Fiennes found herself equally transported by an industrial process. Taking a sailing boat out into Poole Harbour, she landed on Brownsea Island to investigate the production of copperas, or hydrated ferrous sulphate, a green-coloured compound used for dyeing, tanning and ink manufacture:

...the stones being found about the Isle in the shore in great quantetyes, there is only one house there which is the Governours, besides little fishermens houses, they being all taken up about the Copperice workes; they gather the stones and place them on ground raised like the beds in gardens, rows one above the other, and are all shelving so that the raine disolves the stones and it draines down into trenches and pipes made to receive and convey it to the house; that is fitted with iron panns foursquare and of a pretty depth at least 12 yards over, they place iron spikes in the panns full of branches and so as the liquor boyles to a candy it hangs on those branches: I saw some taken up it look't like a vast bunch of grapes...

A cathedral, copperas and water-gardens were the stirring, opening chords of her great work. Episodically, her ingenious itinerary would reveal 'the nature of Land, the Genius of the Inhabitants'. And her purpose? Well, 'to promote and improve Manufacture and Trade suitable to each and encourage all projects tending thereto'. But in parallel with her mission to explore all that was new and worthy in her land, Fiennes had a recurring private quest. In the journal's introduction, she informs her readers that her travels 'were begun to regain [her] health by variety and change of aire and exercise'. Possibly suffering from the effects of an over-rich diet, Fiennes' attempts to sample new medicinal remedies led her further and further from home, and exposed her to situations alien to women of her breeding. On her second recorded journey, she tried out a new healing well in Somerset. Forced to spend the night in Castle Cary, she complained that there was 'no good accomodation for people of fashion', and that the locals were 'a clounish rude people'. In this hellish backwater, she struck off across the fields, for two muddy miles, to a small, stone-lined cavity in the ground, which bubbled with a strong upwelling of water. Since its discovery a decade earlier by a local minister, the saline waters at Alford had become known throughout the region for their extraordinary ability to relieve constipation. Within three years of its discovery, the well was drawing flocks of customers. The queues were infamous. By 1676, its waters were being bottled and sold throughout the West

Country. Alford's spectacular popularity dried up after rumours spread that the well was killing rather than curing; a Dr Pierce of Bath later recorded that indiscriminate consumption had led to patients 'dying almost on the spot'. Arriving some ten or so years after its discovery, Fiennes approached the well with understandable caution. Peering into the clear water, she noted that the bed of the well was composed of 'a sort of blewish Clay or Marle'. She does not record the taste (to an earlier visitor, it had been 'nauseous and bitter'), or how much she imbibed, but notes conclusively that 'it's a quick purger'. Clearly it had been a successful call.

The journey to Alford was immediately followed by a coach ride to Bath. Her description of the five baths is one of the longest in her journals, a reflection of her fascination with water treatments. Nothing seems to escape her eye, from the quality and temperature of the various waters to the construction of the bath houses and the procedures for maintaining decorum. Fiennes approves of the voluminous all-in-one canvas bathing suits used by 'the Ladyes'. In these, 'your shape is not seen', quite unlike those worn by the 'poorer sort that go in their own linning', which tends to 'cling close' in a most inappropriate fashion. Fiennes' account of her exit from one of the baths is an exercise in synchronised de-robing:

> …you still ascend severall more steps, and let your canvass drop of by degrees into the water, which your woman guides takes off and the meanetyme your maides flings a garment of flanell made like a nightgown with great sleeves over your head, and the guides take the taile and so pulls it on you just as you rise the steps, and your other garment drops off so you are wrapped up in the flannell and your nightgown on the top.

The Bath experience could not have been more removed from inhospitable, crude Alford. There are pleasant walks to be taken in King's Mead, the streets are clean and, as in London, there are chairs 'to carry the better sort of people'.

The opening tours through Wiltshire, Dorset and Somerset revealed an England of astonishing diversity, and set the agenda for the next ten years of increasingly adventurous travel. Every day, she harvested the changing forms of passing landscapes, and gleaned insights into the ingenuity and virtue of their populations. On the road to Alford we learn that the downland around Stonehenge is 'most champion and open, pleasant for recreations; its husbandry mostly corn and sheep, the downs though short grass the feed is sweet, produces the finest wooll and sweet meat though but small'. Somerset, however, is very different. Here, the land 'is very fruitfull for orchards, plenty of apples and peares', and yet Fiennes sees scope for improvement. The problem, she thinks, is that the orchard-owners are 'not curious in the planting the best sort of fruite'. This she continues, is a 'great pitty', given the excellent growing season and quantity of fruit the region can bear. Just as careless in their cider production, Somerset's farmers 'press all sorts of apples together'. A more selective attitude, concludes Fiennes, would allow Somerset to match the quality of Herefordshire cider. Already, the England of Celia Fiennes is revealing itself as a deeply inconsistent place. Roads vary from Lyme Regis' vertiginous ascents, strewn with 'large smooth pebbles that make the strange horses slip', to the immaculate 'well pitched' streets of Bath. Dishevelled, timbered Salisbury compares unfavourably with 'neate stone built' Bruton. Buried in this vivid, wilful travelogue is a hint of methodical intent. Each time she crosses a county boundary, it is logged in her journal. But it isn't until her final, 'Great Journey' of 1698, that the reason becomes apparent.

*

After the trip to Bath, Celia took two journeys with her mother into the heartland counties of southern England. Frances Fiennes was well into her sixties, and the itineraries bear an inescapable poignancy. The first of these two journeys took them back to the fortified manor house near Banbury in Oxfordshire that Frances had known as a younger woman. Here, her husband Nathaniel had grown up with his older brother James, and here, their father, the 1st Viscount Saye and Sele, 'Old Subtelty', had provided a secluded tower room for leading Parliamentarians to plot the downfall of their King. Today the house still floats upon its moat in magnificent defiance to the passing of time. In his wonderful revivalist guide, *England's Thousand Best Houses*, Simon Jenkins places Broughton alongside Wilton in the country's top twenty houses, but to Fiennes, its medieval core and centuries of accretions had produced an untidy outcome. Broughton, she notes, is 'an old house moted round and a parke and gardens, but are much left to decay and ruine'. She devotes far more space and enthusiasm to nearby Wroxton House, with its paintings of Queen Mary and Elizabeth, and its new rooms 'built all the new fashion way'.

The last journey Celia undertook with her mother occurred no later than the summer of 1691. Travelling east from Newton Toney to Nursted near Petersfield, they stayed with Frances' youngest sister Margaret, the last surviving member of her immediate family. Margaret and her husband Richard Holt occupied 'a neat new built house with brick and stone', and a garden with 'fine gravel walkes' and 'grass plotts'. From Nursted, they headed for Guildford ('a good town built with stone, the streets are broad'), and then looped around via London, Maidenhead and Cliveden House ('a fine building') to Reading. Here, Fiennes suddenly reveals that they have come to a place with a touching resonance for mother and daughter. 'Redding,' she tells us, 'which is a pretty large place, severall Churches, in one lyes buried one of my sisters that dyed.' It's a moment in the journal when this indefatigable traveller turns to face the reader with a reminder that every journey is guided to some extent by private forces. Ann was the third of Frances' daughters to die. She had been staying with her grandmother in 1675, when she caught smallpox. It's painful to speculate upon the scene, as the two women stood before Ann's 'monument of white marble'. The memorial can still be seen in the church. Of Frances' two surviving daughters, only Mary had married. Shortly after the journey to Reading, in December 1691 Frances Fiennes died.

*

Following her mother's death, Fiennes embraced travel with the passion that many reserve for marriage. She was twenty-nine. A long ride through Buckinghamshire, Oxfordshire, Berkshire, Hampshire,

Sussex ('much in blind dark lanes and up and down steepe hills') and Surrey, was followed by an even longer excursion westward to Herefordshire, and then a ride through the New Forest to the Isle of Wight. Returning through Portsmouth, she managed to be given a conducted tour of both the *Royal Charles* and *Royal James*; '...fine shipps', she notes, 'the Roomes spacious for length and breadth but not high'. By the end of 1696, she had visited over a dozen of England's southern counties.

Then, in spring 1697, Fiennes conceived her most ambitious expedition to date. She called it 'My Northern Journey', and it would take her two-thirds of the way to Scotland. Probably accompanied by her cousin's two daughters, Susanna and Mary Filmer, Fiennes headed first to Cambridge, which she methodically compares to Oxford. The clear winner, incidentally, is Cambridge: Trinity College 'is the finest yet not so large as Christchurch College in Oxford', the library in Cambridge 'farre exceeds that of Oxford', while King's College Chapel 'is the finest building I had heard off'. Fiennes climbed to the roof of the Chapel, from where she could see 'a vast Country round', including the towers of Ely Cathedral – one of the places she would tuck away for a future journey.

As the women continued northward, Fiennes ticked-off the county boundaries: Huntingdonshire, Rutlandshire, Lincolnshire… Nottinghamshire. No longer is Fiennes the twenty-something novice, peeking out from Wiltshire. Now, the journal is enriched with the armoury of comparison: just as Cambridge was weighed against Oxford, Huntingdonshire is described as 'good land and fruitfull and much like Oxfordshire', and Rutlandshire 'seemes more woody and inclosed than some others'. Burghley House, 'eminent for its Curiosity', has the finest situation 'I ever saw', while Nottingham 'is the neatest town I have seen'. Nottingham would become Fiennes' benchmark town. With its lofty, yet 'delicate large', stone-built houses, well-surfaced streets, broad market place, mile-long, collonnaded 'Pyaza' and oustanding ale, Nottingham was a symbol of urban aspiration, and worthy of comparison to London. Suddenly we are in the company of a veteran traveller; a woman who is amassing more first-hand views than Camden himself.

Where the M1 flings motorists northward at fifteen times the speed of a horse, Fiennes and her companions now found themselves meandering through the glades of Sherwood Forest and then joining 'a very heavy sandy way' out of Worksop. 'Musick,' she proclaims, 'wellcom'd us into Yorkshire.' It was Sunday, and the sound of bells carried across the lowlands of the Don.

The largest of the English counties by far, Yorkshire had a magnitude and novelty that made it appear especially foreign. An addicted browser of market stalls, Fiennes rushed from market to market with all the excitement of a child in a chocolate shop. At Ripon, she marvelled at the price of veal and beef. Near Londesborough, she found a fresh salmon 'above 3 quarters of a yard long'. It was selling for only eighteen pence. In Beverley, she was offered 'a large Codffish for a shilling and a good Pearch very cheape'. Three centuries ago, the rivers and seas of the north-east were teeming with delicacies. 'Crabbs,' she exclaims, 'bigger than my two hands, pence apiece, which would have cost 6 pence if not a shilling in London, and they were very sweete.' A Londoner could live well in Yorkshire.

While the city of York had a disappointingly 'meane appearance' (Nottingham, she goads, 'is so farre before it'), the county's waters were in a class of their own. She rode over to Scarborough to sample the mineral waters which seeped from the sands; and at Copgrove she found a bathing well as beneficial as those at Bath. Here, at last, she discovered a cure for her headaches:

> I cannot but think it is a very good Spring, being remarkably cold, and just at the head of the Spring so its fresh which must needs be very strengthning, it shutts up the pores of the body immeadiately so fortifyes from cold, you cannot bear the coldness of it above 2 or 3 minutes and then you come out and walke round the pavement and then in againe, and so 3 or 4 or 6 or 7 as many tymes as you please... I dipp'd my head quite over every tyme I went in and found it eased a great pain I used to have in my head.

In Harrogate, she found four different mineral springs within two miles. It was one of these which extracted from Fiennes her most vivid description of hydrotherapy:

...the Sulpher or Stincking spaw, not improperly term'd for the Smell being so very strong and offensive that I could not force my horse near the Well, there are two Wells together with basons in them that the Spring rises up in, which is furr'd with a White Scumm... it has an additionall offenciveness like carrion or a jakes... its a quick purger and very good for all Scurbutick humours; some persons drink a quart or two – I dranke a quart in a morning for two days and hold them to be a good sort of Purge if you can hold your breath so as to drinke them down...

'Jakes' being a lost word for 'privy', the reader is left reeling with admiration. I drank a small glass of it when visiting Harrogate's Royal Pump Room recently, and reeled into Valley Gardens with breath reeking of rotten eggs and drains. Apparently, it has the highest sulphur content of any mineral water in Europe.

Nearly two months after leaving London, Fiennes and her companions rode their horses southwards out of St Albans to join the route now taken by the M25 (clockwise). Near South Mimms motorway service station, they turned towards the celebrated spa of Barnet, and the capital. Fiennes however was not finished with travelling for the year. Before the summer was out, she was back on her horse for a five-day tour of Kent. It was during this ride that she came across both the finest river she had ever seen (the Medway), and a bridge (at Rochester) which she held to be 'the finest in England, nay its said to equal any in the world'.

That winter was one of the worst in living memory. In November 1697, London was hit by severe frosts, and then sleet and snow. With occasional thaws, the sub-zero conditions lasted for a desperate six months. Deep snow drifts covered England, and rivers froze. In early February, sea ice eight inches thick was reported off the Suffolk coast. As late as May 1698, heavy snow fell from Yorkshire to London. Even within the deep chill of the 'Little Ice Age', the spring of 1698 was the most retarded for forty-seven years.

While all outside was frozen, Fiennes was planning her final journey. It would be the longest and most adventurous of her rides, and it would take her through England's most extensive wetlands, its highest mountains, and its most feared moorlands. It would also take her to the greatest trading centre of the north, and to the two counties most distant from London. As it happened, none of these places could offer Fiennes the pleasures of the 'spaw'. It would be a hard ride.

Plotted on a map, her proposed route was shaped like an enormous, deformed figure-of-eight. On an epic scale, it touched upon the eastern, the northern, the western and southern limits of England. It was almost as if she was beating the bounds of her own nation. And yet this route had another, far grander, purpose. Her discreet intent had been concealed in a trail of clues throughout her journal:

'Nay the Ladies,' she had written in the journal's introduction, 'might have matter not unworthy their observation, some subject for conversation, within their own compass in each county to which they relate; and thence studdy how to be serviceable to their neighbours especially the poor among whome they dwell...'

It took me many years to make the connection between her reference to 'each county', and the methodical logging during her travels of each county-boundary. What finally clinched it was her references to Camden's *Britannia* – the only book to be repeatedly mentioned in her journals. William Camden's county-by-county guide to England, Wales, Scotland and Ireland was a gold-mine of historical, archaeological and geographical information. Within its encyclopaedic scope, readers could investigate matters as diverse as the wines of Gloucestershire, the origins of 'The Picts Wall', and the number of arches under Padstow's bridge. First published in Latin in 1586, *Britannia* had been translated into English by Philemon Holland in 1610. A new edition, heavily revised and updated by Bishop Gibson, had been published in 1695.

The preliminary pages of the 1695 *Britannia* include a section titled 'The General Heads of the Introduction, and Counties of England: A list of the tribes of Ancient Britain', and against them, the counties they occupied. At the time, there was some uncertainty about what exactly constituted a 'county', but Camden's definitive list totalled fifty-three, of which thirty-nine (plus a bishopric and some arsenals) lay in England. By the time Fiennes returned home from Kent in 1697, she had travelled through twenty-six of the counties on Camden's list. Fiennes was riding the pages of *Britannia*! The peculiar, contorted route she had devised for her final tour had been designed to connect, in a single ride, the remaining thirteen counties. These thirteen were grouped in three regions: East Anglia, the far north of England, and the West Country. In crossing the Tamar into Cornwall, she would become the first recorded woman to visit every one of England's thirty-nine counties. The enormous scope of this climactic ride was reflected in the title she wrote into her journal: 'My Great Journey,' she announced, 'to Newcastle and to Cornwall.'

*

Fiennes – like Defoe twenty years later – began her Great Journey with a loop through the counties of East Anglia. And like Defoe, she quickly discovered that she was riding through a region which had profited from the fertility of its soils and its proximity to London and the Continent. Arranged across the level cornlands were busy, heavily populated market towns and centres of local industry. The coast was rimmed with ports. But Fiennes didn't really enjoy East Anglia; it just wasn't very exciting. Where were the new, stone building styles of London and Nottingham? The mineral spas of Yorkshire? The natural wonders of Derbyshire? Elsewhere in England, she had already seen better cathedrals, longer bridges, wider rivers, and newer industries. And it all looked a bit of a mess. Colchester was still much 'ruinated' by the Civil War siege of 1648. Ipswich she found to be 'a little disregarded', blaming 'pride and sloth' for the town's failure to take full commercial advantage of its quayside. Why, she asks, are colliers of 300 tons showing up to deliver coal, then leaving with empty holds?

Riding between East Anglia's towns was not easy, either. Beyond Ipswich, she entered a vague, saturated land, where route-finding was difficult and the roads hazardous. Asking the way was almost futile; the locals, she complains, 'are able to give so bad a direction that passengers are at a loss what aime to take, they know scarce 3 mile from their home, and meete them where you will, enquire how farre to such a place, they mind not where they are then but tell you so farre which is the distance from their own houses to that place'.

Then there was the weather. The appalling winter of 1697–8 had been followed by heavy rains. And in the flatlands of East Anglia, floods took a long time to disperse. When Fiennes eventually reached the county boundary separating Suffolk from Norfolk, she found 'a low flatt ground all here about so that the least raines they are overflowed by the River and lye under water, as they did when I was there'. The road, she reported, 'lay under water which is very unsafe for strangers to pass, by reason of the holes and quick sands and loose bottom'.

Norwich was another East Anglian conundrum. Here, in the heart of the county of Norfolk, she found a 'vast place ... 6 miles in compass', with markets for every product under the sun, and no fewer than thirty-six churches. The textile industry employed men and women 'in spinning knitting weaveing dying scouring fulling or bleaching their stuffs'. The whole city 'lookes like what it is, a rich thriveing industrious place'. And yet Norwich was antique in its fabric. The medieval city walls are 'the best in repaire of any walled citty I know', but 'all their buildings are of an old form', constructed with timber, plaster and lathe, and 'none of brick except some few beyond the river which are built of some of the rich factors like London buildings'. An island in its own flood plain, Norwich seemed immune to modernity.

Getting out of Norfolk was almost as difficult as getting in. West of Norwich, the route to the Midlands was blocked by over 1,000 square miles of impassable Fenland. So Fiennes rode south to Bury St Edmunds and then followed the higher ground across to Newmarket. Her first sight of the Fens came as she made the barely perceptible descent from Chippenham House to the River Snail: 'I passed over a low ground on each side,' she writes, 'deffended by the fendiks which are deep ditches with draines.' The Fens, she observes, 'are full of water and mudd'. For much of the century, Britain's largest wetland had been subject to the largest drainage scheme ever attempted in the country. In one scheme alone, 100,000 acres were drained. Slashed by geometric dykes, Fenland was transformed into the nation's richest farmland. But as the water drained from the Fens, the peat shrank, and the fields subsided below the level of the surrounding rivers. By the late 1600s, nature was reinstating a wetland. Fiennes was amazed by the spectacle of such a vast, watery plain, with its arrow-straight dykes and rows of pollarded willows. It looks, she thought, 'very finely to see a flatt of many miles … but it must be ill to live there'.

The only way to reach Ely was by riding along a seasonal gravel causeway. In winter, it was often flooded, forcing travellers to take to boats. In summer it should have been open, but so much rain had fallen that sections were now completely covered with water, and Fiennes could not see the edge of the embankment. As she floundered towards beleaguered Ely, she came close to disaster. Needing to drink, Fiennes' horse splashed to the edge of the flooded causeway but suddenly found itself 'on the brinke' of a completely submerged dyke. For moments, Fiennes was close to taking a dangerous fall, in heavy clothing, into deep water. It was, she recalls, 'by a speciall providence' that she escaped the fate of so many Fenland travellers.

'Ely', she writes, 'the dirtyest place I ever saw'. The streets have 'not a bitt of pitching', and indeed the whole city is 'a perfect quagmire' and 'a harbour to breed and nest vermin in, of which there is plenty enough, so that tho' my chamber was near 20 stepps up I had froggs and slow-worms and snailes in my roome'.

Not only was this the most disgusting city she had ever seen, but the Minster ('a curious pile of building') offended her particular sensibilities. Ely, fumes Fiennes, 'has the most Popish remaines in its walls of any I have seen, there still remaines a Cross over the alter the Candlesticks are 3 quarters of a yard high massy silver gilt very heavy'.

To gain an aerial view of this decrepit island, Fiennes climbed the eighty or so steps to the Cathedral's octagonal lantern. Looking about her, she appeared to be floating on a vast inland sea. To the south, she could see Cambridge, 'and a great prospect of the country which by reason of the great rains just before laid under water, all the fenny grounds being overflow'd'. The only dry ground was the narrow bank of slightly higher land on which Ely was built. Here, the farmers could drive their cattle to safety during the wet season. Bleakly, she summed up Ely's subsistence economy: she'd found no evidence of any trading in the town, and concluded that 'their maine buissiness and dependance is on draining and fencing their grounds and breeding and graseing cattle.'

Fiennes identified two causes of Ely's woeful state. The first is the absentee Bishop, who 'does not care to stay long in this place not being for his health … it's a shame'. An episcopal presence might make Ely 'better ordered and the buildings and streetes put in a better condition'. The second is Ely's 'slothful' population. The land is so extraordinarily suited to cattle, she observes, that 'in case 6 or 7 wet yeares drown them all', one good year 'repaires their loss'. Why – with their 'vast allowance yearly' of 'at least 3000£' – do they not keep the banks in good repair? 'I wonder,' she asks, 'they have not perfectly runn off the water, and so barracadoed it … they are all a lazy sort of people and are afraid to do too much.' For Fiennes, there was no natural obstacle so great that it could not be overcome by money, machinery and motivation. In the Fens, she happened to come across a community who – for the time being – were losing the battle.

Neither was her escape from Ely without incident. Ten miles west of the city, she found the bridge over the Ouse under water. The road was submerged too, and because its bed was 'so full of holes and quick sands', she was forced to detour to a ferry and pay two pence per horse to cross the flood. For the first time, the phrase, 'I durst not venture' escaped from her pen.

Riding through Leicestershire, Fiennes reached the seat of her uncle Sir Charles Wolseley, where she stayed for six weeks, resting and exploring the neighbourhood. She was also steeling herself for the most difficult section of her itinerary: the journey to the northern limits of England. When she eventually left Wolseley's moated house by the Trent, she headed north-westwards to visit the mineral spa at Holywell in north Wales, and then struck northward for Lancaster and the mountains. She was further from London than she had ever been in the past. Following parts of Fiennes' route through Merseyside and then through Wigan and Warrington, I struggled to recognise her landscapes. Where Fiennes had trotted through fields and villages, I pedalled past chemical works and suburbs. So it was something of a relief when she turned towards the crenellated skyline of Westmorland. However, it wasn't the mountains that appealed to Fiennes.

At the King's Arms in Kendal, Fiennes had come across potted char. The fish was a fairly unusual speciality, even in the seventeenth century, and Fiennes – who reckoned it 'the best of any in the country' – asked the chef, Mrs Rowlandson, where the fish had been caught. She was told that the only place that char could be found was in the 'great standing water' of 'Wiandermer'. Ten miles of very narrow lanes led to Bowness and the shore of the lake. The char were out of season, but Fiennes was amazed by the sight of Windermere. This was the largest lake she had ever seen, and she gazed in wonder at the movements of its surface. 'This great water,' she writes, 'seemes to flow and wave about with the wind or in one motion but it does not ebb and flow like the sea with the tyde, neither does it run.' It was neither river nor lake, and she was mesmerised by its scale.

Further along the lake, water again caught her eye, and then her ear. 'From these great fells,' she writes, there are 'severall springs out of the rock that trickle down their sides, and as they meete with stones and rocks in the way when something obstructs their passage and so they come with more violence that gives a pleasing sound and murmering noise'. This is the same aquatic imagination which had woken to the sound of the water garden at Wilton.

To reach her next county, Cumberland, Fiennes had to cross the Kirkstone Pass, and, rather against her will, she had to engage for the first time with mountains. The crest of the pass, 1,489 feet above sea level, is approached from Windermere by a long, very steep climb known as 'The Struggle'. Forced to dismount, Fiennes took an hour to reach the top, and a further hour to descend the far side. It wasn't a pleasant experience: 'I was walled on both sides,' she recalls, 'by those inaccessible high rocky barren hills which hangs over ones head in some places and appear very terrible.' After a night in a Carlisle brothel, 'with a young giddy Landlady that could only dress fine and entertain the soldiers', Fiennes rode her horse through the quicksands of the Esk estuary so that she could put a toe into Scotland – just as she had with Wales.

From Scotland, Fiennes crossed into Northumberland, the county most distant from London. Ahead of her was a long, hard ride over the roof of the Pennines. Locals up here seemed to be even more misleading with their route directions than those in East Anglia. Troubled by the distances she was being given, Fiennes convinced herself that a 'mile' in Northumberland 'might be esteemed double the number in most of the countys in England'. The 'road' to Newcastle appears to have been little more than sets of hoof-tracks across the peaty hills; 'a sort of black moorish ground and so wet'. The pitched streets of Nottingham were but a distant dream. The high road to Newcastle was not only unsurfaced, but utterly waterlogged. 'I observ'd,' she writes, 'as my man rode up that sort of precipice or steep his horses heeles cast up water every step and their feete cut deepe in, even quite up to the top; such up and down hills and sort of boggy ground it was.'

With night drawing on, and the distance to shelter uncertain, Fiennes found a local guide to lead them around the 'ill places'. But the trials of the day were far from over. Eventually, they reached Haltwhistle, but the owner of the only inn refused to provide hay for the horses, and when Fiennes' servants went out and bought some, the innkeeper got so angry that he ejected Fiennes into the night. 'I was forced to take up in a poor cottage,' she writes, 'which was open to the thatch and no partition but hurdles plaister'd.' Despite the fact that her host brought out her best sheets 'which serv'd to secure my own sheetes from her dirty blankets', Fiennes could not sleep for the smoke of burning peat.

As is so often on journeys, a bad night was followed by a blissful day. At Haltwhistle, the riders had joined the River Tyne. On a sunlit July morning, they followed the river eastwards through Hexham and Corbridge, where they picked up a 'good hard gravelly way'. Fiennes reckoned it was the hottest day on her journey; below the river bluffs, cattle were cooling themselves in the shallows, and the road was busy with strange little carts drawn by combined teams of oxen and horses. All these carts were filled with coal. After a carbonaceous digression of typical thoroughness, Fiennes informs her readers that Tyne coal, by virtue of its small size, blackness and shine, is the best for burning. Coal is everywhere. The air she breathes 'smells strongly to strangers', and from a hill-top, the surrounding country appears 'full of coale pitts'. In these northern hills, Fiennes had come across the fabled source of heat; the place which kept southerners warm throughout interminable winters. Riding this road at around the same time, Defoe wondered where the people were who could consume so many 'mountains' of coal.

Entering Newcastle through Westgate, Fiennes found herself surrounded by the architectural furniture of a truly great city. Wherever she looked, she saw 'lofty and large' buildings, built mostly of brick or stone. The streets were 'broad and handsome, and very well pitch'd'. Repeatedly, she came upon fountains and 'fine Cunduits' feeding water into large stone cisterns 'for every bodyes use'. In these Tyneside water features were all the pleasures of Wilton. Down by the river, she marvelled at the arcaded Royal Exchange, with its stone pillars and huge, civic clock. In front of the building, the quayside was 'soe full of merchants walking to-an-againe' that it looked to Fiennes like an extension of the Exchange. The harbour was 'full of shipps'. Newcastle was her kind of shopping centre, too. Traders exhibited their goods by 'distinct trades, not selling many things in one shop as is the custom in most country towns'. And the markets were individualistic, too, with separate sites for selling corn, and hay. Another area, covering three or four streets, was 'like a faire for all sorts of produce'. It was a Saturday, market day, and Fiennes was able to witness Newcastle at its busiest and most diverse. Browsing the stalls, she came across linen, leather, woollens, 'soft sower things', poultry, cheese, and 'all sorts of stands for baubles'. She snooped on someone buying a quarter of a lamb for only 8 pence. It's a 'noble town', she concludes; 'it most resembles London of any place in England.'

But Newcastle was more than a teeming, wealthy emporium and

trading port. The slopes above the coal wharves revealed all the signatures of civilisation. Just west of the city walls, Fiennes came across a 'very pleasant' bowling green surrounded by gravel walks and a 'fine entertaineing house' – actually a tavern with a viewing balcony. On this blistering July day, she was also pleased by the shade provided by the two rows of trees (limes imported from Holland a decade or so earlier) lining the walks. Out here too was a delightful garden 'where Gentlemen and Ladyes walke in the evening'. On the far side of the city, she visited the Barber Surgeons Hall, with its pretty, walled garden filled with flowers and 'greenes in potts'. Inside the Hall, she inspected skeletons, and a stuffed man used for anatomy lectures. Next door, she paused to admire a row of brand-new, brick-built almshouses, which could boast '2 good roomes a piece' for nearly forty local freemen or their widows. In front of the sunny, south-facing almshouses was an 'open green' and a new water fountain. Today, the fountain is dry, and the Hospital of Holy Jesus has surrendered its serenity – and river views – to the neighbouring multi-storey carpark, underpass, flyover and East Coast mainline. Grimy, yet legible, the Latin inscription on the face of the almshouses recalls that charity was once the greatest civic virtue. Here, at the end of Hadrian's Wall, Fiennes had found the capital of the north.

*

As Fiennes made her way southward towards Leeds, she could congratulate herself on the success of her northern expedition. Since leaving Wolseley, she had visited seven new counties. She only had to visit another three – Shropshire, Devon and Cornwall – and she would have ticked all thirty-nine in Camden's *Britannia*. But a formidable barrier blocked her onward route.

In the seventeenth century there were only three major trans-Pennine routes. Fiennes' most direct means of reaching Shropshire and the West Country was to take the southernmost crossing, from Leeds to Manchester. It may have been direct, but it was also the most hazardous of the three, and notorious for snaring travellers. Between Leeds and Manchester, the Pennines were barely ten miles wide, but the road lurched up to a chilling 1,500 feet, crossed a featureless moor and then plummeted steeply down the exposed, western flank of the range. In his revolutionary new road atlas of 1675, the cartographer John Ogilby mapped the Leeds–Manchester road in great detail, showing roadside hamlets, river-crossings and mileages. Blackstone Edge is depicted as an Alpine range hurdled by a section of road which carries no buildings. Although she never mentions the atlas, Fiennes must have been familiar with Ogilby's *Britannia* – a title he cribbed from Camden. 'Blackstone Edge…' jotted Fiennes, 'noted all over England for a dismal high precipice and steep in the ascent and descent on either end.' In February 1698 – a matter of weeks before Fiennes headed north – the Yorkshire topographer and antiquarian Ralph Thoresby had been caught by the snows on Blackstone Edge, his horse had fallen, and his leg had been crushed. A few months before that, a travelling salesman had his horse shot by a highwayman. Even Daniel Defoe, whose great book *A Tour Through the Whole Island of Great Britain* set him up as the most celebrated traveller of his age, ran into difficulties on Blackstone Edge. With two companions and a pair of servants, he'd begun the ascent on a clear morning, but climbed into falling snow, and then a blizzard. Forced to dismount, they lost the track in the snowdrifts, strayed too close to 'a frightful precipice', and were buffeted by violent winds. Eventually, they battled through the snow to survive what had been a 'troublesome and dangerous' day. For modern readers, the most astonishing aspect of Defoe's account is that the blizzard which caught him on Blackstone Edge occurred in mid-August. The temperature drop which caused the Little Ice Age was just one degree Celsius, but it was enough to trigger extreme weather events.

Modern motorists, thrumming along the six-lane M62 two miles south of Blackstone Edge, hurdle the Pennine backbone in a few minutes of effortless travel. But for Fiennes, this would be the most alarming road she had ever encountered. The climbing began in earnest once she had crossed the pack-horse bridge at Ripponden. Initially, the weather was 'pretty faire', but, as she followed the V-shaped cleft of the Ryburn valley towards the dark moors, conditions deteriorated. Even today, this is a bleak place. Half a mile or so after two columns of pylons stride across the A58, the medieval pack-horse track can be seen cutting up a gully called Rag Sapling Clough. A few minutes up the Clough, the track suddenly steepens and loses itself in interminable peat swamps. It must have been around here that Fiennes noticed 'a sort of mist'. This was followed by 'small raine'. For over a mile, the track climbs up moorland which is completely exposed. There is not a building nor a tree to be seen. She began to worry about the 'very moorish ground all about', and was alarmed by the precarious nature of the 'very troublesome' causeway which carried the track across the bogs. More unnerving still was the mist, and the risk of losing her way. The spattering rain made her 'feare a wet day and that the aire would have been so thick to have quite lost me the sight of the Country'. Fear was not a familiar emotion for Fiennes.

At about 1,400 feet above sea level, the pack-horse track began to level. Off to her left, she would have seen the sombre cliff and tumbled rocks marking the high-point of Blackstone Edge. Beside her (although she doesn't mention it) she would certainly have noticed the Aiggin Stone, a medieval waymark to guide travellers over the moor. She does however record passing the massive cairn (a 'great heap raised up'), which is still there, and notes that it marks the county boundary separating Yorkshire and Lancashire. The passage which follows reads as a deliverance:

> ...the mist began to lessen, and as I descended on this side the fog more and more went off and a little raine fell, tho' at a little distance in our view the sun shone on the vale which indeed is of a large extent here, and the advantage of soe high a high[t] which is at least 2 mile up, discovers the grounds beneath as a fruitfull valley full of inclosures and cut hedges and trees.

The transition from barren, frightening heights to the lovely lowlands took Celia back to her girlhood, and the story her father had told of his own passage over the Alps. 'I could not but think,' she writes of her Pennine adventure, 'this carryed some resemblance tho' in little, yet a proportion to that.' Blackstone Edge was England's most emphatic watershed. This dreary pass separated east from west – and north from south.

Sunnier lands lay ahead, but Fiennes was mistaken if she thought that the dangers were over. Three days after crossing Blackstone Edge, she was riding through the rich cattle country of Cheshire when she ran into the kind of trouble that she must have been expecting for most of her travelling life. Earlier that day, she had passed through Northwich, where she'd spent some time examining the brine pits and learning of the recent discovery of rock-salt in the area. From there, she had taken the main route south across the Cheshire Plain, towards the prominent landmark of Beeston Castle, high upon its isolated sandstone crag.

At the crossroads below the castle, '2 fellows all on a suddain from the wood fell into the road...' Fiennes and her companions held their nerve, as the two men, 'truss'd up with great coates and as it were bundles about them which I believe was pistolls' began to intimidate them. For a while, the men shadowed the travellers, dropping back to mutter between themselves, then riding forward again. Fiennes must have asked their business, for she records that they 'did disown their knowledge of the way'. The men then attempted to isolate Fiennes from her companions, one of them riding in front of her and the other behind, jostling her horse in an effort to force it to one side. Fortunately, it was market day in Whitchurch, and the closer they drew to the town, the busier the road became. Frustrated, the troublemakers eventually lost patience, 'so at last they called each other off and soe left us and turned back'. Fiennes wraps up the incident in a characteristically cool fashion by observing that it had been the only time in her life that she 'had reason to suspect' that she had been 'engaged with some Highway men'.

And that wasn't the end of her trials. The roads in the borders were notoriously bad, and those of Herefordshire, some of the worst in the country. Campaigning here during the Civil War, fifty years earlier, the Earl of Leven had complained that Herefordshire's roads were so difficult to negotiate that his troops could only manage to march eight miles in one day. Rashly, Fiennes decided to take a long detour west from Worcester so that she could visit relations at Stretton Grandison, and see a new house at Stoke Edith. Again, the rains which had hit the country earlier in the year had made the roads – 'which are all lanes full of stones and up hills and down soe steep that with the raines the waters stood or else ran down the hills' – virtually impassable. 'This,' she concluded, 'is the worst way I ever went in Worcester or Herrifordshire.'

*

Late that summer, Celia Fiennes crossed her final county boundary. 'Here,' she records, 'I entred into Cornwall...' England's most western county was still as remote to a Londoner as it had been in John Leland's day. And like Leland, Fiennes found herself describing Cornwall as if it were a strange, unexplored land. Not for the first time, it was the food which quickly tickled her senses. Having searched unsuccessfully for 'West Country tarts' as she rode through Somerset and Devon, she discovered in Cornwall 'the most acceptable entertainment that could be made me ... apple pye with a custard all on the top'. With lipsmacking approval, she records how they 'scalde their creame and milk ... and so its a sort of clouted creame as we call it, with a little sugar, and soe put on the top of the apple pye'.

Travelling, however, was difficult. Ferries had to be used to cross long inlets of the sea, and the incredibly steep roads were either rocky, or filled with 'many holes and sloughs'. The shoes on her horses wore thin and fell off on the stony tracks, and good blacksmiths were hard to find. Alternately battered by rain, hail and strong winds, she struggled on through the worst conditions she had known. Between Looe and Fowey, her horse tripped in a flooded hole and 'had gotten quite down his head and all'. A lesser mortal might have turned back, but Fiennes was determined to investigate the Cornish industry that she'd read about in Camden's *Britannia*.

In the 150 years since John Leland had ridden these roads logging the distribution of tin mines, the extraction and processing of ore had become much more efficient. Fiennes chose a mine near St

John Leland

Celia Fiennes

Gerald of Wales

Daniel Defoe

William Gilpin

Thomas Pennant

William Cobbett

H. V. Morton

✈ Gerald of Wales ✦

LEFT Hergest Ridge, on the road to Radnor

BELOW Gerald claimed that the waters of Llangorse Lake could turn from bright green to scarlet, a phenomenon which has been explained by algae blooms and runoff from adjacent fields of red topsoil. His floating pastures and buildings may have been related to reed-beds and an artificial island that existed in his day

OPPOSITE PAGE Gerald's birthplace: Manorbier Castle, east of Pembroke

INSET Gerald's map of Europe (with the east at the top, and Britain at the bottom)

ABOVE The view north-west from the Black Mountains above Grwyne Fawr

BELOW Llanthony Abbey, in the Black Mountains

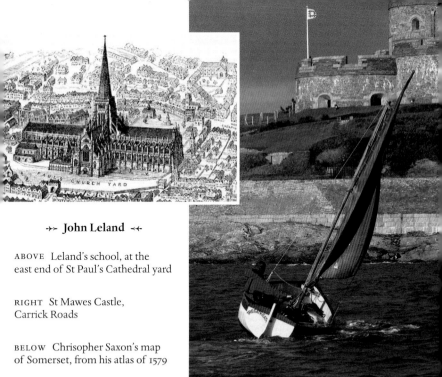

⊱ John Leland ⊰

ABOVE Leland's school, at the
east end of St Paul's Cathedral yard

RIGHT St Mawes Castle,
Carrick Roads

BELOW Chrisopher Saxon's map
of Somerset, from his atlas of 1579

LEFT
Glastonbury Abbey

ABOVE
Dunkery Beacon, Exmoor

BELOW
Hartland Point, north Devon

Airy Point, on the estuary of the Taw

Tin-streaming scars by the source of the Fowey, Bodmin Moor

Austell to record an impression so vivid that the reader is left with ringing ears and stinging nostrils: 'they take oar and pound it in a stamping mill which resembles the paper mills, and when its fine as the finest sand, some of which I saw and took, this they fling into a furnace and with it coale to make the fire, so it burns together and makes a violent heate and fierce flame, the mettle by the fire being seperated from the coale and its own drosse, being heavy falls down to a trench made to receive it, at the furnace hole below; this liquid mettle I saw them shovel up with an iron shovel and soe pour it into molds in which cooles and soe they take it thence in sort of wedges or piggs I think they call them; its a fine mettle thus in its first melting looks like silver, I had a piece poured out and made cold for to take with me.'

With her pannier bags weighed with souvenirs of crushed ore and a tin 'pig', Fiennes continued her survey. From a single roadside vantage point outside St Austell, she was able to count no fewer than twenty tin mines. On the road to Tregony, she passed one hundred mines. This pocked, clamorous, smoky landscape teemed with activity; she estimated that 1,000 men were employed night and day in the pits, furnaces and drainage mills. Excitedly, she noticed that the mills used to drain the mines were like those she had seen around London, Derby and Exeter, powered by water, and 'five tymes more good than the mills they use to turn with horses'. Fiennes couldn't have known that she was witnessing the birth of Cornwall's industrial revolution. At the time, Cornwall was producing a little over 1,000 tons of tin a year, but it would increase tenfold over the following two centuries.

Inexorably, Fiennes was led ever westward, past the River Fal (where she stayed in a relation's fine new house), to Redruth and Penzance ('it lookes soe snugg and warme'), until she was on a road as 'stone and barren as Darbyshire'. Finally, she saw the ultimate point of return: 'I came in sight of the maine ocean on both sides, the south and north sea, and soe rode in its view till I saw them joyn'd at the poynt…'

She had reached Land's End. After a celebratory drink of 'very good bottled ale', Fiennes left her horse, and set off on foot for the furthest tip of land, 'a poynt or peak of great rocks which runs a good way into the sea'. This was the end of her journey. Beyond here, she quipped, her 'horses leggs could not carry me through the deep'. Like millions of travellers since, she was compelled to go right to the end, clambering over the storm-scrubbed rocks 'as farre as safety permitted'.

*

The journey home was tough. Fiennes was weary, and the days were growing shorter; 'the season of the year enclined to raine, and the dayes declineing'. The rains fell, the roads flooded. The day she crossed the border back into Devon was the wettest she had ever known. Towards the end of each day, she would hope to find an inn with a fire, so that she could dry her clothes before supper. The rains followed her through Somerset, where one night's deluge 'put the cattle in the meddows swimming' and prevented her from going to church with her cousin, for fear that the water 'would have came over the windows of the Coach'. In Hampshire, overnight rain turned the chalky tracks to slippery gullies. In one of these miserable defiles, her horse's 'feete failed, and he could noe wayes recover himself'. Fiennes recalls how she was 'shott off his neck upon the bank'. Lesser riders would have been a bundle of broken bones. But Fiennes was unharmed, and her horse rolled himself upright and stood patiently beside his remarkable rider. Several days later, she rode across Hounslow Heath, and into London.

Celia Fiennes had fulfilled her ambition. In sixteen years of travelling, she had visited all the English listed by Camden on the Contents page of *Britannia*. She had seen every one of England's twenty-five cathedrals, sampled twenty-seven healing mineral waters and springs, called at countless country houses and ridden at least 5,000 miles. She must have been one of the best-travelled Englishwomen of her generation.

Some four years after returning from Cornwall, Fiennes decided to compile an account of her journeys. As a feat of authorship, it was just as impressive as her journeys, for the completed journal ran to well over 100,000 words. This was, she claimed, 'never designed, soe not likely to fall into the hands of any but my near relations'. A private document, it was intended to amuse and enlighten those close to her. And yet it is impossible not to conclude that she craved a wider audience. Not only does she refer to her journal as 'this book', but there are moments within it when she appears to be addressing both the nation and women in general. The loudest of these universal appeals appears on the opening page, when Fiennes urges 'all persons' to 'spend some of their tyme in Journeys to visit their native Land'. Two hundred years after she began exploring the English counties, her journal was published. It is still in print, urging new generations of readers to 'cure the evil itch of over-valueing foreign parts'.

DANIEL DEFOE

1724–6

The secret tourist

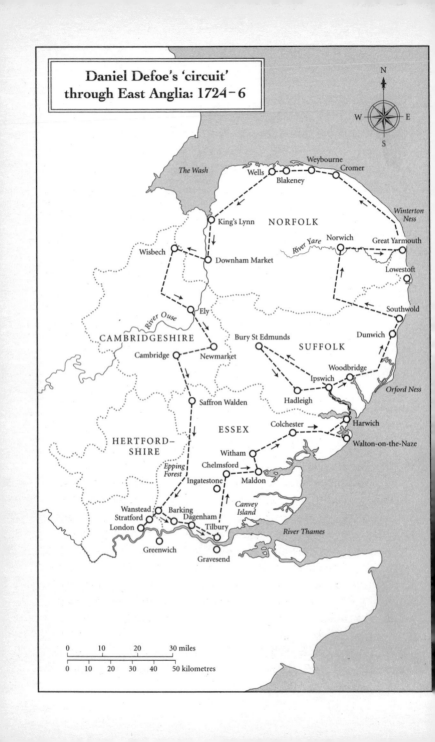

Daniel Defoe's 'circuit' through East Anglia: 1724–6

The Wash

NORFOLK

Weybourne
Cromer
Wells
Blakeney
King's Lynn
Winterton Ness

River Yare
Norwich
Great Yarmouth

Wisbech
Downham Market
Lowestoft

River Ouse
Ely
Southwold

CAMBRIDGESHIRE
Bury St Edmunds
Dunwich
SUFFOLK

Cambridge
Newmarket
Woodbridge
Ipswich
Orford Ness

Saffron Walden
Hadleigh
Harwich
Colchester
Walton-on-the-Naze

HERTFORD-SHIRE
ESSEX
Witham

Epping Forest
Chelmsford
Ingatestone
Maldon
Canvey Island

Wanstead
Stratford
Barking
Dagenham
London
Tilbury
River Thames

Greenwich
Gravesend

0   10   20   30 miles
0 10 20 30 40 50 kilometres

The author of Robinson Crusoe *is perhaps the most colourful writer ever to have saddled a horse and taken to the British byways. He is celebrated for bringing the 'realistic novel' to the English-reading world, and for being the father of modern journalism. Although he was a contemporary of Celia Fiennes, his view from the saddle could not be more different.* A Tour thro' the Whole Island of Great Britain *purports to be a record of seventeen 'Circuits or Journeys' undertaken by an anonymous 'Gentleman' who left London on a quest to reveal 'whatever is curious and worth observation' about his country. Published in three volumes, between 1724 and 1726, the* Tour *was lauded by the historian G.M. Trevelyan as 'an unparalleled survey of Queen Anne's England'. It is still Britain's most spirited guide.*

*

Visit the scene of Robinson Crusoe's shipwreck and you will find a desert of sand backed by a mountainous range of dunes. In winter gales, blonde streamers of sandgrains wave on the beach like wind-blown hair. Even in summer, footprints are rare. At certain times of the tide, an ominous line of breakers can be seen extending far out to sea, as if the swell is tripping on an underwater obstacle. Daniel Defoe plotted the opening passage of *Crusoe* as if he was working from a map. The course of the ship and behaviour of the wind are nautically plausible, the fateful anchorage can be pinpointed on the Admiralty Chart, and the beach where young 'Bob' was washed ashore is on the Ordnance Survey 1:50,000. But why did Defoe wreck Crusoe off Norfolk?

Defoe's reasons for finding East Anglia the most thrilling, lethal region in Britain would emerge in 1724, three years after *Robinson*

Crusoe was published. *A Tour thro' the Whole Island of Great Britain* also opened with East Anglia; at the head of the first chapter, readers were invited to step across the threshold of Britain by way of 'a description of the Sea-Coasts of the Counties of Essex, Suffolk, Norfolk, etc., as also of part of Cambridge-shire'. In subsequent chapters, Defoe would take his readers on a further sixteen journeys, or 'circuits', each contrived to describe a geographical region. In their entirety, they covered the whole of Britain, from the Highlands of Scotland to furthest Cornwall. But he started with East Anglia.

The trail which led Daniel Defoe from his birthplace in London to the byways of Britain is shrouded in estuarine mists. It is known that he was born in the London parish of St Giles, Cripplegate, probably around 1660. His father, James, was a tallow chandler; an upright dependable merchant who belonged to a City livery company. His mother, Alice, has been described by a recent biographer as severe and unapproachable. Both were Nonconformists; Puritans who had learned since the Restoration of Charles II to the throne to live outside the established Church of England. As practising Dissenters, they suffered discrimination and suspicion from an Establishment which sought retribution for the indignities suffered during the Cromwellian Commonwealth. From his earliest years, Daniel was imbued with self-discipline, fortitude and the underdog's drive to succeed in the absence of privilege. He was educated at a special academy for Dissenters' children in Stoke Newington.

These were extraordinary times. Post-war Britain was in the throes of Restoration re-invention and multifarious catastrophe. Defoe was a boy when London was devasted by the Plague and the Great Fire, and he lived through wars with France and Holland, and through the worst storm to strike Britain. At the age of twenty-five, he fought in the rebel Duke of Monmouth's army at Sedgemoor, and he was in the wings during the 1707 Act of Union between Scotland and England. By the time he died in 1731, Defoe had produced over 500 publications and adopted a multiplicity of causes, which he pursued with reckless passion. Reinvigorated Britain, with its ambitious economy, was an exciting playground for a chancer. Defoe was bankrupted twice, fined, pilloried and imprisoned. His occupations ranged from breeding civet cats and running a brick factory to journalism and writing books. He borrowed money to buy a diving bell so that he could recover sunken treasure. At least once, he appears to have been aboard a ship smuggling tin to France, and for a while, he worked as a secret agent. He was a risk-taker and a survivor. And he was a man always on the move, as a soldier, merchant, fugitive, farmer, hack or spy. Habitually secretive, he laid a trail of biographical red herrings. He avoided writing first-person accounts relating to his own life, and often published anonymously (*Robinson Crusoe* was written – according to its title page – 'by Himself'). Subversively imaginative, he inserted invented passages into works of 'non-fiction'. The greatest of those supposedly factual works was his *Tour*.

A Tour thro' the Whole Island of Great Britain was published when Defoe was in his sixties. And it was a characteristically risky venture. At a time when the literary world was metropolitan and classically educated, low-brow Defoe headed off to the regions to write about places that were off the Establishment map. He knew that there was nothing quite like the scent of an untold story. Enormous in its compass and ingenious in its presentation, the *Tour* contained the accumulated wisdom of a lifetime's travel (and a scattering of passages recycled from Camden's *Britannia*). The journeys themselves were less the record of actual itineraries, than a convenient narrative spine on which to hang his encyclopaedic observations. Defoe was clear that the *Tour* was not a geographical compendium. It was, he explained, 'particularly fitted for the Reading of such as desire to Travel over the ISLAND'. The *Tour* was a printed companion for travellers; a guidebook.

*

For Defoe, there was only one place where a journey through Britain could begin. London was the centre of trade; the capital of Protestantism; the heart of the Empire and the standard against which all other cities should be compared. Already the largest city in western Europe, it was still growing. Fifty years after the Great Fire of London, the city had risen from the ashes: 'New squares, and new streets,' rejoiced Defoe, 'rising up every day to such a prodigy of buildings, that nothing in the world does, or ever did, equal it, except old Rome in Trajan's time.' Over the course of several thousand miles of travel, Defoe would demonstrate that every village in Britain was connected by an economic umbilical cord to 'this over-grown city'. Feeding the 'great centre of England', and therefore the rest of the kingdom, was the River Thames.

I joined Defoe on board a recycling and waste-management motor-barge moored just downstream of Tower Bridge. *Tidy Thames* is a neat little ship of around ninety tons, with polished brass in the bridge and a mahogany saloon fully equipped with tea-making apparatus. In front of the bridge windows is a long, rectangular hold, half-filled on this particular day with miscellaneous urban detritus, from paint pots and beer bottles to industrial pallets and black bin bags. Viewed from the bow, *Tidy Thames* looks rather like an incongruous marriage between a rubbish skip and a Victorian conservatory. We untied from the pier as the rush-hour traffic stuttered above our heads, then Colin Murphy, the skipper, spun the spoked wheel and *Tidy Thames* tucked her bow into the ebb tide.

On board the barge was her owner, Chris Livett, a fifth-generation Thames waterman, who runs his company from a cramped suite of cabins below 'X' turret on HMS *Belfast*. Livett's family has worked the river since 1710. 'I came afloat when I was eight years old, with my grandfather,' he told me as Tower Bridge receded. 'I was apprenticed to the Watermens Company, to my father, aged sixteen.' Today, Livett's Launches operate ten pleasure boats and six barges. Livett's river flows through his conversation like a mysterious stream of energy and history, barely sensible to those who had not been born into the world of watermen. 'The smells and the sounds would have been intriguing,' he mused. 'Spices, sugar, tobacco … coal … all the different products coming in, the sounds of oars and flapping sails, the watermen running out, looking for business, throwing up their grappling hooks to the sides of ships, offering their services … quite a lot of banging and crashing as well. Remember the craft in those days were not particularly manoeuvrable. They were all dependent on the tide.' Livett pointed at the muscled eddies on the river: 'The motto of the Watermens Company is "At command of our superiors". That's not the wife or mother-in-law, but the wind and the tide, and the forces that drive them.' Three hundred years ago, there was just one bridge over the Thames in London, and 40,000 watermen servicing the river. Today, there are just over 1,000 Thames watermen, and the river's ferries have been replaced by thirty or so bridges.

As *Tidy Thames* chewed a furrow through the turbid current, Livett pointed to the scattered relics of London's one-time trading artery: the slimy timber 'campsheds' which had once supported barges at low tides; liver-coloured slipways, the renovated wharves, gentrified warehouses and mooring bollards marooned on riverside walks like abstract civic sculptures. Ours was the only vessel moving on a section of river which in Defoe's day was almost rafted with shifting decks. 'I have had the curiosity,' Defoe recalls, 'to count the ships as well as I could, *en passant*, and have found above two thousand sail of all sorts, not reckoning barges, lighters or pleasure boats, and yachts; but vessels that really go to sea.' Between Battle Bridge and Blackwall, he ticked-off three wet docks, twenty-two dry docks and thirty-three shipyards, and that was just for merchant ships. By the early 1700s, London's share of trade was greater than all other British ports put together, with fleets of ships plying the shores of Europe and new trade-routes to North America and the West Indies, Asia and West Africa. Today, Livett told me, the freight on the Thames is rubbish and road aggregate.

Beyond the serene glass stalks of Canary Wharf, *Tidy Thames* thumped past a place Defoe would recognise instantly. It is, he wrote in the *Tour*, 'the most delightful spot of ground in Great-Britain; pleasant by situation, those pleasures increased by art, and all made completely agreeable by accident of fine buildings, the continual passing of fleets of ships up and down the most beautiful river in Europe.' The fine buildings are still there: Queen's House, the Royal Naval College, Flamsteed House and the Observatory. Defoe must have spent many contented hours on the waterfront at Greenwich, lapping up 'the best air, best prospect, and the best conversation in England'.

He clearly loved the place. Defoe's Greenwich was a retirement resort for sea dogs and war heroes; for national treasures. 'Here,' he elaborates, 'several of the most active and useful gentlemen of the late armies, after having grown old in the service of their country, and covered with the honours of the field, are retired to enjoy the remainder of their time, and reflect with pleasure upon the dangers they have gone through, and the faithful services they have performed both abroad and at home.' Reading this passage, it's impossible to see it as anything but a wistful remonstration against the circumstances which had prevented the author himself from enjoying the respectability and contentment of spending his golden years in Greenwich.

Beyond the grubby mushroom of the Millennium Dome, our aquatic skip scooted between the polished cams of the Thames Barrier into less-protected reaches of the river. The tide had caught us now, and shoreline buildings were flicking past at an astonishing rate. Silvertown … Woolwich … Gallions Reach … Barking Creek … Dagenham, port bow, 1117 Greenwich Mean Time. Here, announces Defoe, is 'the famous breach, made by inundation of the Thames, which was so great, as that it laid near 5,000 acres of land under water'.

In October 1707 (just four years after the country had been smashed by the most destructive storm in British history), an exceptional tide had broken through the river embankment at Dagenham. Repeated failures to plug the breach led to it enlarging, and over the following decade, 120 acres of Essex were sucked out through the gap into the Thames, where the silt reformed as a gigantic mudbank which threatened to block the river – and to block London's trade. It took the ingenuity of a Captain Perry, whose reputation had been won whilst working for the Czar of Muscovy on the River Don, to finally block the breach. Defoe's Britain was a buffeted land. Beyond the wars and fires and plagues, the weather was a violent, unpredictable force. Defoe had no way of knowing that he had been born into the coldest phase of the Little Ice Age, and that the chaotic, extreme weather events he took for granted were actually a passing phase, and would ease over the coming centuries. The *Tour* reflects a fascination with Nature's dynamics. It wasn't just the *form* of landscapes which excited Defoe, but the *processes* which could suddenly alter them. Floods, droughts, catastrophic storms and frosts which locked ships into rivers of ice were calamitous. And calamity made good copy.

Livett put me ashore at a concrete pier just downstream of Dagenham. In the early 1700s, this was uninhabited marshland. Today, the equivalent of 40 million bin bags of waste are brought every year to Frog Island, where Britain's first commercial-scale micro-biological treatment site shreds and sorts it all by weight, density and magnetism, then sells it on for recycling or fuel. Investing in garbage (Britain's waste sector is worth around £7 billion a year) would have appealed to Defoe; an impulsive venture capitalist, he lost a whopping £17,000 (over £500,000 today) when a flutter on shipping went wrong and led to his first bankruptcy.

Defoe's Hanoverian view was gloriously unclouded by environmental tipping-points. Poverty could be cured and wealth created simply by relieving the planet of its natural resources and processing them into products which could be traded at markets. The more hands each product passed through, the more money everyone would make. Earth was inexhaustible. The North Sea was overflowing with fish and there was enough coal to keep the country's furnaces and fireplaces glowing for eternity. Some may have warned that Britain's forests were being consumed by iron foundries at unsustainable rates, but Defoe disagreed: 'I must own that I found that complaint perfectly groundless, the three counties of Kent, Sussex and Hampshire … being one inexhaustible source of timber.' Friends of the Earth would have found him tough to conscript.

The key players in this brave new nation were tradesmen, 'these circulators of goods, and retailers of them to the last consumer'. Trade was an ethical, civilising engine of far greater potency than Britain's capricious Navy. The 'rising greatness of the British nation' was not 'owing to war and conquests, to enlarging its dominion by the sword, or subjecting the people of other countries to our power; but it is all owing to trade, to the increase of our commerce at home, and the extending it abroad'. Applied with Puritan diligence, there could be no limit to British fortunes. In Defoe's mercantile world, tradesmen were 'the only gentry in England'.

*

For a vision of the future, Defoe's readers were invited to begin with the site of the 2012 Olympics: 'The village of Stratford,' he marvels, 'the first in this county from London, is not only increased, but, I believe, more than doubled in that time; every little vacancy filled up with new houses.' Take a look at the map (Robert Morden's county map of 1695) and there is Stratford, three miles out in the countryside. Here, and in surrounding villages like Leytonstone, Wanstead, West Ham and Plaistow, property values and rents had soared by as much as a third in twenty years. East of the River Lee, greenfield sites were being gobbled up for housing; Defoe puts the figure at 'above a thousand new foundations' in the area, generally of 'handsome large houses', being let for £20–£60 a year, 'for the habitations of rich citizens, such as either are able to keep two houses, one in the country, and one in the city; or for such citizens as being rich, and having left off trade, live altogether in these neighbouring villages for the pleasure and health of the latter part of their days'. Exploring the packed terraces of E13 today, it's hard to imagine this as a rustic haven for second-homers. The fragments of green space which remain are mostly cemeteries.

East of Dagenham, Defoe's Essex changes character. Villages become more sparse, the marshes broader, and there are secrets to hide. Just before the Thames widens into an estuary, there is an ancient crossing point. On the southern, hilly shore is Gravesend, and on the northern, marshy shore, an isolated fort. In Defoe's day, the ferry between Tilbury and Gravesend made this one of the busiest crossings in the south east; the point at which the Thames intersected the land route between eastern England and Dover. Celia Fiennes was ferried with her horse across the Thames here en route to Canterbury and Dover in 1697, noting the 'fine fort' and 'a great flatt to the land full of watry ditches'. For ships about to leave England, this was where they were obliged to drop anchor for a 'second clearing' by customs officers. Failure to do so could lead to a volley of cannon-fire from Tilbury Fort.

Defoe guides his readers around Tilbury Fort with authority. It is, he says, 'the key of the river of Thames', defended on its landward side by a moat, and on its Thames frontage by a platform arrayed with 106 guns. Its bastions are 'the largest of any in England'. The fort is still intact, its stern angles rising in geometric cliffs over flat marshes slashed by dykes and pylon lines. Around the parade ground, field-guns of various eras have been deposited like items of military lost property. From the grassy rampart at the south-eastern corner of the fort, there is a clear view for three miles downstream.

There has been a fort here since the days of Henry VIII, but the massive structure Defoe described had been built between 1670 and 1683 in response to intermittent, costly wrestles with the Dutch over trade routes and domination of the seas. Three wars with our North Sea neighbours since 1652 had put the Thames and East Anglia in the front-line. War in the east was never far from Defoe's mind. His verdict on Tilbury Fort (sensibly designed by a Dutch engineer who was intimate with both marshland and Britain's foe) was that 'they must be bold fellows who will venture in the biggest ships the world has heard of, to pass such a battery'.

One such 'bold fellow' was Defoe himself, for he describes in 'Letter 2' of the *Tour* how he once sailed past the fort 'with some merchants in a large yacht bound to France'. On board, he said, was 'a great quantity of block-tin … and other goods, which had not been entered at the custom house'. The fog being thick, the captain decided that the ship would not be observed by the customs house. 'As for Gravesend or Tilbury-Fort,' reports Defoe with a smirk, 'they could see no more of us than they could of London-Bridge; and we drove in this fog undiscerned … and went clear away to Caen in Normandy without being visited.' Defoe fails to explain exactly what business he was conducting with the yachtsmen.

Smuggling was not the only questionable activity Defoe had engaged in here. Although he doesn't make any mention of it in the *Tour*, he owned a sizeable chunk of land right beside Tilbury Fort. Contemporary maps show that the fort had been sited at the midpoint of a four-mile stretch of marshland between Thurrock and East Tilbury. According to Defoe it was prized for seasonal grazing: 'It was observable,' he notes, 'that great parts of the lands in these levels, especially those on this side of East Tilbury, are held by the farmers, cow-keepers, and grazing butchers … and that they are generally stocked (all the winter half year) with large fat sheep.' At some point in the mid 1690s, he bought a freehold on West Tilbury Marsh and built himself a brick and pantile works. A map printed in 1777 by John Chapman and Peter André shows only two clusters of buildings on the marsh. One of them is marked 'Milk House'. The other – which appears to consist of three buildings just over half a mile from the fort – is thought to be Defoe's brick and tile works. The Court of Sewers Order Book reveals that Defoe was living on the water's edge; in 1698, he was ordered 'to cope 6 rods of ye sea wall next to Wickss marsh'. The year before, Celia Fiennes must have ridden right past Defoe's door as she headed for the ferry slip beside the fort. Though no record exists of an encounter between the two peripatetic Dissenters, one suspects that Fiennes would have regarded Defoe as a dodgy reprobate of the wrong class.

Having plotted bearings and distances from Chapman and André's map, I pedalled to and fro across this eerie polder searching for remnants of Defoe's marshland acres. His house and works must have stood between Ferry Road and an import terminal. Beside a glittering parade-ground of Korean cars, I eventually found a surviving pasture, still grazed by ponies. Perhaps it was Defoe's land.

*

From Tilbury, Defoe followed the coast of Essex from one muddy estuary to another: from the Thames to the Crouch to the Blackwater. In winter, this can be a spectral hinterland between the grey sea and London's frantic tendrils. I cycled the backroads past mudflat and field as if I was the last person on the planet. The land is so flat that it seems to merge imperceptibly with the sea. It's a coast with two personalities. At high tide, the creeks and flats become blinding mirrors, and every unflooded object shines with reflected light. When the water recedes, wet mud sucks the light from the sky.

Listen, and you can hear the gurgles and pops of dribbling water and escaping methane.

Defoe offers his readers two versions of coastal Essex. On the one hand, the low-lying marshes are 'justly said to be both unhealthy, and unpleasant', with a chronic impact on female mortality: 'I took notice,' he observes, 'of a strange decay of the sex here; insomuch, that all along this county it was very frequent to meet with men that had had from five to six, to fourteen or fifteen wives; nay, and some more; and I was informed that in the marshes on the other side of the river over-against Candy Island, there was a farmer, who was then living with the five and twentieth wife, and that his son, who was but about 35 years old, had already had about fourteen.'

Defoe's informant was 'a merry fellow' who claimed to have had about eighteen wives himself ('though I found afterwards he fibbed a little,' admits the author). Apparently, the men, being bred in the marshland, were adapted to its ills, but they'd taken to sourcing their wives from the hillier, healthier interior of Essex. These 'young lasses', relates Defoe, would leave their uplands 'healthy, fresh and clear, and well', but once they reached the 'fogs and damps' of the marshes, they 'changed their complexion, got an ague or two, and seldom held it above half a year at most'. As each wife died, the bereaved husband would have to 'go to the uplands again, and fetch another'. Clearly a touch sceptical, and observing his informant's mirth, Defoe nevertheless has to agree that 'the fact, for all that, is certainly true'. In coastal Essex, he had noticed that he 'seldom met with ancient people among the poor, as in other places we do', and that a large proportion of the inhabitants had indeed migrated here from other parts of the country. A marshland 'ague' was actually malaria, which was so rife at the time that inhabitants of these estuarine shores had a death rate three times higher than those living inland.

But there was another Essex; an Essex which could make a man rich. This, explains Defoe, is what had attracted so many immigrants to the county. Here, amid the level, lush grasslands, a diligent worker can enjoy 'the advantage of good farms'. The climate is ideal for agriculture, and so is the location, right on London's coat-tails. Essex has the longest shoreline of any county in England. Land and sea ooze with productivity; the Blackwater estuary provides 'the best and fattest, and the largest veal in England, if not in the world'. At the mouth of the Colne, fishermen take 'the largest oysters in England'. Essex estuaries provided London's markets with fish 'night and day'. Near Harwich, Defoe claims that he saw 'such shoals, or hills rather, of mussels that great boats might have loaded with them, and no miss have been made of them'. At Walton-on-the-Naze, copperas lies for the taking, strewn on the beach.

Speculating on natural resources was one of Defoe's particular interests. Had the Restoration dealt in hedge-funds, futures and options, Daniel Defoe would have been in them up to his neck. Coal and timber had made traders their fortunes. Britain's hills and shores were yielding limestone ... lead, tin and iron ... sand ... peat ... rock salt ... copperas, in seemingly inexhaustible quantities. Defoe's own attempt to make money from mud on the Tilbury marshes was yet another of his money-making ventures which didn't quite work; the brick and tile works had gone bust in 1703, when he was arrested for publishing an inflammatory leaflet on Dissenting. But that didn't seem to have restrained him from trying again. The journey through Essex which he made while gathering material for the *Tour*, coincided with a new masterplan: to combine trading with farming on a property outside Colchester.

According to Defoe, he had left London at the start of his great tour, on 3 April 1722. And yet on 6 August of the same year, he concluded negotiations with the Corporation of Colchester, agreeing to pay £1,000 for a 99-year lease on a farm and several hundred acres of land known as the 'Severalls', one mile north of the town in the parish of Mile End. The soil of the 'Severalls' was silty and sandy clay, with substantial stands of woodland. It wasn't a bad bit of real estate; far better in fact than his malarial swamp at Tilbury. And Colchester, a Protestant town in the Civil War, was home-turf for Defoe. He had friends here, one of whom was the Rector of Mile End. William Smythies, a severe critic of the High Church, had retired from his post a couple of years before Defoe bought into Mile End, but William was succeeded by his very able son, Palmer. They would have been neighbours to Defoe, who had typically high ambitions for his new farm. At the Severalls, he intended to market timber for shipbuilding, and to produce cattle and corn, cheese and butter. Later, he used his Colchester estate as a base for trading oysters and honey, metal buttons, tanned leather and imported anchovies. Intriguingly, Celia Fiennes rode past the Severalls ('a sort of deep moore ground and woody') in 1698, as she made her way along the main road from Colchester to Ipswich.

Incomers with new money were changing the social profile of Essex. 'It is observable,' Defoe notes, 'that in this part of the country, there are several very considerable estates purchased, and now enjoyed by citizens of London, merchants and tradesmen.' He goes on to list an iron merchant named Weston, a wholesale grocer called Cresnor, a merchant named Olemus at Braintree and several others who had made a packet from trade. John Eyles, 'a wealthy merchant of London', had erected a 'noble stately fabric or mansion-house' outside Romford. 'I mention this,' continues Defoe, 'to observe how the present increase of wealth in the city of London, spreads its self into the country, and plants families and fortunes, who in another age will equal the families of the ancient gentry.'

The incoming trading classes had adopted the Essex coast as their playground. Osea Island in the Blackwater estuary is 'well known by our London men of pleasure, for the infinite number of wild-fowl, that is to say, duck, mallard, teal and widgeon, of which there are such vast flights, that they tell us the island, namely the creek, seems covered with them, at certain times of the year, and they go from London on purpose for the pleasure of shooting; and indeed often come home very well loaden with game'. There is, of course, a risk associated with gallivanting in the marshes. It must be remembered, warns Defoe, 'that those gentlemen who are such lovers of the sport, and go so far for it, often return with an Essex ague on their backs, which they find a heavier load than the fowls they have shot'. Defoe claims to be no fan of recreation. 'The tradesman that is the lover of pleasure,' he wrote in *The Complete English Tradesman*, 'shall be a poor man.' Osea Island is now the playground of a private landowner who keeps it out of bounds to the travelling classes, but neighbouring Northey Island has become a nature reserve and is currently home to 94,000 ducks, geese and wading birds. Defoe's salt marshes are disappearing at an alarming rate; over one quarter of Essex's salt marshes have been lost since the 1970s, and projections suggest that by 2050, a further third will be swamped by rising sea levels.

*

The Britain portrayed by Defoe is a city state. All roads lead to London, and East Anglia is the pre-eminent province. The *Tour* is both a guidebook and an economic model intended to show 'how this whole kingdom, as well as the people, as the land, and even the sea, in every part of it, are employed to furnish something, and I may add, the best of every thing, to supply the city of London'.

In Defoe's economy, the trickle-down effect from trading would bring wealth to the regions. London's booming population and markets needed 'provisions, corn, flesh, fish, butter, cheese, salt, fuel, timber, &c. and cloths also; with every thing necessary for building, and furniture for their own use, or for trades'. Towns not deriving an immediate income from trade with London benefited from servicing the capital. Brentwood, Ingatestone and Chelmsford all lay on the great road which cut diagonally across the county linking London and Colchester. These, observed Defoe, 'are large thoroughfare towns, full of good inns, and chiefly maintained by the excessive multitude of carriers and passengers, which are constantly passing this way to London, with droves of cattle, provisions, and manufactures for London'.

The key to shifting such vast volumes of produce and people was an efficient transportation network, but the roads were – as Celia Fiennes repeatedly discovered – in an appalling state. Rutted, pot-holed and periodically flooded, they were still preyed upon by highwaymen. Signposts were seldom seen and many rivers still required ferries, or fording. For much of the seventeenth century, road maintenance had been the responsibility of local populations, every able-bodied man being required to devote six days a year, unpaid, to repair work. It was a hopelessly inadequate system. As freight transport boomed, the country's roads disintegrated beneath increasing volumes of hooves and wheels.

At the time, just a scattering of turnpike trusts had been established, but Defoe was convinced that he had seen the makings of a road revolution. In Volume II of the *Tour*, he devoted his one appendix to turnpikes, opening his treatise with 'that great county of Essex', and the arterial highway linking London to Colchester, Ipswich and Harwich. It will come as a surprise to those who sit in tailbacks on the A12, biting their steering wheels, that Defoe rated this as the best road in England. Until the 1690s, this had been the worst road in the country, 'formerly deep' according to Defoe, and 'in time of floods dangerous, and at other times, in winter, scarce passable … the most worn with wagons, carts, and carriages; and with infinite droves of black cattle, hogs, and sheep, of any road (that leads through no larger an extent of country) in England'.

The Turnpike Act which transformed the 'Great Essex Road' was passed in 1695. Initially, toll gates were set up near Mile End, Romford and Ingatestone, which had the reputation (according to Defoe) for being 'the highest rated public toll in England'. Wagons were charged 12d, carts 8d, coaches 6d and single horsemen 1d. Defoe – whose new Colchester estate happened to border the turnpike – was thrilled: the Colchester road was 'now so firm, so safe, so easy to travellers, and carriages as well as cattle, that no road in England can yet be said to equal them'. In 2007, some 4,000 drivers voted the A12 the worst road in Britain.

Defoe's tour through Essex ended at Harwich, whose harbour he reckoned to be 'one of the best and securest in England'. Defended from the Dutch by a fort and battery of guns which overlooked the only deep channel in the estuary, the harbour was strategically located at the busy end of the North Sea and, explained Defoe, 'of a vast extent … safe for all weathers … able to receive the biggest ships, and the greatest number that the world ever saw together; I mean, ships of war'. Defoe knew Harwich from earlier days. 'In the old Dutch War,' he remembered, 'great use has been made of this harbour; and I have known that there has been 100 sail of men of war and their attendants, and between three and four hundred sail of collier ships, all in this harbour at a time.'

Gazing across the water from the old lighthouse on the east side of town, I tried to imagine what a flotilla of 500 sailing ships would look like. While I was there, a wall of white steel slid across the scene. Turning with the slowness of a clock's minute-hand, a gigantic container ship moved with a low rumble towards the battlements of multi-coloured rectangles piled on the far shore. Today, Defoe's mega-harbour is the largest container port in the UK.

Defoe left Essex by boat, boarding a vessel which would ferry him up the River Orwell into Suffolk, while his horse was taken around the estuary by land. As he sailed out into the broad expanse of the harbour, he left behind a county against which none could compare. Essex had it all: fertile land for corn and cattle, abundant fishing, villages suitable for traders and merchants, busy market towns, proximity to the capital, the best road in the country, one of the best harbours and the longest coastline of any county in England. Essex was the county of choice for merchants of fortune.

*

Out on the Orwell, in the space between two counties, Defoe lowered his mask for a moment. As the woods slipped by, the old man thought back to his early years, and the voyage he had taken from Harwich to Ipswich 'about five and thirty years before the present journey' (roughly 1687, then, before his bankruptcies and worst misadventures). The Ipswich coal ships would get laid up each winter while the seas were dangerous and the nights long. Rigging and sails were carried ashore, the topmasts struck, and the vessels moored 'under the advantages and security of sound ground, and a high woody shore, where they lie as safe as in a wet dock'. The sight each winter of 200 sailing ships slumbering on the mud was, thought Defoe, 'very agreeable'. Relieved of their charges, 'the masters lived calm and secure with their families in Ipswich; and enjoying plentifully, what in the summer they got laboriously at sea'. It was, he lamented, 'melancholy to hear, that there were now scarce 40 sail of good colliers that belonged to the whole town'.

Ipswich was still suffering the 'sloth' that Celia Fiennes had detected twenty-four years earlier, so Defoe sets about providing a business plan for the port. The problem, paradoxically, was London, 'which sucks the vitals of trade in this island to itself'. If Ipswich could find 'some particular trade or accident to trade, which is a kind of nostrum to them, inseparable to the place', the town would have an independent source of commerce. By way of exemplars, he cites Yarmouth's herring fishery, Newcastle's coal trade, the Leeds clothing trade, Hull's corn trade, and Liverpool's trade with Virginia and West India. The solution for Ipswich, he concludes, is Greenland. The port, enthuses Defoe, is ideal for building and re-supplying whaling ships; the Orwell has plenty of space for 'the noisome cooker, which attends the boiling their blubber'; the town is conveniently close to the market for the oil; and the same wind which blew ships from the mouth of the Orwell, 'is fair to the very seas of Greenland'.

Fortunately for the local residents, Ipswich never did become Britain's blubber-capital, although the Nova Scotia yard did fit out two whale ships in the 1780s. Eventually, it was the Victorians who revived the port by dredging the river and excavating new docks. Today, Ipswich Docks are being reinvented yet again: the Victorian Customs House has survived, but the mills and warehouses have gone, and the malt house. In their place, tiers of apartments rise above reflections of bistro, brasserie and restaurant. Where sooty colliers moored deck-to-deck, dazzling yachts nuzzle a pristine marina.

Eighteenth-century Ipswich just didn't get it right. Perhaps it was the wrong distance from London; less well placed than Essex to take advantage of the capital's markets, yet too close to generate its own commercial 'nostrum'. It is now thought that ship-building on the Orwell may have subsided because local builders were slower than those on the Thames and the Tyne to respond to the need for the longer, faster bulk-carriers copied from captured Dutch 'fly-boats'. Suffolk's commercial intuition seems to have been sharper inland. It was in this county, Defoe records, that the fattening of sheep and cattle on turnips was first practised, 'to the great enriching of the farmers', and it was Suffolk traders who invented a revolutionary waggon for the mass transportation of turkeys. Instead of marching the birds overland to the capital, the new horse-drawn, four-deckers could 'hurry away the creatures alive'.

*

Travelling back to the coast of Suffolk, an undercurrent becomes detectable in Defoe's excitable economics. To find out why, his readers would have had to explore the first book Defoe wrote. Published in 1704, *The Storm* was Defoe's eyewitness account – corroborated by reports from various parts of the country – of what is still billed as the worst storm in British history. An extra tropical cyclone, it smashed into Britain on 26 November 1703. Over 8,000 people perished and Queen Anne declared that it was 'a Calamity so Dreadful and Astonishing, that the like hath not been Seen or Felt, in the Memory of any Person Living in this Our Kingdom'. Defoe was there. He saw it. The destruction was awesome. He writes of ships thrown into tangled heaps on the Thames; of windmills catching fire because their cogs were spinning so fast; of houses and churches dashed to pieces. Out at sea, there were countless shipwrecks, one of which Defoe would recycle for the opening passage of *Robinson Crusoe*. Once again, East Anglia had been in the front line.

The coast of Suffolk is low and friable, its soft cliffs alternating with muddy inlets and long banks of shingle dumped by the currents. The largest of these shingle banks is ten-mile long Orford Ness, 'a noted point of land', informs Defoe, 'for the guide of the colliers and coasters'. In the twentieth century, the Ness suffered a Cold War takeover by the Ministry of Defence, which constructed a number of concrete 'pagodas' for testing nuclear firing mechanisms. It is one of the strangest places I know in the UK; a seemingly barren stony waste littered with military leftovers. It reminds me of a plain I once pedalled across in the north-western corner of the Gobi Desert. Historic maps show that the Ness grew in length by nearly three miles between the 1530s and 1600, but by 1736, it had mysteriously shortened to its sixteenth-century length. Defoe's 'dreadful tempest' had been so severe that it had wiped out three miles of shingle spit.

Sudden, catastrophic realignments of its shores are part of the East Anglian temperament. It was, after all, the last part of Britain to be connected to the continent by a land bridge. Further up the coast, Defoe called at ruined Dunwich, the Atlantis of the North Sea. Fable had embellished the scale of this disaster. 'Fame reports,' writes Defoe, 'that once they had fifty churches in the town; I saw but one left.' Defoe was right about the nature of the loss, but not the detail. Dunwich once had eight churches (and three monastic houses), and back in the thirteenth century it had indeed been a thriving port, with a fleet of eleven warships, thirty-six trading ships and twenty-four fishing smacks. In a passage which displays Defoe's knack of catalysing a local, topographic description into a broader, universal theme, he attributes the downfall of Dunwich to the fate which can overcome both places and people: 'towns, kings, countries, families, and persons, all have their elevation, their medium, their declination, and even their destruction in the womb of time, and the course of nature.' It's the kind of line which set the *Tour* centuries clear of Camden's and Leland's matter-of-fact topographies.

Dunwich, as it happened, had been built on sand. There is a new urgency along the coast of Suffolk these days: the lighthouse on Orford Ness is expected to topple into the sea in the next ten years, and the Victorian resort of Southwold (where Defoe had amused himself with conjectures on the flight paths of swallows) is bracing itself behind barricades of concrete and Norwegian granite. A mile away, a local resident called Peter Boggis has bulldozed 100,000 tons of sand and earth over the cliff in an attempt to protect his house and those of his neighbours.

*

Defoe ritualised his arrival at Britain's extremities by dipping his foot – or the hoof of his horse – into the sea. Such dippings occurred at South Foreland and Selsey, Land's End and John O'Groats. But the first was Lowestoft, the most eastern point of mainland Britain.

Lowestoft is only seven miles from Yarmouth. The two ports are separated by a county boundary, and by feuding which goes back to at least the Middle Ages. At issue was competition over the market for herrings. The rivalry was frequently violent and caused many a head to be scratched in London. In 1596, Lord Burghley was petitioned by the seamen of Yarmouth for guard-ships, and at about the same time, Camden recorded that Yarmouth had become 'so rich and powerful, that they often engag'd their neighbours of Lestoff … in Sea-fights'. Defoe of course found all this irresistible, relating 'a long and fabulous story' involving battles on land and sea which culminate in defeat for Lowestoft and a terrible geomorphological reprisal: Yarmouth destroyed Lowestoft's trade by damming the mouth of the River Waveney to prevent it from reaching the sea. Today, the Waveney does indeed take a sudden turn to the north, joining the Yare rather than following its own course to the sea. Defoe himself seems to have taken sides in the affair, failing to describe Lowestoft at all, yet heaping paragraphs of gushing praise upon Yarmouth. Could it be that Defoe, who had fought against the King at Sedgemoor, was swayed by the fact that, during the Civil War, Yarmouth had sided with Parliament and Lowestoft with the Royalists? Pedalling through Lowestoft looking for the docks, I found myself held up by traffic on Commercial Road. Right beside me was the boarded premises of 'Biggerland' and a hand-scrawled sign which read: 'SHOP CLOSED DUE TO FIRE PLEASE COME TO GRATE YARMOUTH'.

I spotted *Alert*'s thicket of aerials before I saw her. A Rapid Intervention Vessel, she is the latest ship in the Trinity House fleet, custom-built in Poland to keep Britain's sea-lanes safe and open. As we crashed through seas which periodically washed the bridge windows, Captain Roger Swinney explained why the East Anglian coast was so lethal. It was, he said, a combination of factors: the shallow waters could create steep, broken seas; the sand banks had a habit of moving, so you couldn't trust your charts; and the shoreline was so low-lying that it was difficult to identify landmarks. In a small boat in big seas, you would only glimpse the land as you slid over the peak of a wave. Swinney pulled out an Admiralty Chart covering the Norfolk coast: 'Each of these circles is a wreck. Hundreds of them. There's an awful lot of metal down there.'

Defoe had no doubts about this coast. This is, he writes in the *Tour*, 'one of the most dangerous and most fatal to the sailors in all England, I may say in all Britain'. The reason, he continues, is 'the great number of ships which are continually going and coming this way, in their passage between London and all the northern coasts of Great-Britain'. His impressions of the East Anglian coast had been formed in part by two terrible storms. The first, in around 1692, had wrecked (according to Defoe) 'above 200 sail of ships' and killed 'above a thousand people'. The second had been the meteorological nightmare of November 1703. One of the most graphic descriptions to appear in Defoe's book about this extreme event came from the coast of Norfolk, where 'at least 400 Sail, being most of them Laden Colliers, *Russia* Men, and Coasters from *Lynn* and *Hull*' had anchored in Yarmouth Roads ahead of the 'intolerable Tempest'. The 'Roads' off Yarmouth were one of the most important anchorages on the east coast of England; a deep-water channel between the coast and an offshore sand bank called Scroby Sands. A haven in fair weather, Yarmouth Roads could be a deathtrap in the wrong wind. One of those caught in Yarmouth Roads that November night was the Master of the *John and Mary*, whose account bears an uncanny similarity to the first pages of *Robinson Crusoe*. The *John and Mary*'s skipper (who reckoned this coast to be 'the most dangerous Place between *London* and *Newcastle*') had anchored in Yarmouth Roads because the south-westerly wind prevented further progress towards the Thames. Hindered by a south-westerly, too, the Master of 'Bob' Crusoe's ship had done the same. The scenes are identical: the fleets of ships; the sudden freshening of the wind; the decision to strike topmasts and make 'all tite and fast upon Deck'; the setting of the sheet anchors; the breaking of the seas over the ships 'in such a vast Quantity'; the Mate's urgent requests to cut away the remaining masts ... and the Master's eventual consent. The circumstances around them are similar too: other vessels being swept past, dismasted and sinking; ships firing their guns in distress; a longboat appearing from the maelstrom...

Till this point, Defoe is recording two parallel accounts; one tersely factual, the other grippingly fictional. Both come from the same source: the Master of the *John and Mary*. But with the appearance of the longboat, the two versions diverge. As the Master of the *John and Mary* recounts, what actually happened was that the longboat was swept from the night to collide with his ship, whereupon it was 'stav'd to pieces with the Blow' and its crew drowned. In *Robinson Crusoe*, the longboat miraculously manages to rescue the entire crew of Bob's ship, and then to row them towards the shore of Norfolk.

Numbed 'partly with fright, partly with horror', Bob clings to the longboat as it is driven by the wind towards the shore 'almost as far as *Winterton Ness*'. On the sands, he can see figures running to assist the stricken boat as it is tossed towards land. But Bob and his shipmates are swept north-westwards, 'till being past the light-house at *Winterton*'. Here, observes Crusoe, 'the shore falls off to the westward towards *Cromer*, and so the land broke off a little of the violence of the wind.' In the lee of the Ness, the exhausted sailors are able to beach the longboat, 'tho' not without much difficulty'. Staggering ashore, they stumble along the coast to Yarmouth, where they are received 'as unfortunate men', and 'used with great humanity as well by the magistrates of the town, who assign'd us good quarters, as by particular merchants and owners of ships, and had money given us sufficient to carry us either to *London* or back to *Hull*, as we thought fit'. Crusoe, of course, heads towards London.

Out on *Alert*, it struck me that there is nothing comfortable, or scenic, about the North Sea in a Force Six. We were only a couple of miles off the coast, but I found it quite impossible to recognise any of the features I selected from my Ordnance Survey map. All I could see was a very thin, dark smear trapped between a vast expanse of lurching grey waves and an implacable, grey sky. It was more reassuring to watch the instruments. On various screens, *Alert*'s location was being continuously updated in 3D against the coast and the sea floor. Passing over the end of Scroby Sands, the ship's scanners showed that the bank had shifted by fifty metres since the publication of the most recent Admiralty Chart.

Somewhere around 52 degrees 45 minutes north, Swinney turned *Alert* towards the coast. 'That,' he said, pointing towards the blurred shore, 'is Winterton.' Squinting through the spray out on the wing of the bridge, I could just make out Winterton church, poking like a piece of pencil lead above an indistinct skyline. I stuck my head back inside: 'Where's the Ness?' Swinney pointed over my shoulder: 'There. The surf.' Just a few hundred yards off our starboard beam was a long, dirty scratch across the chipped slate of the sea. Through binoculars, the standing waves looked big enough to flip a lifeboat. We were right above the spot where young Bob had been rowing for his life after watching his ship sink at the beginning of *Robinson Crusoe*. 'Have you ever run aground?' I asked Swinney. 'I have, yes,' he replied. 'Checking to find a shingle bank, and we found one. Quite successful really.'

Viewing it from the lurching deck of *Alert*, I could scarcely comprehend how sinister this coast seemed. I knew it well, but from the other side. When I was young, the place where Bob had stumbled ashore blinded by salt and fear was a perpetually sunny paradise, with tidal lagoons for paddling and hours of sand to run across. I still go back, but it has changed. The cliff has moved so far inland that the cafe now hangs above an abyss, and the concrete tank obstacles which used to stand back from the cliff-edge are strewn on the beach like scattered dice.

Riding his horse along the shore from Winterton to Cromer wrenched from Defoe one of the most melancholic passages in the *Tour*. By the roadsides of this 'most dangerous and most fatal' coast, he found that 'the farmers, and country people had scarce a barn, or a shed, or a stable; nay, not the pales of their yards, and gardens, not a hogsty, not a necessary-house, but what was built of old planks, beams, wales and timbers, &c. the wrecks of ships, and ruins of mariners' and merchants' fortunes.' Maritime disaster had a poignant resonance for Defoe: his first bankruptcy had been triggered by the loss of goods at sea.

This shoreline of summery innocence is still on the front line. It was here, in 1953, that the sea broke through the dunes and drowned seven residents of Sea Palling. By the time the winds abated, the worst storm to hit Britain in the twentieth century had killed 307 people. The physical damage was colossal: 24,000 homes were damaged, gas works, power stations, oil refineries, cement works and 180,000 acres of land flooded. In King's Lynn, the water rose by an astonishing 2.97 metres. With sea levels rising, and the incidence of severe storms projected to increase, Crusoe's coast is horribly exposed to more catastrophe. The defences are conceptual, rather than real. Scroby Sands, the offshore sand bar which used to shelter Britain's coastal shipping, has a different role today. Protruding from the grey waves is a plantation of wind turbines intended to provide enough power for 41,000 homes. Where hundreds of sailing ships once rode out storms, the wind is being farmed for the chance it offers of averting climate events far more extreme than those witnessed by Defoe.

Darkness had fallen by the time *Alert* sailed slowly into the welcoming arms of Yarmouth's harbour moles. Unlike Lowestoft, Yarmouth's harbour is actually a two-mile section of river, lined on both sides by berths and occasional grand façades. Arriving from the black night of the North Sea, I could sense the source of Defoe's excitement. Here, running through the centre of this 'beautiful town', he found 'the finest quay in England, if not in Europe, not inferior even to that of Marseilles itself'. Tweaking the steering joystick with his fingers, Swinney eased *Alert* against the deserted quayside and the props ceased stirring the inky water. 'The ships ride here so close,' records Defoe, 'and as it were, keeping up one another, with their head-fasts on shore, that for half a mile together, they go across the stream with their bowsprits over the land, their bows, or heads, touching the very wharf; so that one may walk from ship to ship as on a floating bridge.'

*

Nowhere in England were two trading centres of such importance so close together. Thirty-five miles up river from Yarmouth lay the city of Norwich. From all corners of Europe, ships could sail into the heart of Norfolk, to its seething, industrious capital. Today, it is one of the calmest river journeys in Britain. For mile after mile, the river meanders in disorienting loops through a wetland of marsh and dyke and whispering reeds. Paddling a canoe, I was moving so slowly, so low on the water, that the land, that engineered platform crammed with buildings and highways, ceased to exist. Not a single road bridge crosses the Yare between Yarmouth and Norwich. Only fifty years earlier, I might have been overtaken by a freighter or two heading inland on the tide. Beyond Reedham, I had to drift for a moment while a raft bearing a couple of cars was hauled across the river. A sugar-beet factory sidled out of the Fen. Eventually, I sneaked into Norwich past the football stadium, new apartment blocks and a derelict warehouse lined with grimy iron bollards. A flaking sign instructed ships' masters to take care with the wash from propellors.

Given that Norwich was second to London in size and importance, Defoe's description of the city is curiously brief. But it seems there was a creditor to avoid. As it happened, Norwich was at the peak of its provincial success, with around 12,000 looms and 70,000 workers employed in the wool trade in and around the city. This was no cultural backwater, either. It was here, twenty years before Defoe peeped cautiously over the city walls, that the first provincial newspaper in the country appeared. By the end of the century, industrious Norwich, and flat-as-a-map Norfolk, would begin to succumb to the powerful water mills, cotton-spinners and coal fields of the north. But for the time being, Defoe can only see 'a face of diligence spread over the whole country'. It has all the virtues Defoe admires: Norfolk is densely populated, with 'great and spacious' market towns and farms which are 'exceeding fruitful and fertile, as well in corn as in pastures'. He was also thrilled to see large numbers of pheasants in the stubble, testimony, in his eyes, 'that the country had more tradesmen than gentlemen in it'. Gentlemen, you see, would have been wasting time shooting game. 'Indeed,' continues Defoe, 'this part is so entirely given up to industry, that what with the seafaring men on the one side, and the manufactures on the other, we saw no idle hands here, but every man busy on the main affair of life, that is to say, getting money.'

Out on the coast again, we pick up Defoe's hoof-prints at Cromer as he rides his horse 'on the strand or open shore to Weyburn Hope, the shore so flat that in some places the tide ebbs out near two miles'. Five hundred years after Gerald of Wales rode the sands of South

Wales, some of Britain's 'coast roads' still ran below the tide line. Beyond Weybourne, he picked up the road to Cley ('where there are large salt-works, and very good salt made, which is sold all over the county, and some times sent to Holland, and to the Baltick'), to Wells ('a very considerable trade carried on with Holland for corn'). Out of sight of London, Defoe nods knowingly at 'the great trade' of smuggling between England and Holland. In Wells, he must have passed the new Customs House, which still has a wooden relief above the door depicting a customs officer with a drawn cutlass, leading his Revenue men in a charge towards a group of smugglers who are unloading a smack onto pack horses. Throughout Norfolk, Defoe finds markets, industries and ports that are trading as never before. Records for the 'Glaven ports' of Blakeney, Cley and Wiveton show that the number of ships leaving for London each year had more than doubled between 1700 and 1722, from fourteen to thirty-four.

Up here in North Norfolk, there is a sense that Defoe has found what he is looking for: a level, productive land being tilled by diligent Puritans who feed the fruits of their labour to a network of active market towns and secure trading ports. His dreamscape was a world of visible endeavour. He liked his landscapes to seethe with motion and his coasts to be crowded with rigging. The landscapes he came to hate later in the *Tour* were the very ones which are treasured today for their undeveloped, natural state. Show Defoe a National Park, and he would have retched. Westmoreland is 'a country eminent only for being the wildest, most barren and frightful of any that I have passed over in England'. The horror he felt for Britain's uplands was exacerbated by the effects of the Little Ice Age, which frequently inflicted wintry conditions on travellers, even in high summer. Crossing the Pennines in August, Defoe was caught by a snowstorm. Riding past the Lake District, he miserably noted the 'unpassable hills, whose tops, covered with snow, seemed to tell us all the pleasant part of England was at an end'. The further south he is, the better his outlook.

Defoe's coastal tour of East Anglia conveniently produces the perfect port. King's Lynn is 'rich and populous and thriving'; it is

⤛ Celia Fiennes ⤜

ABOVE Low tide on the River Esk

RIGHT Bath, the Queen's and King's Bath

BELOW Salisbury Plain

'The Struggle', Kirkstone Pass

Blackstone Edge (at top of central strip) in John Ogilby's *Britannia* of 1675

→→ **Daniel Defoe** ←←

18th-century Greenwich

LEFT Defoe's rebuilt London, 'the great centre of England'

CENTRE The River Blackwater, Essex

BELOW Salt marshes near Northey Island, Essex

Happisburgh, Norfolk

Brown and Hogenberg's copper engraving of Norwich, 1581

⊶ **Gilpin** ⊷

◁ LEFT The source of the River Wye,
on Plynlimon

BELOW LEFT Scaleby Castle, Cumbria

▽ BELOW The Wye, from Yat Rock

The old wharf, Brockweir

ABOVE Near Ross-on-Wye   BELOW The Wye, downstream of Bredwardine

'beautiful, well built, and well situated'; it is militarily secure, and it has the best social scene in Norfolk: 'Here,' applauds Defoe, 'are more gentry, and is consequently more gaiety in this town than in Yarmouth, or even in Norwich it self; the place abounding in very good company.' (One wonders what Dan got up to in Lynn.) Situated at the mouth of the River Ouse, Lynn has unparalleled access to the heavily populated hinterland of eastern England. In this era before the canal revolution, inland freight was restricted to roads and rivers, and so Defoe is able to claim that Lynn has 'the greatest extent of inland navigation ... of any port in England, London excepted'. From the Wash, a complex, dendritic system of navigable rivers squirms through the Fens, tapping into countless markets. Lynn's merchants are in a class of their own, supplying (claims Defoe) 'about six counties wholly, and three counties in part'. One of the most important river systems feeds barges up the Ouse, through Downham Market and the seasonal swamps of Whelpmoore, to Ely and into the River Cam, which leads (after 15 miles of Fenland meanders) to 'the very edge of the fair' – in Cambridge.

The 'fair' is Stourbridge Fair, 'not only the greatest in the whole nation, but in the world'. Defoe devotes three times more space in the *Tour* to Stourbridge Fair, than he does to Cambridge and its University. Not even the international fairs of Leipzig or Frankfurt, or Nuremberg or Augsburg, can – Defoe crows ('if I may believe those who have seen them all') – better Stourbridge Fair. Here on the meadows beside the Cam are arrayed 'goldsmiths, toyshops, braziers, turners, milliners, haberdashers, hatters, mercers, drapers, pewterers, china-warehouses, and in a word all trades that can be named in London; with coffee-houses, taverns, brandy-shops, and eating houses, innumerable, and all in tents, and booths'. Stourbridge was a lot more than an open-air superstore; this was Britain on exhibition; the trade fair and showcase for a modern economy.

The Fair can still be traced on the streets of suburban Cambridge. The Wool Fair and White Leather Fair are beneath the scrap yard and railway line by Swann Road. The Horse Fair took place on the southern side of Stourbridge Common. The Oyster Fair has been buried by the tarmac of what has become 'Oyster Road'. The main street which used to run through the heart of the Fair is now a residential road named 'Garlic Row'. If the ghost of Daniel Defoe is to be found anywhere, it is here on the banks of the Cam, recording the fruits of diligence. He died in debt, and on the run, five years after the final volume of the *Tour* was published.

Trailing Defoe back towards London and the end of his first 'Letter', I felt as though I'd been riding with the master of creative travel; a writer who knew better than any how to tease a story from every turn in the road. The *Tour* is a profoundly optimistic, imaginative work written by an outsider who felt compelled to see the best in his country. He had survived more catastrophes than can usually be compressed into a single life, and he rode the shires with the joyful curiosity of a traveller who knew he was lucky. Britain's natural resources and entrepreneurial spirit appeared unlimited. In the golden dawn of the 1720s, anything and everything appeared possible for 'the greatest trading country in the world'. Defoe's dream came true. We dug, forged, manufactured and traded our way to economic supremacy. And then environmental exhaustion. Faced with the challenge to promote a sustainable economic system, this wonderful, tempestuous man would be sharpening his quill.

WILLIAM GILPIN

1770

One man in a boat

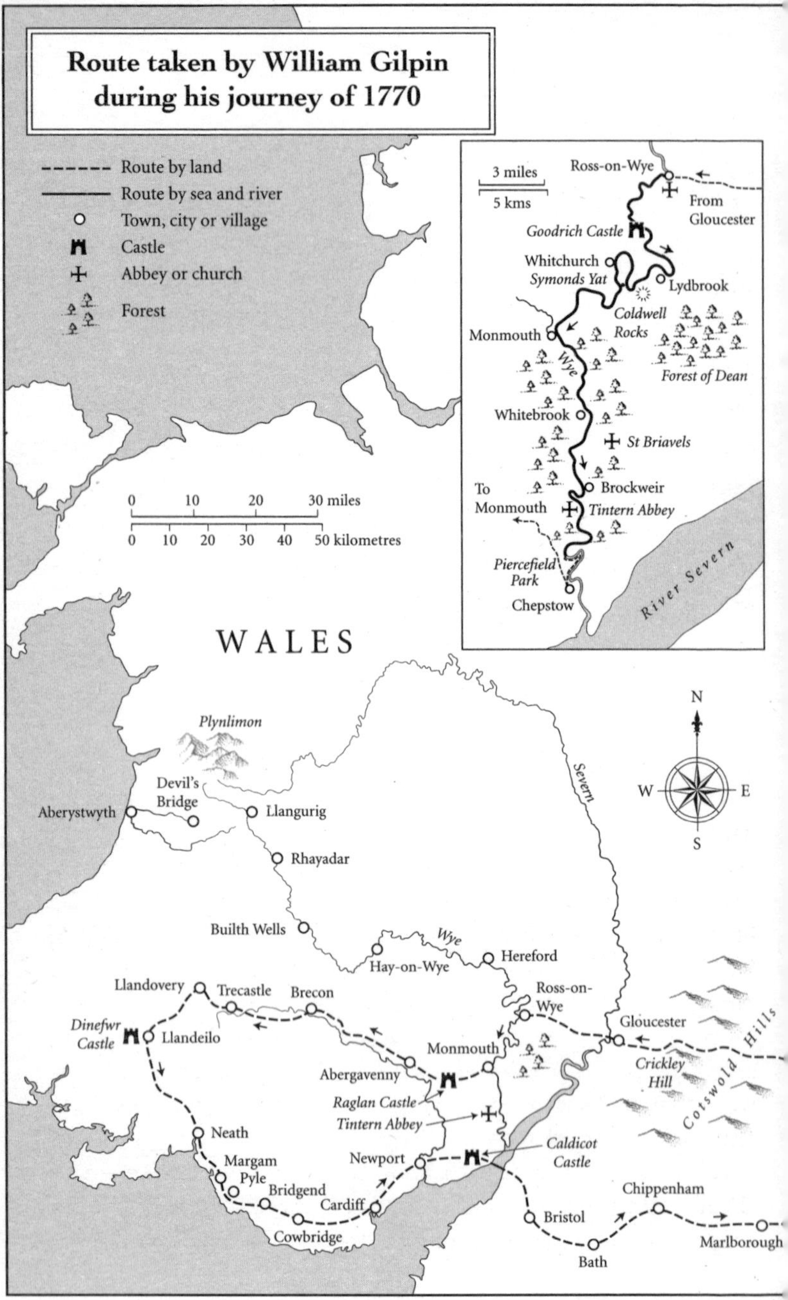

Route taken by William Gilpin during his journey of 1770
Route by land
Route by sea and river
Town, city or village
Castle
Abbey or church
Forest
0 10 20 30 miles
0 10 20 30 40 50 kilometres
3 miles
5 kms
Ross-on-Wye
From Gloucester
Goodrich Castle
Whitchurch
Symonds Yat
Lydbrook
Coldwell Rocks
Monmouth
Wye
Forest of Dean
Whitebrook
St Briavels
Brockweir
To Monmouth
Tintern Abbey
Piercefield Park
Chepstow
River Severn
WALES
N
W
E
S
Plynlimon
Devil's Bridge
Aberystwyth
Llangurig
Rhayadar
Severn
Builth Wells
Wye
Hay-on-Wye
Hereford
Llandovery
Trecastle
Brecon
Ross-on-Wye
Gloucester
Dinefwr Castle
Llandeilo
Monmouth
Abergavenny
Crickley Hill
Cotswold Hills
Raglan Castle
Tintern Abbey
Neath
Caldicot Castle
Margam
Pyle
Newport
Bridgend
Cardiff
Chippenham
Bristol
Cowbridge
Marlborough
Bath

*W*hen the Reverend William Gilpin *stepped aboard a rowing boat at Ross-on-Wye in 1770, he had no idea that his adventurous river voyage would lead to his ordination as 'The High Priest of the Picturesque'. The coldest period of the Little Ice Age had ended half a century earlier, the furnaces of the Industrial Revolution had just been fired, and Britain's landscape was entering an era of cataclysmic change. In shaping the taste for nature and for ruins, Gilpin accidentally became one of the most influential travellers of the eighteenth century. Published in 1783,* Observations on the River Wye *prepared the way for 'the Romantics', and allowed the Wye to stake its claim as the birthplace of British tourism.*

*

Ten days after seeing the Wye trickle from a spring in the mountainous heartland of Wales, I angled the prow of the canoe towards a dark arrowhead in the current and felt the hull surge towards the jaws of the gorge. Reefs of rocks reached out from each bank towards a space where the river appeared to fall over an edge. The little boat tilted and bucked. Water slopped inboard. Trees and rocks flashed by. Then all was calm. From somewhere in the sheer woods came the hollow knocking of a woodpecker. For two other-worldly miles, the Wye twisted through a green chasm. Each side of the river, tiers of foliage and rock scrambled skyward for 600 feet. There were no roads, and except for a couple of buildings and tracks, little sign of human presence.

I knew just then that I'd caught a glimpse of my visionary guide. 'The first source of amusement to the picturesque traveller,' he had written, 'is the *pursuit* of his object – the expectation of new scenes continually opening, and arising to his view.' Gilpin's traveller was an explorer. He was searching for beauty. And the essence of that beauty could be found in nature. The more natural the landscape, the closer you were to the object of your quest. 'We suppose the country to have been unexplored,' he wrote. 'Under this circumstance the mind is kept constantly in an agreeable suspence. The love of novelty is the foundation of this pleasure.'

The man who'd brought me to the Wye has been caricatured as one of the most incompetent travellers ever to grace an English byway. In the course of his various misadventures, he topples into mud and water, mistakes a gentleman's house for an inn, is pursued by a bull, and gets tied to a tree by highwaymen. Memorably, he is duped into buying a blind horse, and of course he gets lost. 'Dr Syntax' was the creation of Thomas Rowlandson and Dr William Combe; in Syntax, the old travelling elite could amuse themselves with the quaint notion that the middle classes had discovered tourism. Syntax was well-meaning, sensible, and yet doomed to ridicule by the absurdity of his quest:

> *I'll make a* TOUR – *and then I'll* WRITE IT,
> You well know what my pen can do,
> And I'll employ my pencil too:-
> I'll ride and *write*, and *sketch* and *print*,
> And thus create a real mint;
> I'll *prose* it here, I'll *verse* it there,
> And *picturesque* it ev'ry where,
> I'll do what all have done before;
> I think I shall – and somewhat more.

Most who bought *The Tour of Dr Syntax in search of the Picturesque* knew that the catastrophe-prone curate was based upon the one-time vicar of Boldre and 'apostle of the Picturesque'.

William Gilpin was born in a castle of blood-red sandstone in sight of the Lake District. Scaleby's gentle vale has been altered somewhat by Carlisle Airport and the M6, but if you know which roads to take, there are still corners of eighteenth-century tranquillity.

A third-generation artist, young Gilpin knew the vale well. Beyond the copses and fields of barley and oats, Hadrian's Wall ran along the far side of Brunstock Beck, just a mile from the castle's dishevelled walls. Scaleby had been battered during the Civil War, and partially restored by the time Gilpin was born in 1724. On a clear day, young William would have seen the southern horizon crinkled with Lake District peaks. He was schooled locally in Carlisle, then sent to the Free Grammar School at St Bees on the Cumberland coast, and finally to Queen's College, Oxford. Coincidentally, Gilpin left Oxford in the year – 1744 – that a young Welsh gentleman called Thomas Pennant matriculated at Queen's. Neither student appears to have drawn measurable benefit from University, Gilpin regretting the time 'squandered on the appearance of doing something more', while Pennant failed to graduate at all. Between them, this pair of drop-outs would play a leading role in forming a bridgehead between Britain's 10,000-year history of exploration, and the age of tourism.

Two years after graduating, Gilpin was ordained as a deacon and appointed curate of Irthington, the neighbouring village to Scaleby. It was an exciting time to move in ecclesiastical circles; the securities offered by the Toleration Act of 1689 had given Britons an extraordinary liberty of worship. A heretical spirit was sweeping the country, and Christianity was being exchanged for a new belief in the divinity of nature. In Gilpin's low-Church, liberal perspective, proof of God's existence could be found in the natural world, rather than through scripture alone. Like many of his age, he had been influenced by the amiable philosopher Lord Shaftesbury, to whom the universe exhibited all the signs of divine design. God, the artist-creator, had brought 'beauty' to Earth through harmony, proportion and order. Freed from the old rigidities of religion, Britons turned to their landscapes. In literature, and in the arts and design, nature would set the agenda for the next hundred years. Gilpin found himself in the midst of a spiritual revolution.

One of the most exciting laboratories for exploring nature's rela-tionship with the divine was a garden in Buckinghamshire. In verdant farmland, Stowe's owners had created an incredible themed park dotted with classical temples, bridges, lakes and a 'Shrine of British Worthies'. Visitors were enchanted, and educated. Accessible from London, and vigorously promoted through its own guidebook and the engravings of Jacques Rigau, Stowe was a must-see for England's elite. Here, one's taste – and moral worth – could be improved and updated in a single, fashionable ramble through a terrestrial paradise. Stowe was a thrilling work-in-progress. When Celia Fiennes called by fifty years earlier, she had found Sir Richard Temple's new gardens pleasant, if unremarkable ('replenished with all the curiosityes or requisites for ornamental pleasure and use'), but between 1712 and the 1740s, Temple's son, Viscount Cobham, had devoted his wife's brewing fortune to transforming the estate. Cobham and his designer, Charles Bridgeman, broke all the rules, and invited nature into the garden. They achieved this with a 'ha-ha', an ingenious new type of barrier which allowed unobstructed views to be appreciated from a house through to the countryside beyond. Instead of by fences and hedges, livestock was excluded from the man-made gardens by a hidden, steep-sided ditch. Cattle and sheep could be seen grazing in what appeared to be an extension of the gardens. At Stowe, the ha-ha was just the start. Cobham had banished all the formalities inherited from Versailles. Out went symmetry and manicured topiary; in came serpentine paths and constant references to the natural form of the landscape. The carefully sited monuments and temples expressed the ideals of his time. Stowe's head gardener since 1741 had been a Northumbrian called Lancelot 'Capability' Brown, who had been working with Cobham for several years on the 'Grecian Valley', an ambitious plan which included a grass amphitheatre and a Greek temple. Brown's 'great merit', Gilpin would write later, 'lay in pursuing the path which nature had marked out.' One of Stowe's many fans was the poet of the age, Alexander Pope, whose *Epistle to Cobham* made Stowe a focal point of literary Britain. 'All gardening,' declared Pope, 'is like landscape painting.' For its genteel visitors, Stowe was a window on nature. Safely behind the ha-ha, the leisured classes could observe the form of the countryside without the risk of stepping in mud.

Inevitably, Gilpin found his way to Stowe, visiting the gardens in 1747, shortly after returning to Oxford for his MA. He left Buckinghamshire as an author, and as a visionary:

> Our Gardens for the most Part were laid out in so formal, aukward, and wretched a Manner, that they were really a Scandal to the very Genius of the Nation... But Stow, it is to be hoped, may work some Reformation: I would have our Country Squires flock hither two or three times in a Year, by way of Improvement, and after they have looked about them a little, return Home with new Notions, and begin to see the Absurdity of their clipped Yews, their Box-wood Borders, their flourished Parterres, and their lofty Brick-walls.

Published anonymously in 1748, when Gilpin was just twenty-four, *Dialogue upon the Gardens of the Right Honourable the Lord Viscount Cobham at Stowe* was a sixty-page, trial airing of his views on the nature of landscapes.

Gilpin's 'new notions' were nourished over the next twenty years in the theatre of education, first as a teacher and then as headmaster of Cheam School for Boys in Surrey. Despite the fact that his *Dialogue* was re-published in 1749 and 1751, he seems to have been reluctant to return to print. Devoted to his family and his school, he preferred to circulate his various authorial 'amusements' in manuscript form among friends and relatives, rather than hawk his wares in the market place. 'The hazard and expense,' he explained, 'had rather a formidable appearance.' When one of his fans, the Duchess of Portland, sent Gilpin a generous subscription of one hundred pounds, he squirmed free of her financial embrace: 'I could not accept her grace's kindness,' he recalled, 'as I was still afraid of an *engagement with the public.*'

Eventually, in 1768, aged forty-four, Gilpin was persuaded to send one of his manuscripts to the London publisher J. Robson. *An Essay upon Prints* was a remarkable little book. Confident, authoritative, and written with flair and clarity, it was the first English guide to print collecting, and one of the earliest publications to address engraving as a fine art. Again, Gilpin declined to put his name on the title page, and the preface – written apparently by a third party

– is almost apologetic: 'The following work,' it begins, 'hath lain by the author at least fifteen years, in which time, as nothing had appeared upon the subject, he took the liberty to offer it to the public with whatever faults it might have.' Tip-toeing towards the art fraternity, he unfurled his intention to 'put the elegant amusement of collecting prints upon a more rational footing'. He began by listing the terms which should be used to describe prints: 'Composition', 'Design' ... 'Expression', 'Effect', 'Spirit' ... 'Manner' and 'Picturesque'. This was Gilpin's first use in print of the word. Until then, 'picturesque' had been taken to mean 'graphic' or simply 'pictorial'. A couple of years later, when Pennant referred to the 'picturesque and magnificent scenery' beside the river at Dundonnell, he meant that it looked like a picture. But to Gilpin, the word was fundamentally associated with the wonder of God's Creation.

In the pages which followed, Gilpin slashed and hurrahed his way through Europe's great masters. Rembrandt's landscapes had 'very little to recommend them'; Berghem had 'genius truly pastoral' when it came to cows; Sadler's landscapes were 'picturesque and romantic', although their manner was 'dry and disagreeable'; Piranesi was unbeatable for his ability to capture 'a defaced capital, a ruined wall, or broken fluting'. Claude Lorraine may have been surprised to learn that his etchings were 'below his character'; his talents, opined the Reverend Gilpin, 'lay upon his palette'. Who, then, won the 'landskip' contest? Well, it was Anthonie Waterloo. 'Waterlo,' announced Gilpin, 'is a name beyond any other in landscape.' The Flemish etcher knew nature like no other: 'His subjects are perfectly rural,' enthused Gilpin. 'Simplicity is their characteristic... A coppice, a corner of a forest, a winding road, or a straggling village... Every object that he touches, has the character of nature.'

An Essay upon Prints was a runaway success. Translations into French, German and Dutch followed, and Gilpin's 246-page guide became a standard reference for print connoisseurs. A copy even made its way into the library of Thomas Jefferson. Fashionable society seemed ready for some rules.

*

Gilpin took to the road the summer that his bestseller began pouring from London bookshops. In 1768, he toured Kent. In 1769, he toured Essex, Suffolk and Norfolk. Then in 1770, he headed west, to the river Wye and south Wales. Other tours covered Cumberland and Westmorland, the Scottish Highlands, south-west England and Wales.

Britain was now in the throes of unprecedented change. The Industrial Revolution had kicked into gear in the 1760s and – encouraged by a surge in food supply and mass production of everyday necessities – cities and towns were expanding fast: between 1750 and 1800, the population would soar from around 6–7 million to 9 million. As James Cook set sail for the Antipodes, and Thomas Pennant sailed off to explore the Highlands of Scotland, England discovered tourism. With much of the continent a war zone, the Grand Tour of Europe was being spurned in favour of domestic adventures. England offered brisk, low-risk, affordable encounters with an exciting range of unfamiliar landscapes.

'We travel for various purposes,' explained Gilpin, 'to explore the culture of the soils, to view the curiosities of art, to survey the beauties of nature, and to learn the manners of men, their different politics and modes of life.' On the itineraries of these summer tours of enlightenment would be Benedictine ruins and megalithic stones, industrial works, natural wonders, houses and gardens. Typical among these pioneers was the Honourable John Byng. After twenty years in Guards regiments, he landed a second career with the Inland Revenue, which gave him the chance to take two- or three-month tours each summer. Byng lived for his travelling: 'Oh, that I had stayed in London till this day,' he exclaimed after six weeks on the road, 'and that now my holidays were to begin, for this was a summer's day, with a high and blue sky.'

Conditions for travel in England had never been better. The Little Ice Age had thawed in the early 1700s, and the travelling season was longer than it had been for Fiennes and Defoe. The road network was enjoying an unprecedented makeover, with the four middle decades of the eighteenth century seeing an explosion in turnpike trusts. When Defoe was travelling in the 1720s, the average number of turnpike acts passed each year by Parliament was a little over eight. In the twenty years from 1751, the annual figure rose above forty. Provincial cities like York and Exeter, which used to be three or four days' travel from London in the 1720s, were suddenly little more than twenty-four hours away. The rate at which horse-drawn coaches could travel also increased with the introduction of Arab bloodstock, while comfort (and speed) was increased as flexible steel springs gradually replaced leather braces. With improving roads came better inns and a range of travellers' aids. 'We are tolerably well accompanied,' observed Byng as he set out in June 1781, 'with touring, road books, maps etc.' It is a measure of just how far and fast you could travel that Gilpin undertook his 1770 tour of the Wye and south Wales in just a fortnight, during which time he covered around 400 miles.

Gilpin returned from his summer tours with copious notes and sketches which he assembled into finished manuscripts. *On the Lakes and Mountains of the Northern Parts of England* grew into an eight-volume monster containing 830 pages and 249 sketches. He was a publisher's nightmare: 'I have not the most distant idea of printing them,' he informed London publisher William Mason, the man who would eventually tease Gilpin into print again. Mason encouraged Gilpin 'to make an essay in a smaller work of the same kind'. The 'smaller work' Gilpin chose to present to Mason was the account of his journey of 1770 down the River Wye. Included with the text were fifteen prints derived by Gilpin's nephew from original sketches. Nevertheless, it wasn't until 1783 that the first one appeared (the date on the book's title page is 1782, but publication had been delayed due to problems with the aquatint illustrations). *Observations on the River Wye and Several Parts of South Wales, etc. Relative Chiefly to Picturesque Beauty* would change the way Britons viewed their landscapes.

*

Gilpin's quest for the picturesque began at Heathrow: 'Crossing Hounslow Heath from Kingston in Surrey,' he writes, 'we struck into the Reading road...' With pauses to condemn the 'heavy' beeches dotted around Capability Brown's park at Caversham House, and to scrutinise views of the Thames ('nothing very interesting'), he passed through Oxford and began the long, gentle climb westward on the Gloucester turnpike, through the Cotswolds, until the land abruptly fell away to reveal a breathtaking panorama. Here, on Crickley Hill, Gilpin presented his readers with a prospect of the journey ahead.

Crickley Hill had been a vantage point for thousands of years before Gilpin peered over its brow. A sharp, triangular promontory formed from Jurassic coral beds, it juts west from the scarp slope of the Cotswolds, 600 feet above a vast green vale. The remains of Stone Age ramparts – scattered with arrowheads and carrying evidence of a burned palisade – lie beneath one of the highest surviving Iron Age bulwarks in Britain. By the 1770s, the view from Crickley Hill was familiar to any on the London–Gloucester coach road who'd dared to snatch a glance from the carriage window before tipping over the edge and skidding alarmingly into the Vale of Gloucester. But few would have dismounted and asked themselves what they were looking at. 'I know not,' Gilpin pens, 'that I was ever more struck with the singularity and grandeur of any landscape.'

Gilpin recognised the Cotswolds as an unusual landform. Where many hill ranges had slopes of equivalent gradient on both sides, the Cotswolds were different. The beds of hard limestone which overlay this part of England have been tilted downward to the east and south-east, and raised in the west, where the underlying softer rocks have been eroded to create an asymmetric hill range. When nature, explains Gilpin, 'raises a country through a progress of a hundred miles, and then breaks it down at once by an abrupt precipice into an expansive vale, we are immediately struck with the novelty and grandeur of the scene.' You only have to compare his spirited response to Gloucestershire's geology with that of the Honourable John Byng to see the novelty of Gilpin's viewpoint. Arriving at the same spot eleven years later, the retired Lieutenant Colonel reacts rather differently: 'This is a truly fine prospect,' he concedes, 'yet prospects please me but for an instant, for they fatigue my eyes and flurry my nerves, and I always wish to find myself in the tranquil vale beneath.'

In an age before aerial views, it was the sheer immensity of the panorama which so moved Gilpin. 'Perhaps nowhere in England a distance so rich,' he avowed, 'and at the same time so extensive, can be found.' What he could see was perhaps a twenty- or thirty-mile stretch of the Vale of Severn: 'The eye was lost in the profusion of objects which were thrown at once before it, and ran wild over the vast expanse with rapture and astonishment…' Two or three miles to the north, the town of Cheltenham lay spread beneath their boots. Far up the vale rose the twin eminencies of Bredon Hill and the Malvern Hills, and between them Tewkesbury's church, 'bosomed in wood'. On a clear day, fancied Gilpin, one might even spy the towers of Worcester. To the west lay Gloucester, also between two hills. But the furthest and most inviting objects in this enormous prospect were far to the west, where 'a distant forest-view' and a thin line of Welsh mountains united the '*determined form*' of a slender, yet discernible, body of water; 'an arm', ventured Gilpin, 'of the sea'.

This Cotswold scarp was England's Darien peak; the natural barrier dividing the waters of the Thames from those of the Severn. Crossing the watershed, Gilpin clattered down the turnpike into Gloucester, where he took a quick look at the cathedral, and then pressed on towards the river which had lured him from London.

*

Those of watery sensitivities still lose their hearts to the Wye. Geology and climate have given it beauty, and the currents of human affairs have given it a story to tell. Although Gilpin's tour concentrated on a thirty-eight-mile section of the lower Wye, he managed to include the entire river in his book, by recycling a description from a borrowed journal.

The river rises in the heart of Wales, on (according to Gilpin's source) 'vast, wild, and unfurnished' Plynlimon. This remote massif rears in massive shoulders to 2,467 feet and is marked on the medieval Gough map as a huge, green blob. Just two miles across the mountain's upper slopes from the rising of the Wye, are the sources of the River Severn: 'The two springs,' records Gilpin, 'are nearly alike, but the fortunes of rivers, like those of men, are owing to various little circumstances, of which they take the advantage in the early parts of their course.'

Tumbling down its rocky bed from Plynlimon, the Wye clatters through Llangurig to Builth Wells, then at Llyswen its southerly flow is blocked by the Black Mountains and it swerves towards England. Gilpin wondered whether this upper section of the river might be the most beautiful part of the entire Wye, and in many ways, he was right. Until it turns to skirt the Black Mountains, the river still behaves like a mountain stream, running fast and clear through wooded clefts. When it's not jostling over shingle, or falling over lips of bedrock, the river tends to pond into black pools where salmon rest in the shadows of overhanging trees. I have never seen trees like the oaks on the Wye; they seem as old as the river itself, with immense, complicated crowns which seem to reflect the Wye's own, infinitely complex, dendritic capillaries. Fed by ever-smaller tributaries, they reduce to invisibility somewhere in the Welsh heartland. It is in his depiction of trees, decided Gilpin in his *Essay upon Prints*, that his great hero, Anthonie Waterloo, 'particularly excels'.

The character of the Wye is changing by the time it ripples across the border at Hay, and begins to meander uncertainly eastwards past Clifford Castle and Merbach Hill, to the red-brick bridge at Bredwardine. After cutting under the precipitous cliff known as 'The Scar', even lazier loops unravel past Capability Brown's park at Moccas, to Hereford, where another change of direction sets the Wye on a collision course with a band of limestone, and a spectacular rejuvenation. This is the section of the river towards which Gilpin was headed.

When Gilpin first caught sight of the river, that summer's day in 1770, the Wye was a little-known backwater. Gerald of Wales described the course of the river so accurately from its source on Plynlimon, past the castles at Hay and Goodrich to the Forest of Dean ('full of deer and where iron-ore is mined'), that he seems to speak from first-hand knowledge. But Celia Fiennes never saw the river, and Daniel Defoe had been unable to reach the Wye on his great tour because of 'the badness and danger' of the ferries over the River Severn. Instead, he had relied on memories from an earlier visit; and those memories were not going to trigger a rush of well-heeled sightseers. 'Hereford,' he warned, 'is truly an old, mean built, and very dirty city, lying low, and on the bank of the Wye, which sometimes incommodes them very much, by the violent freshes that come down from the mountains of Wales.' The Wye's huge drainage area of 1,609 square miles, and various constrictions, cause wildly temperamental water levels; droughts can reduce the river to a placid stream, while downpours in the Welsh hills can fill myriad tributaries to brimming and turn the Wye into a solid, brown torrent. Bridges over the river are infrequent, and high-arched. In Leland's day, there were no bridges at all between Builth Wells and Hereford, and only one – at Monmouth – between Ross and the sea; Chepstow's timber bridge had been torn away. Despite the roads revolution, the Welsh border in Gilpin's day was an infamous brown hole on the transport map. Pack horses, rather than waggons, were still being used to shift goods across Herefordshire, and most of the roads were medieval sloughs. When the agricultural writer Arthur Young came this way shortly before Gilpin, he warned that the roads from Chepstow were 'mere rocky lanes, full of hugeous stones as big as one's horse, and abominable holes'. Another traveller, attempting to reach Tintern Abbey overland from Monmouth in the late 1700s, complained of 'hollow and uncouth tracks, seldom attempted by any carriage but those of the natives'.

One of the few border routes to have been improved was the main road between the cathedral cities of Gloucester and Hereford, and it was a small town on this road which would soon claim its title as the tourist capital of the Wye. Ross-on-Wye had developed and prospered around one of the rare bridging points on the river, and in the 1720s, it became one of the first market towns in England to be connected by turnpike to a city. Ross, recorded Defoe, was renowned for its cider, its iron-ware, and for its 'monstrous fat woman' whose waist measured three yards. Defoe – who could never resist a revolting aside – added that Ross-on-Wye's giantess 'was obliged to have a small stool placed before her, to rest her belly on, and the like'. Reading Defoe, eighteenth-century travellers could be forgiven for thinking that the Wye was the home of the grotesque, rather than the picturesque. But Defoe had missed the town's star turn. If he'd managed to reach Ross during the travels which formed the basis of his great *Tour*, rather than used recollections from an earlier visit, he'd have met an extraordinary man called John Kyrle. Kyrle had devoted himself to the welfare of Ross, distributing alms, improving the education of children, arbitrating in squabbles, embellishing the town with gardens, and aiding the construction of a new, taller church spire. Immortalised as 'The Man of Ross' in 1732 by Alexander Pope, Kyrle had died in 1724, the year Defoe's *Tour* was published. Admirers of Pope's *Moral Essays* knew Kyrle as the standard bearer for civic philanthropy. In an era of broadening spiritual perspectives, Kyrle had unwittingly laid the foundation stone for Christian tourism on the Wye.

When Gilpin's coach rumbled along the turnpike into Ross in 1772, the landmark he first spotted was Kyrle's slender church spire rising like a beacon above the flood plain. In the footsteps of Pope, Gilpin walked through the churchyard to Kyrle's 'Prospect' and gazed for the first time upon 'an easy sweep of the Wye'. Modern visitors making the same pilgrimage will be disappointed: the view-point on The Prospect is structurally unsafe, and inaccessible behind temporary fencing; elsewhere, roofs and trees block all but broken glimpses of the Wye's famous meander. Actually, Gilpin wasn't that impressed, anyway. While conceding that the churchyard commanded 'many distant views', and that they were 'indeed very amusing', the outlook was 'not picturesque'. The problem was that the view contained 'no characteristic objects' and that it was 'broken into too many parts'. The most commendable feature was Pope's 'heav'n directed spire'.

Poke about on the banks of the Wye at Ross and you can still find reminders of its one-time role as the launch-slip of the 'Wye Tour'. On the outside curve of the horseshoe bend are fragments of old wharf, and in one place, the ribs of an old boat. In front of the Hope and Anchor, concrete steps lead down the bank where timber skiffs once waited for customers.

By the time Gilpin came down to the water, the Wye Tour had been growing in popularity for some years. In 1745, a local rector called Dr John Egerton had constructed a sightseeing boat so that he could take his guests on summer trips down the river. Egerton's boat rotted in the mud after he left the borders in 1756 to become Bishop of Bangor, but around 1760 a local basket maker called James Evans had begun hiring out boats. By the 1760s, the river had been spotted by the scribe of the gardens movement, Thomas Whateley. His descriptions of New Weir and Tintern Abbey were published in *Observations on Modern Gardening*, which appeared in 1770, the year Gilpin headed west.

Gilpin hired a covered boat, with a local crew of three men. His plan was to use the boat for just one day, disembarking twenty miles downstream at Monmouth, where a chaise would be waiting to take him on by road to Tintern and Chepstow. Gilpin quickly found himself in a riparian paradise. The early moments of a river journey can be charmed with a kind of magical incredulity. Left behind is the tumult and visual chaos of road travel, with its discomforts and unwanted decisions. In its place is a gentler, simpler form of movement. Pause on the oars, and the silence can turn a boat into an innocuous leaf, borne upon the current. Landscapes glide by at a rate which permits appreciation, and there are no options to weigh, for there is only one, and it ends at the sea.

When you take to the lower Wye in a small boat, the first thing you notice is the height of the banks. Set deep between sharp, parallel edges, the watercourse could have been carefully excavated by a cosmic trowel. Gilpin needed no further evidence of God's handiwork: 'The channel of no river,' he announces shortly after boarding at Ross, 'can be more decisively marked than that of the Wye.' Here in Herefordshire was evidence of Creation: 'A nobler *water-course* was never *divided* for any river than this of the Wye,' he continues, 'we see a channel marked with such precision, that it appears as if originally intended only for the bed of a river.'

Gilpin introduces his picturesque system cautiously, explaining that nature works, 'no doubt harmoniously', on such a vast scale that it is 'beyond human comprehension'. In the meantime, the artist 'is confined to a *span*' and 'lays down his little rules, which he calls the *principles of picturesque beauty*, merely to adapt such diminutive parts of nature's surfaces to his own eye as come within scope'. More simplistic and accessible than the intensely stirred emotions of the Sublime, the Picturesque was intended to rationalise the appreciation of nature.

The first few miles from Ross were a calm prelude to the spectacle soon to erupt from the river banks. Gilpin used this stretch of river to rehearse the Picturesque's 'little rules'. The perfect river-view, he explains, is composed of 'four grand parts': the river itself in the foreground, the two 'side-screens' formed by the opposing banks, and finally the 'front screen', which is the onward view of the 'winding of the river'. Perspective would be led by the pair of side-screens. Amplifying himself, Gilpin points out that a long, straight Dutch canal would have no front screen, while its side-screens would taper to a point. What makes the Wye so unusual is the extraordinary diversity of its screens. Such is the 'exceedingly varied' nature of the river that one bank can be lofty and precipitous, while the other can be level. Or both can be precipitous, or both flat. Further variations are created by 'the folding of the side-screens over each other', which have the effect of hiding from view the onward winding river, the 'front screen'. Lest readers think it's *too* simple, Gilpin appends 'complex' variations, such as side-screens composed of both lofty and level banks. And that is just the start.

To the compositional screens can be added four types of embellishment which he terms 'ornaments'. These are ground, wood, rocks and buildings. All will be revealed in the first couple of hours on the river. 'Ground', explains Gilpin, can range 'from the steepest precipice to the flattest meadow', while a sub-category of 'broken ground' offers a wide range of surfaces from 'naked soil' to waterfalls and dry, stony channels. Bald downland is particularly unattractive, and drystone walls 'the most offensive separation of property'. The colour of broken ground is a significant picturesque element too, and the Wye can produce a palette which ranges from 'the yellow or the red ochre, the ashy grey, the black earth, or the marly blue', while the 'intermixtures of these with each other, and the patches of verdure, blooming heath, and other vegetable tints, still increase the variety'.

The other three ornaments are defined in similarly specific terms. Unaware of the havoc about to be wreaked on the countryside by the Industrial Revolution, Gilpin sees the destruction of woodland through rose-tinted eye-glasses. The Wye's woods, he states, are made more picturesque by the partial felling for the 'many works carried on by fire', which lead to 'a kind of alternacy' in the tree cover. Industry itself can be picturesque: 'One circumstance attending this alternacy is pleasing. Many of the furnaces on the banks of the river consume charcoal, which is manufactured on the spot; and the smoke issuing from the sides of the hills, and spreading its thin veil over a part of them, beautifully breaks their lines, and unites them with the sky.'

The third ornament, rock, is an element rare to large English rivers. Gilpin was no fan of rock in its 'bleak, naked and unadorned' form. Put him in a raft down the Grand Canyon, or on a ledge in Yosemite, and he'd have been appalled by the ugliness. Tint the same rock with mosses and lichens however, and you have 'a degree of beauty'. Adorn it with shrubs and 'hanging herbage', and 'you make it still more picturesque'.

Gilpin's list of picturesque buildings includes abbeys, castles, village spires, forges, mills, and bridges. The lower Wye is rich in this ornament: 'One or other of these venerable vestiges of past, or cheerful habitations of present times, characterise almost every scene.' Buildings, thinks Gilpin, are not necessary for us to appreciate the full wonder of a natural landscape; forests and lakes, rock and mountains are more than enough to 'furnish an inexhausted source of pleasure'. But once such views are contained within a frame, some types of buildings become important: 'Indeed the landscape painter seldom thinks his view perfect without characterizing it by some object of this kind.' Unacceptable buildings include industrial sites and profusions of whitened houses.

So much for the theory. The reality was rather more testing. Shortly after Gilpin left Ross, it began to rain. This was not what the Reverend had planned. In another age, he might have logged onto the Met Office website from an hotel in Ross, and waited for an incoming high-pressure. But he was 200 years too early, and he was in for a soaker. 'I must, however, premise,' he apologises, 'how ill-qualified I am to do justice to the banks of the Wye, were it only from having seen them under the circumstance of a continued rain, which began early in the day, before one third of our voyage was performed.' Having followed Gilpin's wake down this wonderful river, beneath a Mediterranean ceiling, I can sense the anguish in his words. Of his own bad luck, Gilpin can only offer a plaintive line upon the effects of falling rain on the picturesque: 'It is true, scenery at *hand* suffers less under such a circumstance, than scenery at a *distance*, which it totally obscures.' It must have been absolutely pelting down.

In that first hour or so before the first drops of rain pocked the river surface, his boat slid downstream to the rhythmic creak and plash of heavy, wooden oars. Just before Pencraig, the river twists through a double-bend, and Gilpin was able to observe the pictur-esque effects of the river surface: 'The bank,' he notes, 'soon began to swell on the right, and was richly adorned with wood. We admired it much; and also the vivid images reflected from the water, which were continually disturbed as we sailed past them, and thrown into tremulous confusion by the dashing of our oars.' Reflections, like memories, had a beauty of their own: 'A disturbed surface of water endeavouring to collect its scattered images and restore them to order, is among the *pretty* appearances of nature.'

Almost anywhere he looked, Gilpin could find elements of beauty. 'Even the rain gave a gloomy grandeur to many of the scenes,' he noted, 'and by throwing a veil of obscurity over the removed banks of the river, introduced, now and then, something like a pleasing distance.'

In the course of his two days on the river, Gilpin would muse on many views, but three of them stood out as exemplars. Four miles downstream of Ross, the first 'grand view' began to appear in the distance. From an implacable stream, they watched a fractured tower rise above the trees. 'A reach of the river, forming a noble bay, is spread before the eye,' observes Gilpin. 'The bank, on the right, is steep, and covered with wood; beyond which a bold promontory shoots out, crowned with a castle, rising among trees.' Due to the heavy rain, Gilpin was advised not to land and attempt the slippery ascent to the castle. But he hastily sketched the scene: 'This view, which is one of the grandest on the river, I should not scruple to call *correctly picturesque*, which is seldom the character of a purely natural scene.'

Goodrich ticked the boxes: the 'parts are few; and the whole', concluded Gilpin, 'is a simple exhibition'. Visiting the same spot in a canoe, I spent an energetic hour or so criss-crossing the river, then wading upstream, hauling the boat against the current, in a futile attempt to match Gilpin's aquatint with the actual landscape. Gilpin's version of Goodrich has an elegant, eroded profile, with a staircase of battlements ascending to a pair of noble turrets. Below the gaunt walls is a formidable cliff adorned with vegetation, and a massive, sculptural rock reflected in the still, deep-looking waters of a narrow river. It looks a bit like a gorge in the upper Rhine, decorated with a borrowed Byzantine citadel. The effect is undeniably pleasing, but untrue. Gilpin re-engineered the castle, invented the cliff (and the rock) and halved the width of the river. 'I am so attached to my picturesque rules,' he admitted later to an indignant William Mason, 'that if nature gets it wrong, I cannot help putting her right.' Gilpin never meant his hasty sketches to be factual representations: 'I did all I could to make people believe they were general ideas, or illustrations,' he explained.

It's not difficult to sympathise with Gilpin. Most landscape photography is an exercise in omission; a tilt or shift of focal-length craftily cutting from view the dumped fridge or ubiquitous queue of cars. Perhaps a modern qualification is needed, though. Today, it's not so much nature that 'gets it wrong', as *human* nature. Since the beginning of my Wye journey on Plynlimon's windy shoulder, I'd gathered a mental scrapbook of rustic discordancies: massive, flat-pack farm buildings; crude, concrete bridges; Brobdingnagian pylons; rashes of roadsigns; architectural aberrations. In the overall picture, they were but flashes of unsightliness, but they were matched by equivalent assaults on the ear. On the slopes of Plynlimon, where the Wye trickles from a cushion of sphagnum moss, the air was torn by fighter-bombers, and then by rally cars.

From the mountain's foot to Llyswen, the river is shadowed by the A44 and then by the A470, so cars and trucks are an almost constant, ambient soundtrack. For precious miles north of Builth, the 470 is forced away from the river, but it is a rare segment of tranquillity. From Kerne Bridge, the river acts like the slow lane on the B4234. Motor vehicles flash past unconcerned herons. The picturesque depends on selective use of a single sense: sight. Gilpin's idealised views tell you nothing of the true state of nature: the pollutants in the water, the collapsing salmon population, the anguish that can attend modern farming.

An hour or so after leaving Goodrich, Gilpin's boat rounded a sweeping, right-hand bend and he was confronted by his first sight of modern industry: 'All has thus far been grandeur and tranquillity,' he muses. 'It continues so yet; but mixed with life and bustle.' The source of this activity was the long wharf on the outer bend of the river at Lydbrook, where coal from the Forest of Dean was shipped out to Hereford and beyond. Horses and carts were grinding up and down the long, diagonal roadway cut into the river bluff between the moored vessels and the mines. The novelty of fossil-fuel extraction appealed to Gilpin: 'Here the scene is new and pleasing,' he writes. 'The contrast of all this business, the engines used in lading and unlading, together with the variety of the scene, produce all together a picturesque assemblage.' Detached from the sweat and curses of the toiling men by the river, Gilpin was able to view the scene with Breughelesque amusement.

*

The greatest physical spectacle on the Wye begins as a tease. Gilpin describes their approach as if he's unveiling his 'screens': the front screen appearing as a wooded hill, 'swelling to a point' and then changing again into a lofty side-screen, 'while the front unfolds itself into a majestic piece of rock-scenery'.

They had reached the 'Yat', or gate.

At Coldwell Rocks, the river performs one of its most extreme meanders, taking a four-mile loop northward out of the hills, only to return to within 500 yards of its earlier course. Gilpin had intended to disembark at Coldwell, and to hike over the steep ridge at the 'neck' of the meander. He'd been promised 'very noble river-views' from the top of the climb, but once again, the rain forced him to stay on the boat. He'd have found the climb quite an adventure. Seventy years later, Louisa Anne Twamley recorded 'toils and tumbles' as she climbed up to 'the platform of rock crowning the narrow ridge'. Today, a footpath scrabbles upward through the foliage to a vast car-park furnished with public conveniences and a cafe. Yat Rock, once a precarious slab poised above the abyss, is now rimmed with a stone wall and polished by millions of shoe-soles. On summer weekends, it looks like the deck of a cruise ship entering port. The view is still astonishing: far below, the river unwinds through a wooded gorge which opens like a flower into decorated farmland.

Denied his aerial view, Gilpin emerged from his four-mile detour to be confronted by the river's greatest natural wonder, 'the second grand scene on the Wye'. Since picturesque tended to diminish with elevation, he had missed little by failing to reach Yat Rock:

> The river is wider than usual in this part; and takes a sweep around a towering promontory of rock; which forms the side-screens on the left, and is the grand feature of the view. It is not a broad fractured face of rock; but rather a woody hill, from which large rocky projections, in two or three places, burst out; rudely hung with twisting branches and shaggy furniture, which, like mane around a lion's head, give a more savage air to these wild exhibitions of nature. Near the top a pointed fragment of solitary rock, rising above the rest, has a rather fantastic appearance; but it is not without its effect in marking the scene.

Gilpin was reminded of Virgil's description in *The Aeneid* of the dizzy needle of rock toppled by Hercules as he demolishes the horrid lair of Cocus. From the hamlet on the bank facing Yat Rock, 'volumes of thick smoke, thrown up at intervals from an iron forge, as its fires receive fresh fuel, add double grandeur to the scene'. Beneath the gauzy precipice is, continues Gilpin, 'a circumstance on the water'.

Approaching the rapid at Symonds Yat in a canoe, you are aware of an odd shift in the river's perspective, as if the scene has been scissored in two and then incorrectly joined. This was probably the first rapid Gilpin had shot:

> The whole river at this place makes a precipitate fall; of no great height indeed, but enough to merit the name of a cascade; though to the eye, above the stream, it is an object of no consequence. In all the scenes we had yet passed, the water, moving with a slow and solemn pace, the objects around kept time, as it were, with it; and every steep and every rock which hung over the river, was awful, tranquil, and majestic. But here the violence of the stream and the roaring of the waters impressed a new character on the scene: all was agitation and uproar; and every steep and every rock stared with wildness and terror.

This was as wild as the Wye could get. For a few seconds, the Reverend Gilpin was tossed about as the timber rowboat bucketed down the cataract. Whether it really was the rock which stared with 'terror', or Gilpin himself, is hard to say. In the 1700s, shooting rapids was not standard practice among clergymen. Today, running the Yat's rapids is literally child's play; during holidays, Gilpin's 'precipitate fall' bobs with plastic kayaks.

It is below the rapids at Symonds Yat that the river takes its secretive, two-mile excursion away from humanity. Allowing the current to take the boat, I drifted with the river, suspended in a kind of aching tranquillity. These moments occur infrequently. Several days into a journey, when the unshackled imagination has begun to fill the diurnal cycle with so many sights and thoughts that life begins to seem infinite, windows can open on the soul of a landscape. Below the falls, the river had lost itself in a chasm of almost silent, sunlit trees. As the canoe yawed gently on the deep, black current, a woodpecker knocked. The vast, muffled forest had shut out all sound but its own. The peace was so spacious that the little boat seemed to shrink to a speck between the blanketing tiers of trees. Generally, Gilpin had found the Wye overburdened with trees, and complained that they tended to block the view and to disturb a sense of distance. Particularly problematic were clumps of trees on the river bank, and trees which occupied too much foreground. These, he ruled, 'cannot be suffered'. Gilpin had compared the quest for the picturesque to the 'pleasures of the chase'. We can tramp and paddle every landscape, but never quite touch our quarry: 'Every distant horizon promises something new; and with this pleasing expectation we follow nature through her walks. We pursue her from hill to dale; and hunt after those various beauties, with which she everywhere abounds.'

Sliding downstream, I knew beauty would slip her bonds; I'd seen the map. And sure enough, the sounds of the A40 soon began to stain the murmuring stream. The last two miles into Monmouth were short on enchantment: the canoe seemed to be dragging a sea anchor, and all the while the road roared above my right shoulder.

By the time Gilpin's crew of weary boaters floated down the interminable straight into Monmouth, the sun had set. Their chaise was waiting for them, but when Gilpin inquired about the road route to Chepstow, he abruptly changed his plan. It seemed that the river would provide better 'amusement' than the road. A new agreement was negotiated with the boatmen, with the intention of sailing next morning for the third and final 'grand view'.

*

Fortune favours the opportunistic traveller, and Gilpin's decision to stay on the water repaid him with serene weather: 'the sun shone; and we saw enough of the effect of light in the exhibitions of this day, to regret the want of it the day before.' As it happened, the day I travelled this section of the river, it rained so heavily that my canoe kept filling like a bathtub. Below the gloomy forest, Berghem's inscrutable cattle watched my passing with no obvious signs of compassion.

The river here looks much as it did in Gilpin's day. As the Reverend says, the banks 'consist almost entirely either of wood or pasturage'. This suited Gilpin's vision of the picturesque, for there was nothing less helpful to a painter than arable farmland.

'Furrowed lands and waving corn' were 'charming in pastoral poetry', but 'ill accommodated to painting'. A picturesque landscape had to reflect the glory of God's creation; it had to 'approach as nearly as may be to nature'. And that meant grazing land: 'Pasturage not only presents an agreeable surface; but the cattle which graze it add great variety and animation to the scene.'

Along with his distaste of arable farmland, Gilpin's enthusiasm for industry was selective. The day he left Monmouth, he floated down one of the main arteries of the awakening Industrial Revolution. The Wye had all the requisites for heavy industry: accessible coal reserves in the Forest of Dean, fast-running streams for power, plentiful timber for fuel, and a river to ship raw materials and finished products. When Gilpin refers to other boats on the river, 'whose white sails passing along the sides of woodland hills were very picturesque', he's glancing at the surface of the scene. These were industrial barges, and in side valleys such as Whitebrook, paper-mills were thundering.

At Brockweir, I landed with difficulty on an old cobbled slipway inches deep in gelatinous mud. Beside the slipway, a short stretch of dressed stonework led past an unsightly rubbish skip to a flight of steps leading back down to the water. It was an old quayside. This, perhaps, was one of the riverside vignettes Gilpin had meant when he wrote of 'harbours in miniature, where little barks lay moored, taking in ore and other commodities from the mountains'. Once again, he's glossing the scene. Brockweir had a raucous reputation, for this was a major transhipment point for goods being taken down the Wye. Ships were built here, there were several pubs and a motley population of watermen who unwound after a long day on the wharf, by drinking and cockfighting. The boats tied up at places like Brockweir were indicators to Gilpin that his river was undergoing one of its episodic changes of character. 'These vessels,' he continues, 'designed plainly for rougher water than they at present encountered, shewed us, without any geographical knowledge, that we approached the sea.'

There was one other indicator of the approaching ocean, though Gilpin seems to have missed it. Between Monmouth and Brockweir, the river becomes tidal. The mud dumped all over Brockweir's slipway had been left by the last tide, and while I was wandering about the old wharf, I was able to watch the bizarre spectacle of the small rapid beneath the nearby road bridge change directions. One moment, it was a clear cataract flowing southward, and the next it reversed into a brown flood, heading north.

The climax of the Wye Tour was hidden a mile beyond Brockweir. From water level, it's impossible to see 'the most beautiful and picturesque view on the river'. And landing here is not easy, for the ferry slipway has been replaced by a near-vertical flood defence. On all fours, I clawed up a wall of slimy mud and lurched like a chocolate-coated puppet into a huge car park.

Gilpin's initial reaction to Tintern is that of a pilgrim who has stumbled by chance upon the holiest of shrines. The abbey looked absolutely enormous, even in its ruinous condition. Dwarfed by 800 foot hills, it rested like a shattered reliquary on a velvet pasture beside the streaming Wye. The Cistercian principle that abbeys should be founded 'far from the concourse of men', in 'a kind of second paradise of wooded delight' are echoed by Gilpin's delight that Tintern should be so well 'hid in the sequestered vale'. The composition is made perfect by the river, as it 'winds its course' through the view. At Tintern, Gilpin finds the perfect expression of God's wondrous design. Enraptured by the scene, he drifts off in monkish reverie: 'Every thing around bears an air so calm and tranquil, so sequestered from the commerce of life, that it is easy to conceive a man of warm imagination, in monkish times, might have been allured by such a scene to become an inhabitant of it.'

Tintern is not quite perfect, though. The all-important pictur-esque 'ornaments' are present and correct, among them ivy 'in masses uncommonly large', and mosses 'of various hues', together with lichens, maiden-hair, penny-leaf 'and other humble plants' which had 'overspread the surface, or hung from every joint or crevice'. With some in flower and others in leaf, the effect 'gave those full-blown tints which add the richest finishing to a ruin'. The only thing which spoiled an otherwise perfectly picturesque ruin was the state of the abbey itself. Because the tower had collapsed, it had removed 'form and contrast' from the surviving buttresses and walls, leaving 'the whole ill-shaped'. Particularly offensive were the remaining gable ends, which 'hurt the eye with their regularity, and disgust it by the vulgarity of their shape'. Gilpin had a solution: 'A mallet judiciously used (but who durst use it?) might be of service in fracturing some of them; particularly those of the cross-aisles, which are both disagreeable in themselves, and confound the perspective.' The image of a middle-aged Reverend knocking lumps off Tintern Abbey with a mallet was a gift to eighteenth-century caricaturists.

As he wandered about the exterior of the abbey, Gilpin eventually settled upon a viewpoint close to the rutted road which passed down the vale. The actual spot is now blocked by the second-storey bedroom of an hotel, but it seems that Gilpin was standing on what is now the small lane cut into the hillside behind the hotel. From this point, he sketched the abbey, removing with his pen what he wished to do with a mallet. Gilpin's Tintern is missing two of its gables. And he omitted the neighbouring iron works.

His visit to the abbey's interior forces him to engage for the first time with the reality of nature. As Gilpin steps through Tintern's shattered west wall, beauty and horror become inseparable: the scale of the abbey church is staggering. The west front soars skyward like a fretworked cliff, its slender bar tracery thickened with centuries of ivy. Everywhere there are columns, 'noble columns', rising from a carpet of close-cropped turf to meet a long-gone roof. The eye, gasps Gilpin, 'was above measure delighted with the beauty, the greatness, and the novelty of the scene.' But humankind had infiltrated this ruin of 'most perfection'. Lurking within the walls were the abbey's wretched inhabitants, foul-smelling and ragged, begging for alms. Their shelters were scattered about the crumbled church and cloisters, 'little huts, raised among the ruins'. One of these impoverished souls, a woman, led Gilpin and his companions to the monk's library. 'She could scarcely crawl,' observes Gilpin, 'shuffling along her palsied limbs and meagre contracted body by the help of two sticks.' Through an old gate 'overspread with nettles and briars', the old woman revealed her shelter. 'I never saw so loathsome a human dwelling,' continues Gilpin, who describes it in detail: 'It was a cavern loftily vaulted between two ruined walls, which streamed with various coloured stains of unwholesome dews. The floor was earth; yielding through moisture to the tread. Not the merest utensil or furniture of any kind appeared, but a wretched bedstead, spread with a few rags, and drawn into the middle of the cell to prevent its receiving the damp which trickled down the walls. At one end was an aperture, which served just to let in light enough to discover the wretchedness within.' The Picturesque wasn't equipped to deal with the awfulness of human existence, but Gilpin's own humanity obliged him to find the words for this distressing scene. There are no hovels or beggars in the aquatint.

Just before the tide turned, I left Tintern on water the colour of oxtail soup. Rafts of debris glided upstream as if carried on an aquatic conveyor-belt. The canoe's hull bumped against knotted tangles of foliage and dead wood. A table passed by, legs skyward, and then a dead salmon, as thick as my arm. Rain had begun to fall again, and the river was stippled with dark roundels. Mist seethed through the trees on the valley sides. Rounding a bend, half-a-dozen herons took to the air, flapping like pterodactyls towards the seeping vapours. Presently the tide rested, and the debris slewed to a halt. The river was very quiet, and enormous. Clamped between walls of smoking jungle, I felt as if I had paddled through a spatial warp into an Amazonian backwater.

Gilpin's voyage down the Wye finished close to this spot. He disembarked beneath the 700-foot wall of the river's final gorge, at a place called Piercefield, a 300-acre estate owned by a Mr Valentine Morris. 'We pushed on shore close under his rocks,' writes Gilpin, 'and the tide being at ebb, we landed with some difficulty on an oozy beach. One of our bargemen, who knew the place, served as a guide; and under his conduct we climbed the steep by an easy regular zig-zag.'

Traces of the 'regular zig-zag' can still be seen, though once again I found myself clawing upward coated in the Wye's peculiarly sticky mud. Piercefield was – as Gilpin noted – 'generally thought as much worth a traveller's notice as anything on the banks of the Wye'. Along with Mount Edgcumbe, Stowe, Stourhead, Hagley and the Leasowes, it was a compulsory sight for modern tourists. The procedure for gaining admission to these gardens took the form of an eighteenth-century right-to-roam. D.C. Webb noted in his *Observations and Remarks during Four Excursions*, published in 1812, that 'the only ceremony required' to gain admittance was 'that of setting down your name and address in a book kept for that purpose at the Porters Lodge'. After this minor formality 'you are permitted to stroll through the park and grounds'. While other gardens were embellished with grottoes, Chinese pavilions and Gothic alcoves, Piercefield's attraction lay in a range of artfully devised views which could be enjoyed from a series of paths and belvederes constructed along the edge of the precipice. Poor Mr Morris had got it wrong, though. The views themselves were 'enchanting', and 'extremely romantic', but Gilpin could not, he decided, 'call these views picturesque'. The vantage points were too high; the planted shrubbery interfered with 'the grand beauties of nature', and the paths were marked by 'a degree of tediousness'.

Piercefield today has been reclaimed by nature and by the local population; it is a Grade I Registered Historic Park and Garden. The precipice path is in daily use by dog-walkers and ramblers, but the ornaments Morris constructed are crumbling or hidden by undergrowth. The Grotto is throttled with laurel, and the dam, where a hydraulic ram pumped water into a pool, is lost to sight in regenerated woodland. Only the Giant's Cave, where a cannon was sited so that tourists could experience echoes, is in its original, rock-cut condition. Morris's great house is a precarious shell, stripped of its stone staircase and choked with rubble. In this ruined, semi-natural state, perhaps Gilpin would have been more lenient with Piercefield.

Gilpin's summer tour continued on land, through south Wales, but it was his two days on the Wye which came to define the picturesque 'movement'. By the end of the century, the forty miles of river between Ross and Chepstow were one of the most celebrated landscapes in Britain. Among those who followed were J.M.W. Turner,

Paul Sandby, Thomas Hearne and William Wordsworth, whose 'Lines, written a few miles above Tintern Abbey' came to mark the poetic response to the Wye. Fleets of boats were operating by then, some of them bearing twenty passengers at a time, on cushioned seats. Awnings protected them from the worst of the weather, and tables were provided for the maps and books, barometers and telescopes. And the Gilpin-effect spread far beyond the Wye. Through his simple system of aesthetic appreciation, he removed the wall of incomprehension which had previously surrounded 'untamed' Britain, and replaced it with a virtual ha-ha. Where Defoe and Pennant wrote through fear of mountains that were 'horrid and frightful', or 'naked, rugged' and 'dreary', Gilpin's looking-glass perspective insisted that there were 'orders of architecture in mountains as in palaces'.

Gilpin was not the first to gaze up at Goodrich, or to shoot the rapids at Yat Rock, or to gawp at Tintern, but his simple, accessible 'rules' provided the first generation of English tourists with the means to detect 'that peculiar kind of beauty' which can make a traveller smile or cry. Gilpin took the terror out of wilderness, and replaced it with wonder. The reverence he placed on picturesque views helped train a nation to value its landscapes. His rules are still in everyday use, in picture postcards and paintings, in planning departments, and in our choices when we plan holidays and choose homes. The Picturesque never could describe the real landscape, but in identifying its most pleasing features, Gilpin seems to have touched a craving deep in all of us.

THOMAS PENNANT

1772

Highlands and islands

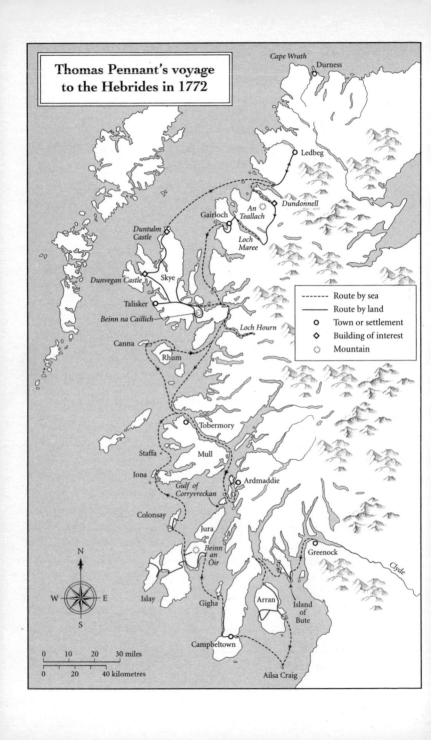

Thomas Pennant's voyage
to the Hebrides in 1772

Cape Wrath

Durness

Ledbeg

Dundonnell

An Teallach

Gairloch

Duntulm Castle

Loch Maree

Dunvegan Castle   Skye

Talisker

Beinn na Caillich

Loch Hourn

Canna

Rhum

Tobermory

Staffa   Mull

Iona   *Gulf of Corryvreckan*   Ardmaddie

Colonsay

Jura

Beinn an Òir

Greenock

Islay   Arran   Island of Bute

Gigha

Campbeltown   Ailsa Craig

Clyde

- - - - Route by sea
——— Route by land
○ Town or settlement
◇ Building of interest
☼ Mountain

N
W   E
S

| 0 | 10 | 20 | 30 miles |
| 0 | 20 | 40 kilometres |

T *he planet's wildest places remained secret till the last. In Britain, that wilderness lay in the far north-west, where mountains, sea and climate conspired to make travel — and existence itself — extremely challenging. As late as the eighteenth century, the highlands and islands of Scotland were a mystery to most who were not natives. Thomas Pennant's journey of exploration in 1772 opened the door to tourists like Dr Johnson, who claimed that Pennant was the 'best traveller' he had 'ever read'. Packed with insight, danger and uncomfortable truths,* A Tour in Scotland, and Voyage to the Hebrides; 1772 *is the work of an explorer and natural historian who found himself on a mission to alleviate the suffering of an oppressed population.*

*

On a crystalline autumn evening, I followed Thomas Pennant's route up Beinn na Caillich. The 'hill of the old hag' is a massive, curved bulwark which occupies the full width of the island of Skye, between the salt waters of Loch Slappin and Caolas Scalpay. To Pennant, on the deck of his ship, Beinn na Caillich was 'one of those picturesque mountains that made such a figure from the sea'. He liked his mountains to be rounded, or 'mamillary', as he put it. Today, few mountaineers give this 2,400-foot hummock a second glance as they speed along the coast road towards the chiselled spikes of the Cuillins. Pennant climbed from the east, an energetic scramble up tongues of scree and heather, with no apparent path and plenty of opportunities for twisting an ankle. I couldn't help wondering whether I had got the right mountain, but once the gradient eased and the stones thinned to gale-rubbed turf, I recognised Pennant's summit, 'flat and naked, with an artificial cairn, of a most enormous size'. With the wind rattling my jacket, I dropped my pack at the foot of the cairn and turned to the four points of the compass. Northward, an arm of platinum sea ran between Raasay and the Applecross peaks towards The Minch. Southward, I could just see the island of Rhum, a boulder resting on polished slate. To the east, lights were beginning to twinkle on the darkening mainland. But westward, backlit by a bleeding sun, a ferocious palisade of ancient rock was ripping low-flying cloud into tattered streamers. 'The prospect to the west,' Pennant had written with awe, 'was that of desolation itself; a savage series of rude mountains, discoloured, black and red, as if by the rage of fire.' There are parts of Scotland that have not changed for thousands of years.

You only have to look at the emergence of Scotland from the last Ice Age to detect a spectacle in the making. The glaciers pulled back to expose tottering walls of rock, serrated ridges and immense U-shaped valleys streaming with meltwater. Vast areas of the far north had been levelled by the ice into polished plateaux, strewn with rubble. This frigid tundra was gradually colonised by hardy little shrubs such as juniper and willow, and prowled by wandering herds of bison, woolly rhinoceros, giant elk and mammoth. Scotland's first trees were birch, followed by hazel and then the big pines, elm and oak. As the forests rooted and thickened, the lumbering beasts of the tundra were squeezed into extinction, and new species of quicker, smaller animals – wolves and wild boar, bears and deer – stalked the glades. Red squirrels bounced among the boughs and freshwater lakes filled with fish. But of all the species to colonise post-glacial Scotland, the most successful by far was a nomadic hominid.

The humans who undertook the first seasonal treks into these northern lands were the greatest explorers to have trodden British soil. With its impassable cliffs, lethal cataracts and dense forests, Scottish terrain was as tough as it gets. But it was also a gigantic game park, and there is evidence that the highlands and islands of the far north were being explored within a couple of thousand years of the ice sheets melting. Near the outfall of a river on the east coast (at a place now called Cramond, on the north-western outskirts of

Edinburgh), some of these pioneering hunter-explorers left the remains of a temporary shelter, and a dump of hazelnut shells which have been radiocarbon dated to around 8,500BC. At the time, there were probably no more than 2,500 people in the whole of Britain, so the total number of hunters in Scotland would have been counted in hundreds. They knew better than any of their descendants how to live with the land. Their axes, hammers, bows and arrows were fashioned from carved wood and knapped stone. They knew where to find caves for overnight shelter, or they constructed bivouacs from timber and skin. Some of them built seagoing boats capable of braving the fierce tides and winds of the west coast, paddling to the Orkneys and to many of the islands of the Inner Hebrides. As early as 7,500BC, they reached Rhum. On the island of Oronsay, archaeologists have found Mesolithic stake holes which may have supported windbreaks around open hearths.

For the best part of 8,000 years, the highlands and islands released their secrets with extreme reluctance. Snippets appeared in the work of early Greek and Roman writers, but the first real insight into this isolated, extraordinary land was written by Cornelius Tacitus in around AD 98, compiled from stories brought back to Rome by the victors of the battle of Mons Graupius. For the Roman army, the conquest of Scotland was both a military necessity and a journey of exploration. 'These remotest shores,' proclaimed Tacitus, 'were now circumnavigated, for the first time, by a Roman fleet, which thus established the fact that Britain was an island.' Tacitus wrote for Romans who believed they had found a new land, rather than invaded an old one: 'The farthest boundary of this land, which they only knew by report or rumour, we hold in our grasp with arms and fortresses. We have both explored and conquered Britain.'

The Scotland of Tacitus was unlike the rest of Britain. For the Romans, the isthmus between the Clyde and the Forth separated two lands. North of this 'narrow neck of land' was, wrote Tacitus, 'virtually another island'. Tacitus doesn't even begin to comprehend the form of this distant land. It's merely 'a huge and shapeless tract of country, jutting out to form what is actually the most distant coastline and finally tapering into a kind of wedge'. In this land of extremes, the shores were 'beaten by a wild and open sea' and the hinterland was rendered all but impassable by 'the perilous depths of woods and ravines', and an obstacle course of 'marshes, mountains, and rivers'. In the eve-of-battle speech by the Caledonian commander Calgacus, the Romans are caricatured as 'a scanty band, scared and bewildered, staring blankly at the unfamiliar sky, sea, and forests around them'. The Highlands are a labyrinth known only to her native warriors, who had 'hidden away in her most secret places'.

Tacitus' fearsome description of northern Scotland – revived during the Renaissance – informed prejudices for 1,700 years. Other writers did little to encourage colonisation. In Donald Monro's sixteenth-century *Western Isles,* the myriad islands are depicted as a hunter-gatherer's paradise, but a seafarer's nightmare ('…very perillous for schippis be reason of the starknes of the stream'). The mainland was scarcely any safer. Readers turning to Camden's *Britannia* of 1586, and Joan Blaeu's atlas of 1654, found that northern Scotland was infertile due to the cold climate, which had also led to the region being devasted by wolves. Timothy Pont, whose sketch maps had been used by Blaeu for his atlas, had labelled the far north: 'Extreem Wildernes'. The description of Scotland in Mercator's famous *Atlas* was no more encouraging: 'Those who inhabit the western coast,' he wrote, 'are called *Hechtlandmen*, that is "higher" Scots and speak Hibernian, and are fierce enemies of the lowlanders who use the English language.' Through to the 1740s, perennially feuding clans, and the Jacobite uprising, successfully repelled most southerners. 'The Highlands,' observed Captain Edmund Burt, an English military engineer posted to Inverness in the late 1720s, 'are but little known even to the inhabitants of the low country of Scotland… But to the people of England, excepting some few, and those chiefly the soldiery, the Highlands are hardly known at all.' Burt's contemporary, Daniel Defoe, felt equally ill-informed: 'Our geographers,' he complained of 17th-century mapmakers, 'seem to be almost as much at a loss in the description of this north part of Scotland, as the Romans were to conquer it; and they are obliged to fill it up with hills and mountains, as they do the inner parts of Africa, with lions and elephants, for want of knowing what else to place there.' Nearly 10,000 years after Rhum was first sighted by Mesolithic explorers, the Highlands and islands were still a mystery to southern Britons.

*

Into the void stepped a Welsh ornithologist. Thomas Pennant had been born in the summer of 1726, the year after Daniel Defoe completed the book that would become *A Tour Through the Whole Island of Great Britain*. Although the two men shared a passion for the geography of Britain, they were utterly dissimilar in background and temperament. A gentleman of means, Pennant could trace his family's presence at their seat at Downing, on the coastal plain of north Wales, back to David Pennant ap Tudur ap Ithel, in the 1440s. Where Defoe matured into bankruptcy and the pillory, Pennant would be elected to Royal Societies and become High Sheriff of Flintshire. In his autobiography, Pennant recalled how a boyhood gift had set him on the road: 'A present of the ornithology of Francis Willughby, esq. made to me, when I was about the age of twelve,' he declared, 'first gave me a taste for that study, and incidentally a love for that of natural history in general.'

First published in 1676, *The Ornithology of Francis Willughby* revolutionised ornithological taxonomy, and it woke young Pennant to the joys of fieldwork. Willughby and the naturalist John Ray had spent four years travelling through Britain and Europe observing 'all the birds hitherto known'. Instead of organising their findings according to the alphabetical order of their names – as was the accepted method – they had arranged their species by physical characteristics. The relationships between species were clear on every page. Illustrated with eighty exquisite engravings, Willughby and Ray's 441-page *Ornithology* was the world's first systematic classification of birds, and it marked the beginning of scientific ornithology as we know it today.

To the detriment of his education at Wrexham, Pennant was soon collecting and cataloguing flora and fauna. In 1746 or '47, he left Oxford University without graduating and took off to Cornwall, where – inspired by Dr William Borlase, the vicar of Ludgvan and 'father of Cornish archaeology' – he developed 'a strong passion for minerals and fossils'. Then in his fifties, Borlase had amassed a vast collection of fossils, and his devotion to God had been accompanied by research into the natural history of Cornwall. In no apparent hurry to reveal himself as a serious investigator of natural history, Pennant spent the 1750s indulging his gentlemanly enthusiasms; in the summer of 1754, a boozy journey to Ireland failed to deliver any useful fieldwork, 'such was the conviviality of the country'. More productively, he opened a correspondence with the Swedish botanist, Carl Linnaeus, whose new system of classification had revolutionised botanical understanding. Finally, in 1761, Pennant began work on the book he would title *British Zoology*. Two years later, Pennant's world shook on its axis. In 1763, his father died, leaving him responsible for the Downing estate. And then, the following year, his wife of only five years, Elizabeth Falconer, also died.

Two deaths and an inheritance must have played a part in Pennant's decision to depart in 1765 for the continent on a Grand Tour of influential thinkers. First, Paris, where he found himself 'happy in the company' of the celebrated naturalist Comte de Buffon, who was then nearing completion of his mammoth *Histoire Naturelle*. Then to the Alps, where he called on 'that wicked wit', Voltaire. Back on the North Sea coast, he enjoyed a 'momentous' meeting with the German naturalist Peter Pallas, who would soon leave the Low Countries to explore Russia's Urals, the Altai mountains on the frontier with Mongolia and western Siberia.

To Pennant, it must have seemed that everyone he met was caught in a thrilling centrifuge of exploration and discovery. And then one of them came knocking at his door. On 19 March 1766 (a date meticulously recorded in his autobiography), a wealthy young botanist called Joseph Banks called at Pennant's lodgings and presented him with a valuable copy of William Turner's sixteenth-century work on ornithology – the first printed book entirely devoted to birds. Days later, Banks sailed for Newfoundland on a plant-collecting expedition. He returned early in 1767 with no fewer than 340 specimens. In August 1768, Banks sailed again, but this time with one Lieutenant James Cook, on a round-the-world expedition. Banks bankrolled the £10,000 expedition himself.

While those about him explored distant shores, Pennant turned his eyes to his own isles. He had, at last, decided to mount his own, amateur expedition: 'This year,' he recalled of 1769, 'was a very active one with me; I had the hardiness to venture on a journey to the remotest part of North Britain, a country almost as little known to its southern brethren as Kamtschatka.' Thomas Pennant was going to explore Scotland.

★

Pennant rode his horse across the border at the beginning of July 1769. It was rather too late in the travelling season to embark upon such a journey, and Pennant later suggested that it had been a fairly impulsive decision, following the long-awaited publication of *The British Zoology*. Comparing himself to a traveller who discovers that, in order to see a country, it is 'preferable to travel by day than by night', Pennant declared:

> I cannot help making this applicable to myself, who after publishing three volumes of the Zoology of Great Britain, found out that to be able to speak with more precision of the subjects I treated of, it was more prudent to visit the whole than part of the country: struck therefore with the reflection of having never seen SCOTLAND, I instantly ordered my baggage to be got ready, and in reasonable time found myself on the banks of the Tweed.

Scribbling as he travelled, Pennant followed the least-difficult route northward, through Edinburgh and Aberdeen to Inverness, and then on to Caithness. With the exception of a diversion through the Grampians, he clung to the low-lying land of the east coast, recording everything from farming practices to local geology and the treasures of country houses. The return journey southward gave him the chance to ride General Wade's military road alongside Loch Ness, and to visit the awesome chasm of Glencoe.

A Tour in Scotland was published in 1771. To many, it was a ground-breaking book. Pennant's Scotland was a country of staggering physical diversity and huge natural resources. Edinburgh, he announced, was a city 'that posseses a boldness and grandeur of situation beyond any that I had seen'. Here, at last, raved *The Scots Magazine*, was a work which broke the political fashion 'to ridicule and vilify the Scots and Scotland in the keenest and grossest manner'. The 'more candid, the more gentleman-like' Pennant would, continued the reviewer, 'excite an earnest desire in his readers to make the same excursion … to the mutual advantage, perhaps, of both nations'. Thus did a Welshman find himself cast in the role of literary healer between the English and the Scots.

But Pennant knew that the tour of 1769 was incomplete. Shortage of time, and the timidity of a first-time visitor, had restricted him to riding Scotland's safest routes. The various deficiencies of the journey filled him, he admitted, with 'that species of restlessness that infects many minds, on leaving any attempt unfinished'.

The remedy for that restlessness would be a return to the far north. But this time, it would be a full-blown expedition, with its own ship, and a systematic programme of research. Using horses, a manoeuvrable cutter, rowing boats and his own two feet, he planned to push far beyond the reach of military roads, to explore the most remote region in Britain: the Hebridean islands and the north-west coast of mainland Scotland.

Pennant's expedition was an ingenious hybrid. Travelling with a small team of hand-picked specialists, he would record observations, interview 'the natives', collect samples, take measurements, make sketches and so on. But he would also take advantage of the fact that the *The Scots Magazine* penetrated parts of the Highlands beyond the reach of convenient travel. Through the letters' page, Pennant attempted to recruit a dispersed team of voluntary researchers who would accumulate information in advance of his visit. He advertised his intentions in a letter dated 27 January 1772:

It has now become fashionable among the English to make a tour into Scotland for some few weeks or months; and there is a moral certainty of this fashion increasing, as the foolish prejudices against the country and its inhabitants daily decrease. But it is to be regretted that an intelligent curious traveller from England has no proper helps to assist him; so that it often happens, that many return without having seen one third of what is most curious in the country...

To this end, Pennant announced that the journey would result in the publication of 'a new tour ... in two pocket volumes'. Prejudice would not be allowed to corrupt the findings. The greatest care, he insisted, 'should be taken to keep clear of all party-work, either in religion or politics, because such peculiarities will disgust some readers, and thereby effectually condemn the work'. A eulogy upon the beauty of the Highlands followed, and then the sting in the tail: a list of no fewer than ninety-seven 'Queries' addressed 'to Gentlemen in the several parts of Great Britain'. Covering fields as diverse as the materials used to construct the local church, road communication, the price of rabbits, the presence of barrows and tumuli, the methods of tillage and the number of fishing vessels, Pennant was requesting his gentleman-readers to furnish descriptions of their localities so thorough that Camden would look like a beginner.

Pennant's principal companion on this epic odyssey would be the Rev. John Lightfoot, of Shalden in Hampshire, who would contribute botanical observations. Accompanying the pair as translator would be a Gaelic expert, the Rev. John Stuart, who would provide 'a variety of hints, relating to customs of the natives of the Highlands, and of the islands'. Recording the expedition with sketches would be Pennant's servant, the 'able artist' Moses Griffiths. Bringing the total to eight men would be two further servants, a fowler and a groom. In a letter written to the Scottish antiquary George Paton, three weeks before he left home, Pennant referred excitedly to his team as 'my troop'. They were a tight-knit group, and appear to have enjoyed each other's company. The distance Pennant intended to travel was around 2,000 miles.

★

Pennant set off from Chester on Monday, 18 May 1772. He was forty-five years old. Many months later, when he came to tackle the structure of his book, he portrayed his first day on the road as a sunlit prologue. Chester rises from the page as an exemplary British city, 'a city without parallel' for its neat and congenial layout; a model emporium then trading with Guinea and the Baltic. In keeping with Pennant's new role as a trans-national mediator, Chester is 'a *place d'armes*, a great thoroughfare between two kingdoms, and the residence of a numerous and polished gentry'. The city is also an example of humanitarian munificence. Here, in Chester (with mortality rates to prove it), is the best poorhouse in the land. 'Might I be permitted to moralize,' warns Pennant, 'I should call this the reward of the benevolent and charitable disposition, that is the characteristic of this city.'

Departing this peerless city, Pennant rides across the Cheshire Plain to Halton Castle, where the countryside appears as an eighteenth-century Garden of Eden: 'From the castle is the most beautiful view in Cheshire; a rich prospect of the meanders of the Mersey, through a fertile bottom; a pretty wooded peninsula jutting into it opposite Runcorn; the great country of Lancashire, filled with hedgerow trees; and beyond soar the hills of Yorkshire and Lancashire; and on the other side appears Cheshire, the still loftier Cambrian mountains.'

Pennant's inaugural day of wonders closed at one of the greatest industrial crossroads west of the Pennines. Warrington was where transport between Cheshire and Lancashire – and all the traffic using the east coast route between London and Scotland crossed the busy Mersey. Here, Pennant found 'long, narrow, ill-built' streets 'crowded with carts and passengers' engaged in the manufacture of products which ranged from pins, locks and hinges to cast iron, glass and sugar. Nearly half of the navy's sail-cloth came from Warrington. Warehouses and cranes lining the wharves of Bank Quay serviced eighty-ton vessels bound for distant markets. The town had doubled in size in the past twenty years. Warrington even had its own publisher, W. Eyres, who would issue a new edition of *The Agricola*, to coincide with the publication of Pennant's new book. That night, the travellers slept at the family seat of John Black-burne, whose collection of hardy exotics and hothouse plants was, claimed Pennant, 'at least equal to that at Kew'. Blackburne was celebrated for being 'the second in these kingdoms that cultivated the pineapple'. By the end of Day One, readers had been introduced to Pennant's model of benevolent, charitable civilisation. By the end of the journey they would have visited a land of Swiftian horrors.

From Warrington, Pennant made his way through the Lake District and southern uplands of Scotland to Greenock, on the Clyde, where he boarded *Lady Frederic Campbell,* a ninety-ton sailing cutter skippered by Archibald Thompson. An outstanding sailor, Thompson would be taking his ship to one of the most treacherous coasts in Europe.

The voyage got off to a slow start. In the absence of any wind to propel the ship, *Lady Frederic Campbell* resorted to the ebb tide, slipping slowly away from Greenock at the speed of the outgoing current. Unlike a journey on land, where itineraries could be planned with a degree of reliability, this would be a sea voyage, governed by the wind and tide. Pennant would soon get used to abandoning plans and modifying ambitions, for this would be a narrative written by meteorology and the moon.

The first few days on board set the tone for the expedition. Here, for example, is Pennant's account of their departure from East Loch Tarbet, on Loch Fyne:

> In the afternoon attempt to turn out, but am driven back by an adverse gale. Get out early in the morning… Most of the morning was passed in a dead calm: in the afternoon succeeded brisk gales, but from points not the most favourable, which occasioned frequent tacks in sight of port: in one broke our topsail yard.

After he had investigated the islands of Bute and Arran (where he measured a harpooned basking shark), and then the isolated bird-encrusted rock of Ailsa Craig, the ship was once again becalmed as she attempted to round the Mull of Kintyre. Issuing Thompson with instructions to wait by the island of Gigha, Pennant took to the ship's boat and rowed for seven miles to Campbeltown, where (according to local custom) he consulted the Oracle of the Bottle about his future voyage (he fails to pass on what the Bottle predicted). After exploring Gigha 'in a rotten, leaky boat', Pennant was back on board, preparing to sail for Islay: the 'capital' of the Hebrides: 'The weather extremely fine,' he wrote in his journal, 'but so calm that Mr Thompson is obliged to tow the vessel out of this little harbour.' A short while later: 'Attempt to steer for the island of Islay, but in vain …' About noon, a breeze sprang up, and the ship was moving again, towards the island of Jura, which they collided with, lightly: 'About one o'clock on June 30, receive notice of getting into the harbour of the small isles of Jura, by the vessel's touching ground at the entrance.'

They had reached the Hebrides.

*

Unable to begin his Hebridean odyssey on Islay as he had planned, Pennant opens his account with Jura, 'the most rugged of the Hebrides'. Procuring local horses, he set off with Lightfoot and the tick-list of 'Queries', recording Jura's physical characteristics, its produce, its wildlife (which included wildcats, otters, stoats and rats, and about one hundred stags), the health of its population, its superstitions (old women still preserved a stick of the wicken tree, or mountain ash, as a protection against elves), and its local diseases (a nasty flesh-worm curable only by a poultice of cheese and honey). They also came across a 'grotesque group' of shelters being used as a summer camp by the families that were tending cattle in the mountains. Jura would be Pennant's portal into unknown Scotland. But before he left the island, he decided to climb a mountain called Beinn an Òir.

Beinn an Òir is one of Jura's 'Paps', the distinctive range of conical peaks which run down the spine of the island. They are a captivating sight, and as Pennant observes, 'perfectly mamillary'. From afar, their flanks appear smooth and symmetrical; up close, it becomes apparent that the Paps are sheathed with interminable screes of angular blocks.

Pennant's motives for mountaineering were not those of today. In the absence of surveyed charts, the only way Pennant could anticipate the form of the coast he was exploring was by climbing to a vantage point and making his own survey.

But Pennant may have had other reasons for attempting the ascent. The Welsh explorer had taken the mountain's name – Beinn an Òir – to mean 'the mountain of gold', and it seems plausible that his considerable efforts to investigate the peak may have been associated with the belief that its slopes hid veins of gold. During the ascent, he paid particular attention to the geology of Beinn an Òir's rocks. Sadly for Pennant, 'mountain of gold' is a mis-translation; the 'Òir' in its name is more likely to be the Gaelic word for 'edge' or 'side'. 'Mountain of the Edge', or 'Boundary Peak', would fit with the Gaelic tradition of topographic nomenclature, for the mountain occupies a distinctive position in the Paps, where the range turns a sharp corner as it runs down the spine of Jura. As the highest summit in the range, Beinn an Òir would have been a natural territorial marker. Topographically, it separates the grazing and hunting lands of the north-west of the island from those of the south-east. (The 'Hanging Rock' performs a similar role at a kink in the border between Scotland and England.)

Beinn an Òir is not the easiest of climbs. I've tried a couple of different routes to the summit, and both involved a fair bit of boulder-hopping. If you imagine trying to scramble up a downward-moving escalator whose steps are made of loose, sharp-edged rocks, you'll get the picture. Gratifyingly, Pennant found the climb 'a task of much labour and difficulty'. The screes have been prised from tilted beds of quartzite which were laid down over 600 million years ago as horizontal layers of loose material – gravel and pebbles, sand, mud – on the bed of a shallow sea. Compressed and heated by the shifting of the earth's crust, this slop of debris has turned into the kind of rock which can strip an ankle to the bone. Pennant relished the ascent. 'The stones of this mountain,' he scribbled, 'are white (a few red), quartzy and composed of small grains; but some are brecciated, or filled with crystalline kernels, of an amethystine colour.'

He also spotted a strange feature on the north-western flank of the mountain, 'a narrow stripe of rock, terminating in the sea, called, the Slide of the Old Hag'. This is Sgriob na Caillich, 'The Old Woman's Slide', marked on OS maps as a runway-straight band of stones extending for over a mile up the mountain. From above, it looks as if millions of tons of quartz have been laid in a deliberate alignment. Compared to the quartz, the 'slide' is a relatively recent feature. It dates back to the last Ice Age, when huge westward-grinding glaciers were forced to part when they collided with Beinn an Òir. Where the tongues of ice converged again on the west side of the mountain, they dumped their cargoes of suspended rock in a long 'medial moraine' which points out to the warm Atlantic. Although he doesn't record it in his journals, Pennant may have been told by his guides that the 'Old Hag' was the infamous witch of Jura who used her ball of thread to snare those straying near the Paps. When Macphie of Colonsay found himself well-and-truly snagged, he snitched the hag's secret hatchet and cut himself free and sailed as fast as he could for Colonsay. Spying the departing Macphie from the summit of Beinn an Òir, the desolate witch repeatedly tried to reel him in, but each time the thread caught him, he slashed himself free with the hatchet. In a final act of desperation, Jura's witch leapt from the summit and skidded down her Pap leaving a mile-long trail of stones; the 'The Old Woman's Slide'.

When Pennant reached the summit ridge, he found others had been there before. Arrayed along the whaleback were several enormous cairns, 'not', he decided, 'the work of devotion, but of idle herds, or curious travellers'. The ridge is a wonderfully airy amble, and still carries its string of cairns and a couple of more recent features: the remains of a stone hut, and a long 'causeway'. A report in the September 1894 edition of the Scottish Mountaineering Club Journal recorded 'stone houses' up here, and a 'well-made causeway', apparently built by 'Ordnance Surveyors'. On the second of my two ascents, I was told by my local guide that the causeway had been built over a hundred years ago by the laird, who liked to take his horse to the summit. It's not impossible that some of this stone architecture had been raised by the Rev. Dr John Walker,

➤➤ Pennant ◄◄

ABOVE The Inner
Sound, Skye

RIGHT Glencoe,
a romanticised view,
circa 1675

BELOW Warrington, 1772

ABOVE Beinn an Òir,
The Paps of Jura

LEFT The schooner,
Spirit of Fairbridge

BELOW Briis-mhawl,
near Talisker, on Skye

RIGHT The east coast of Scotland, from James Dorret's map of 1761

CENTRE An Teallach
BELOW Strath na Sealga

⇥ **Cobbett** ⇤

ABOVE Portsmouth Harbour
from Portsdown Hill,
circa 1814–25

LEFT The turnpike gate
on what is now Kensington
High Street

BELOW The National Trust's
19th-century farmhouse
at Emley, Surrey

TOP One of Cobbett's byways, Hampshire

CENTRE LEFT
Pre-enclosure map of 1653,
showing fields outside
Nutley, Hampshire

CENTRE RIGHT
The edge of the hanger,
near Hawkley, Hampshire

RIGHT The Avon Valley,
Wiltshire

⇥ **Morton** ⇤

ABOVE Glen Trool,
Galloway Forest Park

LEFT A Bullnose Morris,
touring in the '30s

BELOW The open road,
in a 30mph sofa

RIGHT Skye and the Black Cuillins, *The Times Contour Motoring Map of Scotland*

CENTRE Leaving Rothiemurchus Forest bound for the Pass of Lairig Ghru

BELOW The Stacks of Duncansby, by John O'Groats

ABOVE The Black Cuillins, from Druim Hain

LEFT The quay, Portree

BELOW Morton's road over 'the roof of the Highlands', and the reservoir which flooded Glen Loyne

who climbed with a Torricellian barometer to the summit of Beinn an Òir eight years ahead of Pennant (Walker calculated the peak's altitude at 2,340 feet, 231 feet short of its actual height). Pennant makes no mention of Walker's considerable achievement, perhaps because it would have detracted from his own. Britain is absolutely plastered in Beinn an Òirs; natural features which have accumulated layer upon layer of fable and fact during thousands of years of post-glacial history. Archives, libraries and recalled local histories from the likes of shepherds and land- owners can embellish a seemingly featureless landscape with an extraordinary human geology.

'Gain the top,' gasps Pennant, 'and find our fatigues fully recompensed by the grandeur of the prospect from this sublime spot.' Jura was spread before him, 'a stupendous scene of rock, varied with little lakes innumerable'.

Turning to all points of the compass, Pennant logged the geography of the surrounding Highlands and islands:

> To the south appeared Ilay, extended like a map beneath us; and beyond that, the north of Ireland; to the west Gigha and Cara, Cantyre and Arran, and the Firth of Clyde, bounded by Airshire; an amazing tract of mountains to the north-east, as far as Ben Lomond; Skarba finished the northern view; and over the western ocean were scattered Colonsay and Oransay, Mull, Iona, and its neighbouring group of isles; and still further the long extents of Tirey and Col just apparent.

Thomas Pennant had good reason for feeling on top of the world. His Hebridean adventure had begun very satisfactorily; he'd under-taken a succcessful audit of lowland Jura, and although he hadn't found gold on Beinn an Òir, he had reached the island's highest point. Later, when he came to write his book, he couldn't resist taking a gentle sideswipe at one of his fellow explorers, young Joseph Banks. As it happened, Bank's second expedition with Captain Cook had fallen through, and the botanist had instead mounted an expedition to Iceland. Two months after Pennant had ridden north from Cheshire, Banks had sailed from Gravesend on board a 190-ton brig accompanied by ten fellow-scholars and their manservants. Banks' brig called at Islay a month or so after Pennant left, and they too decided to climb one of the Paps of Jura. Banks went for Beinn a'Chaolais. 'Mr Banks and his friends,' smiled Pennant, 'mounted that to the south, and found the height to be two thousand three hundred and fifty-nine feet: but Beinn-an-Òir far overtopped it.' Shortly after leaving Jura, Joseph Banks pulled off an exploration scoop of such magnitude that Pennant would have to ask the botanist for permission to use his description.

*

Returning to Islay, Thomas Pennant made a distressing discovery:

> A set of people worn down with poverty: their habitations scenes of misery, made of loose stones; without chimneys, without doors, excepting the faggot opposed to the wind at one or other of the appertures, permitting the smoke to escape through the other, in order to prevent the pains of suffocation. The furniture perfectly corresponds: a pothook hangs from the middle of the roof, with a pot pendent over a grateless fire, filled with fare that may rather be called a permission to exist, than a support of vigorous life: the inmates, as may be expected, lean, withered, dusky and smoke-dried.

Famine would have been inevitable, writes Pennant, 'but was prevented by the seasonal arrival of a mealship'. The contradiction was all too evident; despite the 'excellency of the land', people were starving. Pennant quickly found the reason. Cattle. Land grazed by cattle made more money for the laird than land under corn. Pennant discovered that Islay was exporting around 1,700 cattle each year, at a price of fifty shillings each. In fact, the island was so overstocked with cattle that 'numbers died in March for want of fodder'. To a man from the edge of the Cheshire Plain, it made no sense: 'The country is blessed with fine manures: besides sea-wrack, coral, shell-sand, rock and pit-marl, it possesses a tract of thirty-six square miles of limestone. What treasures, if properly applied, to bring wealth and plenty to the island.' It would become a debilitating refrain. A staggering 7–8,000 people were living on the island. The population today is half that number.

From Islay, *Lady Frederic Campbell* sailed northwards, calling at the twin islands of Oronsay and Colonsay, then Iona, Canna, Rhum and Skye. Each island was subjected to the same methodical scrutiny. On Oronsay, Pennant found that good management, and a mix of pasture and arable, provided for the entire population. Two hundred yards across the water, Colonsay's greedy proprietor had reduced the population to starvation, on an island which had good soil, excellent pasturage, plenty of limestone, sufficient peat, and a sea 'abounding in fish'. For the first time, Pennant allows anger to break across the page: 'How inadequate then is the produce of cattle, and how much more so is that of corn!'

On Canna, the plight of the islanders was heartbreaking. As *Lady Frederic Campbell* anchored in Canna's sheltered natural harbour, the shores 'appeared pleasing to humanity; verdant, and covered with hundreds of cattle … the natives soon dispelled this agreeable error'. Bread and meal had run out some time ago, and with their stock of fish hooks almost exhausted, the islanders' plight was now desperate. Pennant suddenly found himself utterly inadequate to the task: 'The ribbons, and other trifles I had brought would have been insults to people in distress. I lamented that my money had been so uselessly laid out; for a few dozen of fish-hooks, or a few pecks of meal, would have made them happy.' Why, he wondered, could not emergency 'magazines of meal' be established on the islands?

Despite the human misery, Pennant and Lightfoot gathered useful data on the island's natural resources and impoverished economy. Before leaving, they also investigated Martin Martin's bizarre claim that there was a 'high hill in the north end' of the island, where the compass needle 'instead of settling towards the north, as usual … settled here due east'. By the 1700s, this hill had acquired the name 'Compass Hill', and testing their own compass, Pennant found that the needle did indeed 'vary a whole quarter'. And Compass Hill is still playing its tricks. During one of my visits to Canna, I climbed up to the island's eastern highpoint, and after an hour or so traversing the gale-swept cliff-tops, I did locate the exact spot: a patch of sodden turf and rock just a few metres square, where the compass needle suddenly lurched a full ninety degrees off magnetic north. As Pennant had concluded, the cause is an area of rock so rich in iron that it overrides the earth's magnetic field.

Sailing on northward, each island produced a wealth of material. On Rhum, Pennant listened to tales of second sight, and learned of a woman called Molly MacLeane who could foresee the future 'through a well-scraped blade-bone of mutton'. Unlike Gerald of Wales, who wrote 600 years earlier of Flemings in Dyfed who could perform the same trick with the shoulder blades of rams, Pennant was sceptical. Skye, however, produced some real science.

Earlier in the voyage, Pennant had been disappointed when bad weather had prevented him from landing on Staffa and examining the basalt columns. But on Skye, he had the good fortune to be directed to a mountain he calls 'Briis-mhawl'. Pennant's mountain can be found just south of Talisker. Here, he discovered 'a fine series of genuine basaltic columns, resembling the Giant's Causeway'. The entire western side of the mountain is lined with faceted columns, which are so geometrically precise that they defy the normally chaotic rule of mountain-building. To Pennant, 'these were the ruins of creation: those of Rome, the work of human art, seem to them but the ruins of yesterday'.

On local horses, Pennant rode to the northernmost tip of Skye, where he found *Lady Frederic Campbell* anchored in Duntulm Bay. He had now reached the furthest extent of the Inner Hebrides. His plan had been to cross The Minch to the Outer Hebrides, but stories had been circulating on Skye of a 'putrid fever' that was raging on the Hebridean island of Lewis.

As the cutter rode at anchor off Skye, Pennant made a decision which would alter the course of his expedition. 'It was our design,' he reveals, 'to have penetrated by land, as far as the extremity of the island.' It was an audacious and undoubtedly hazardous twist to the itinerary. Pennant planned to sail *Lady Frederic Campbell* to the mainland, and then to ride horses overland to the north coast of Scotland. Why? Well, Pennant doesn't elaborate, but it's possible to put forward a couple of suggestions. He knew well that the risk and effort would be rewarded with recognition. No published account existed of the overland, western route to the 'top' of Scotland. This was, after all, the region that Timothy Pont had labelled 'Extreem Wildernes'. And Pont was rare among mapmakers for having actually visited the north of Scotland. If Pennant succeeded, and returned to tell the tale, he would be applauded for his scientific endeavour.

Secondly, the remote, far north-western tip of Scotland had become a kind of mythical El Dorado; an inaccessible wilderness fabled for natural riches (and wolves). Camden's *Britannia* had popularised the myth with stories of iron ore and pearls in furthest Sutherland, together with coal, freestone, limestone and slate, apparently 'in abundance'. More tantalisingly, *Britannia* also reported that Sutherland had silver, and that 'it is supposed that there is *Gold* in *Durinesse*'. Durness is one of Britain's most remote communities; the closest village to Cape Wrath.

Hauling the anchor on 24 July at two in the afternoon, *Lady Frederic Campbell*'s crew were wafted on an 'easy breeze' into The Minch on a course for Loch Kanaird. They sailed all night, and when Pennant climbed on deck at daybreak, he found the ship taking endless 'teasing tacks' through the Summer Islands. The anchorage, in the lee of Isle Martin, is a fiercely intimidating spot. Looming over the far side of the bay are the southern cliffs of Ben Mor Coigach, which appear to fall straight to the sea from a 2,000-foot summit. The reader can almost sense Pennant shivering with apprehension as he describes the 'vast and barren mountains' which blocked the view northward. The heights were, he noted, 'patched with snow' – a spectacle which seems extraordinary in this era of summer heatwaves.

The explorers had effectively landed on another island, for the whole north-west corner of mainland Scotland was cut off from eastern Scotland by belts of mountains. It was easier to travel by sea than by land. Ominously, the weather had broken: 'Still on board,' notes Pennant tersely. 'The weather very bad.' Waiting on his creaking cutter, Pennant had all too much time to brood upon the challenge he had set himself. Everything Pennant had read, or heard, had prepared him for what he knew would be the greatest physical – and navigational – challenge of his life. James Dorret's map of 1761 described a region strewn with formidable obstacles. Between Loch Kanaird and the north coast lay numerous mountains, and four long sea-water inlets, each fed by sizeable rivers. Not one road was marked on Dorret's map between the Kyle of Localsh, opposite Skye, and Cape Wrath. To Camden, this was the most impoverished, remote region in mainland Britain, crippled by infertility due to the harsh climate, and plagued by 'very rapacious wolves'. Of Eddrachillis, the parish Pennant would have to cross on his way north, Blaeu had warned of it being 'impassable because of deserted cliffs'. But there was a prize for the taking: Pennant knew that if he could push northward to the Kyle of Durness, the sea loch adjacent to Cape Wrath, he would have pioneered a route which connected the west coast of the Highlands with the east coast.

The weather eventually eased, and Thompson was able to put his expeditioners ashore. In Strath Canaird, Pennant managed to procure some horses. They were diminutive beasts, unshod, but sure of hoof. The climb from the valley began encouragingly: 'Kindreds and hospitality possess the people of these parts. We scarce passed a farm but the good woman, long before our approach, sallied out and stood on the roadside, holding out to us a bowl of milk or whey.'

To a man who had ridden, sailed and walked all the way from the Welsh border, 'the extremity of the island' must have seemed enticingly close: no more than sixty miles on horseback. But the climb from Strath Canaird went on for five miles, and rose to almost 1,000 feet above sea level; it would have been the longest climb Pennant had ridden on his entire journey. 'Ascend a very high mountain,' he notes, 'and pass through a birch wood, over a pretty little loch…'; this was presumably Loch Cul Dromannan, whose magical waters still reflect the ridges of Coigach.

The going was abysmal: 'a variety of bog and hazardous rock, that nothing but our shoeless little steeds could have carried us over'. Today, the crest of the pass is marked by a loop of abandoned single-track road, curving in a forgotten arc through the bog. Look west from this point and the prospect is dissuasive. A peaty track (similar, probably to the one Pennant was attempting to follow) meanders off towards the dark bulk of Cul Beag, while the foreground is puddled with random lochans. In low cloud and slashing rain, this is a grey and frightful place, with no shelter and a sense of utter isolation. Somewhere among the heathery mounds and sucking mosses, there is a parting of the waters, for one side of this vast bog drains southward towards Strath Canaird, while the other side dribbles northward into the vast parish of Assynt. For Pennant, it would be a watershed too far.

As the riders began the long and difficult descent on the far side of the pass, they had to creep beneath a sheer cliff whose footings were strewn with fallen rock: 'Pass under some great precipices of limestone,' notes Pennant (correctly identifying the rock of Knockan cliff), 'mixed with marble.' To his left, he could see 'a most tremendous view of mountains of stupendous height'. Nowhere else in Britain do mountains present themselves in such singular magnificence. Cul Beag, Stac Pollaidh, Cul Mor, Suilven and Canisp appear as a series of sheer-sided peaks, each separated from its neighbour by U-shaped gulfs which seem to plummet to sea-level. There was little in this view to comfort Pennant and his companions. 'I never saw,' shudders the explorer, 'a country that seemed to have been so torn and convulsed: the shock, whenever it happened, shook off all that vegetates.' At the foot of the peaks, he continues, 'the blackness of the moors by no means assisted to cheer our ideas'.

The riders descended into a desperate land. Assynt, a vast, bleak, parish of some 1,700 unhappy souls, blocked the route that led to the north coast. As the sodden track picked its way through a dejected landscape, an anguished howl is released onto the page:

This tract seems the residence of sloth; the people almost torpid with idleness, and most wretched: their hovels most miserable, made of poles, wattled and covered with thin sods. There is not corn raised sufficient to supply half the wants of the inhabitants: climate conspires with indolence to make matters worse; yet there is much improveable land here in a state of nature: but till famine pinches they will not bestir themselves: they are content with little at present, and are thoughtless of futurity; perhaps on the motive of Turkish vassals, who are oppressed in proportion to their improvements. Dispirited and driven to despair by bad management, crowds were now passing, emaciated with hunger, to the eastern coast, on the report of a ship being there loaden with meal. Numbers of the miserables of this country were now migrating: they wandered in the state of desperation; to poor to pay, they madly sell themselves for their passage, preferring a temporary bondage in a strange land, to starving for life in their native soil.

As evening drew in, the small troop of horsemen made their way over the mosses of the Ledmore valley, and then turned left to follow a tributary up towards the next watershed. A short way up this tributary, they came to a small, dishevelled township perched on the exposed ramp of moorland. The township was called Ledbeg – 'small slope'.

Pennant's Ledbeg has disappeared, except for a white-painted house on the far side of a tumbling river. Today, it is thought to be the oldest inhabited house in Assynt. It was built in around 1740 by a tacksman farmer, Alexander Mackenzie of Ardloch. Pennant makes no mention of what he found here, but a survey carried out in the summer of 1774, two years after Pennant's visit, has survived. Charged with assessing the Sutherland estate, John Home recorded that there were seven families, consisting of thirty-five people, living at Ledbeg, and that among them were 'Ardloch & Lady & 9 Serts' [servants]'.

Pennant's bleak note, that they 'obtained quarters, and rough hospitality' at Ledbeg, suggests that Mackenzie of Ardloch hardly made them welcome. This cannot have been a happy encounter, for Mackenzie was presumably one of those lairds whose 'bad management' had driven the local population to despair and emigration. Overnight, Pennant's plans unravelled. Perhaps the misery of his circumstances had sapped his spirit. Perhaps – after nearly three months of travel – he was tiring. On most arduous journeys, there

comes a point when the sum of imagined difficulties launches a
surprise attack on the will to continue. It takes a doughty spirit to
ride it out; to push on when all appears impossible. Pennant provides
no insight into his own state of mind. He merely states that they
'were informed' that the route to the north coast 'was impassable
for horses'. The explorers seem to have considered continuing on
foot, but this too was deemed too difficult, for they were also advised
'that even a Highland foot-messenger must avoid part of the hills
by crossing an arm of the sea' – a reference perhaps to the long
tentacle of Loch a' Chàirn Bhàin, which reaches far inland from
Eddrachillis Bay, to join with Lochs Glendhu and Glencoul, all of
them hemmed-in by formidable mountains. Until a concrete bridge
was opened in 1984, all west coast traffic had to cross by ferry from
a slipway at Kylesku.

Defeated, Pennant and his companions turned, and retraced their
route through bog and rock, and over the appalling pass to Strath
Canaird. 'At length,' notes Pennant with relief, 'we arrive safely on
board the ship:

> *A wond'rous token*
> *Of heaven's kind care, with necks unbroken.*

*

Lady Frederic Campbell probably left Isle Martin on the last day of July.
With his failure to reach the north coast, the expedition was now
homeward bound. 'Weigh anchor,' Pennant wrote, 'and sail with
a favourable breeze towards the mouth of the bay, with a design on
returning south...'

But as the cutter sailed clear of the Summer Isles that evening, the
wind changed and they were struck by 'cold weather and hard
adverse gales'. With the crew at the ropes, Thompson was forced to
change course and tack into the mouth of Little Loch Broom,
unaware that he had sailed into the jaws of a trap.

Lady Frederic Campbell sought shelter in the lee of a gigantic mountain which Pennant calls 'Tallochessie'. It 'may vie', he thought,
'with the highest I have seen'. 'Tallochessie' can only be mighty

An Teallach, 'the forge' – a name thought by many to derive from the smoky mists which often writhe from its tortured summit ridge. An Teallach is one of the largest, and most spectacular peaks in the Scottish Highlands, a massif of enormous spurs rising to a bristling spine of pinnacles. Protected from the worst of the wind, the explorers diverted themselves for a couple of hours by fishing with hand-lines. Little Loch Broom quickly yielded plentiful cod, some dogfish, 'and a curious ray'.

With darkness falling, Thompson decided to remain at anchor. For those who knew its confined waters (and Thompson clearly did not), Little Loch Broom was – and still is – prey to its own, extraordinary weather system. The sheer bulk of An Teallach, rising straight from the waters of the loch, had the nasty habit of converting easterly or southerly winds into chaotic downdraughts which could blast a ship onto its beam.

During the night, the wind picked up again, and as the gusts increased, Thompson began to fear that the cutter would drag its anchors and fetch onto the rocky foreshore, or worse, onto an unseen reef. Unsurprisingly, all on board now seem to have been awake. Rather than drag the anchors, Thompson considered cutting his cables. Better to risk the ship in the open sea than to be driven ashore and wrecked. Neither option was particularly attractive, and Pennant remarks with amusing detachment that 'the circumstances of a black night, a furious storm, and rocky narrows, did not contribute to the repose of freshwater seamen'. The situation, he concludes, 'was disagreeable.'

As it happened, the storm seemed to subside, and by the time Thompson decided to weigh anchor, the wind was merely 'moderate', and Pennant was sufficiently in command of his observational faculties to note that the anchor chain reappeared from the waters of the loch clustered with 'several very uncommon asteriae'. It was, however, a deceptive moment of calm. As soon as the anchor was lashed to the gunwhale, they were struck again by the curse of Little Loch Broom:

'No sooner was our anchor on board,' writes Pennant, 'but a furious squall arises, and blows in blasts like a hurricane, driving us before it at a vast rate.' Unable to regain the open sea, the cutter was hurled into the throat of the loch, a narrow constriction no more than 1,000 metres wide. Beyond the constriction, the loch widened slightly to run inland between rocky shores for over seven miles. On the northern side of the loch, the mountains rose to 1,500 feet; on the southern shore, An Teallach topped 3,000. *Lady Frederic Campbell* was trapped. With little room to manoeuvre, Thompson struggled in vain to sail his way out of trouble. The further the ship was driven inland, the closer the mountains loomed, and the greater the downdraughts. Careering out of control, the ship 'arrived within a mile of the bottom of the loch'. Thompson realised that they were about to run aground and for a second time, ordered his crew to the anchor. Pennant's own words more than adequately describe the cutter's struggle for survival:

> Drop anchor, but without effect; are obliged to weigh again, while the furious gale engages an attention to the sails, and flings us into a double perplexity in this narrow strait, where for an hour our tacks were almost perpetual, and the vessel frequently in no small danger. The blasts from the mountains were tremendous, not only raising a vast sea, but catching up the waves in eddies, and raising them up in the air to a surprising height.

The 'waterspouts' Pennant describes are well known on the loch, and it was a miracle that the cutter did not run into the rocks.

'At length,' he continues, 'we were relieved from our distress by a successful anchorage, under a high and finely wooded hill, in eight fathoms water, but within a small distance of eighty.' The wooded hill was probably Torr Garbh – 'rough mound'. With *Lady Frederic Campbell* riding securely at anchor, the travellers were rowed ashore. Yet again, Pennant's expedition was about to take an unexpected turn.

★

The tempest could not have cast Pennant ashore at a more propitious spot. No sooner were they safely on dry land, than horses were provided for them 'by favour of Kenneth Mackenzie, Esq., of Dundonnel'. Mackenzie was both the local landowner, and a man whose reputation and influence carried far beyond the shores of Little Loch Broom. For over forty years, he had been developing and enlarging his father's land-holding around the loch.

Riding along the side of the hill towards the head of the loch, Pennant came to a broad, flat-bottomed valley, '…a small but fertile plain, winding amongst the vast mountains, and adorned with a pretty river and woods of alder'. After the storm, and the horrors of Assynt, the travellers could scarcely believe their eyes. For the first time in weeks, they were gazing upon enclosed fields: 'Here,' continues Pennant, 'we rejoiced with the sight of enclosures long strangers to us: the hay was good, the bere and oats excellent…'

This was all the work of Mackenzie's tenants. Three miles from the head of the loch, Pennant came to Mackenzie's house. Built only five years earlier, it was an imposing, two-storey building, five windows wide, rising beside the river in the sheltered neck of the strath. In such fearsome surroundings, it is still a sublimely calm haven. 'We found ourselves,' writes Pennant, 'seated in a spot equalised by few in picturesque and magnificent scenery. The banks of the river that rushes by the house is fringed with trees; and the course often interupted by cascades.'

Pennant had much to share with Kenneth Mackenzie, who had devoted considerable effort to improving the returns from his estates. Mackenzie recognised that the land and waters of the western Highlands could be made productive through investment. Besides his commercial cattle interests, he had also tried to turn herring into an income, hiring a cooper to make barrels, and commissioning a skipper to ship the fish to market. In 1758, he had applied to the Forfeited Estates Commissioners for financial assistance to construct a road to Loch Broom, and he had also paid to repair the local church. He was described by one who knew him well as 'a man of real worth', as prominent 'among his Neighbours as the full moon among the stars in a frosty night'.

Like Pennant, Mackenzie had high expectations, and would proudly boast that of his seven sons, one was in Virginia, one in Holland, one in London, one in Edinburgh, one at home and two at school. However, his concern that there was 'neither Chief or Leader in this Country, particularly in our Name, to take any Concern with the growing generation' proved to be well founded. Although his son George was to be a very able custodian of the estate, the Mackenzie dynasty ran out of luck in 1813, when George's son Kenneth took over. Kenneth, who did not do well at school, developed a passion for the supernatural, and for hens. The estate was sold in 1834, for £22,000. By the 1990s, Dundonnell House and its enormous holdings were owned by lyricist Sir Tim Rice (whose extensive musical credits include the song 'No Chicken').

Pennant's unplanned call at Dundonnell opened the door to a second foray into the mainland's interior. 'Determined,' he announces, 'to go by land to visit Loch Maree, a great lake to the south: and direct Mr Thompson to sail, and wait for us at Gairloch.'

Given his experiences in Assynt, this was a courageous – and perhaps foolhardy – idea. But he may have deemed it less unpleasant than another encounter with Little Loch Broom. To reach Gairloch overland, he would have to trek for twenty miles through the mountains and then find a boat to carry him the length of Loch Maree. Pennant left Dundonnell early in the morning with Mackenzie, one of the laird's sons, 'and another gentleman of the name' – perhaps another son. Of Pennant's team, only Lightfoot seems to have participated in the adventure.

On a day of buffeting wind and horizontal rain, I followed Pennant's mountain traverse. In any weather, this is an absolutely stunning hike. Coming down the zig-zag track into the head of Strath na Sealga, sunlight suddenly touched every fleck of water in the glen. Streaming slabs dazzled, and the river looked for a few moments like a serpent of molten metal. During the hike, I was able to identify most of the features Pennant describes. The 'vale with birch trees thinly scattered' is clearly Strath na Sealga; 'Loch Nanniun', or 'the lake of birds' is the Ordnance Survey's Loch an Nid, the 'loch of the nest'; the 'amazing mountain' whose flanks 'appear like an enormous sheet of ice' is Mullach Coire Mhic Fhearchair, whose wet, tilted slabs do indeed look like ice sheets. If you look in the bed of the stream beyond the slabs, you can even find chunks of the 'red and white marble' Pennant came across.

Shortly after this, Pennant's party reached Bealach na Croise, 'the pass of the trouble'. In mist, this is a notorious spot for getting lost; the correct route from the pass cuts slightly upward, across a vast, slanted peat bog. Scrambling up and down the peat hags, soaked and covered in black slime, I found it impossible to comprehend how Pennant managed to negotiate the slope with a horse. As if this section of the route could not be more tricky, the map leads you straight to the brink of a gorge into which are funnelled all the waters collected in the mighty corrie on the south side of Mullach Coire Mhic Fhearchair. The only safe way to cross is to follow the lip of the ravine downstream, descend to the bed, hop across the boulders and then return up the far side to regain the compass bearing across the peat bog. Pennant did at least concede that the going wasn't easy… 'The way horrible,' he notes, 'broken, steep and slippery.' He too, had trouble with the ravine: 'but our cautious steeds tried every step before they would venture to proceed'.

He must have been as glad as I was to see Loch Meallan an Fhudair sitting like an inky puddle in the peat below the crags of Sithean Biorach; there are few sights more pleasurable than a recognisable landmark on a misty mountain. Above the lochan is a slight levelling on the mountainside. At around 1,600 feet, it is the highest point on the trek. Far below, Lochan Fada's wrinkly shores run along beneath the massive bulk of Slioch. Mountains fill every horizon. It is a liberating, wild place, and about as far from a road as it is possible to be on mainland Britain.

A natural ramp of stone leads down the mountainside rather like a pavement. From the foot of this descent, there are no more navigational hazards. 'Dine on the side of a rill at the bottom,' notes Pennant, 'on plentiful fare provided by our kind host.' Kenneth Mackenzie bade farewell and set off back towards Dundonnell, leaving the two younger Mackenzies to guide Pennant and Lightfoot 'to the next stage'. Another seven miles of rough track led the travellers down to the 'meadowy plain' of Kinlochewe, where Pennant was set on procuring a boat, and pressing on down Loch Maree. But the weather turned 'wet, and tempestuous', and they decided to defer the voyage and take shelter in a 'whisky house'. For a man who professed to disapprove of such distillations, Pennant seems to have enjoyed this odd billet:

> Mr Mackenzie complimented Mr Lightfoot and me with the bedstead, well covered with a warm litter of heath: we lay in our clothes, wrapped ourselves in plaids; and enjoyed a good repose.

Before dropping off to sleep, Pennant was amazed to observe the manner in which the two Scotsmen prepared their bed:

> Our friends did not lose their sleep; but great was our surprise to see them form their bed of wet hay, or rather grass collected from the fields; they flung a plaid over it, undressed, and lay most comfortably, without injury, in what, in a little time, must have become an errant hotbed: so blest with hardy constitution are even the gentlemen of this country!

By seven the next morning, Pennant and Lightfoot were climbing into a six-oared rowing boat. It wasn't until they had rowed some distance down the loch that Pennant's attention was drawn to 'a young man of good appearance', who was running along the shore 'hailing the boat in Erse language'. Thinking that he was trying to hitch a lift in the fully loaded boat, Pennant ignored him. It was only after the young man had raced after them for two miles, 'through every difficulty', shouting dire threats as he did so, that one of the rowers informed Pennant that he was actually the owner of the boat, and merely wanted the honour of taking the place of one of the rowers. 'Instead of insulting us with abuse, as a Charon of South Britain would have done,' muses Pennant, 'he instantly composed himself, and told us through an interpreter that he felt great pride in finding that his conduct gained any degree of approbation.'

Hugging the north shore, where the looming cliffs of Slioch leapt straight up from the water for 3,000 feet, the rowing boat inched westward. It wasn't until I rowed a heavy wooden boat into the centre of Loch Maree that I sensed its disquieting power. A vast body of water (the fourth largest freshwater loch in Scotland), pinched by sombre peaks, it can make a small boat seem microscopic. Like Little Loch Broom, the surface of Loch Maree can be stirred by violent squalls to a howling fury of white-capped waves. On a grey, gusty day with ice in the air, it is difficult not to row with a certain urgency.

In equivalent distance, Pennant and his crew were attempting to row nearly two-thirds of the way across the English Channel. Two hours of hard pulling would have placed Pennant's boat in sight of the waterfall which tumbles down the crags of Letterewe. Above the boat's bow he would have seen Loch Maree's archipelago of thirty or so islands, scattered as if a giant had snatched a chunk of Slioch and hurled its shards at the loch. Yet in the detail of the islands, in their pebbled coves and stands of pine, he might have sensed a still, and almost shocking, beauty.

'Land on that called Inchmaree, the favoured isle of the saint,' begins Pennant, 'the patron of all the coast from Applecross to Loch Broom.' It was of course this stretch of coast which had come so close to wrecking *Lady Frederic Campbell*. Inchmaree is the only island which has a clear line of sight to both ends of the loch. It is a sacred place. Barely 200 metres across, it looks from an approaching boat like a verdant fragment of Amazonia. At the western end is a tiny shingle beach. Pennant and Lightfoot leapt ashore and picked their way through 'a beautiful grove of oak, ash willow, wicken, birch, fir, hazel and enormous hollies'. In the midst of the island, the explorers found 'a circular dike of stones, with a regular narrow entrance'. It is still there. And so are the medieval cross slabs, side-by-side among the fallen leaves. The slabs are said to mark the burial places of a Norwegian prince and his wife. Pennant conjectures that Saint Maree had practised pagan rites here 'as the readiest method of making a conquest over the minds of the inhabitants'. (Bulls were still being sacrificed on the island as late as the 1670s.) To the visitors, the 'curiosity of the place' was the well of

Saint Maree, whose waters were known for their 'power unspeakable in cases of lunacy'. Pilgrims finding the well full could expect their onward journey to be propitious, but if it was empty, they could expect to proceed with 'fears and doubts'. Pennant fails to record the water level. Today, it is permanently dry.

Five miles beyond the end of the loch, Pennant and Lightfoot found *Lady Frederic Campbell* riding at anchor on the south side of Gairloch's bay. Blessed by 'a good breeze', the ship sailed away from the troublesome northern coast of Scotland.

Lady Frederic Campbell would take ten days to sail southward from Gairloch to Ardmaddie, where Pennant's Hebridean expedition would end. With the ship headed towards safer, more familiar waters, the tension on board lifted, and Pennant produced some of his best work. Two days after leaving Gairloch, the cutter anchored off Skye, and Pennant took the ship's boat ashore to gather information on the parish of Glenelg, and to examine two brochs which had been described fifty years earlier by Alexander Gordon. A few miles south of Glenelg, the ship dropped anchor in Loch Hourn, and Pennant took the ship's boat eight miles up the loch, where he chanced upon a fleet of one hundred herring boats, and a shore station constructed from 'multitudes of little occasional hovels and tents'. For Pennant, Loch Hourn was a happy epiphany:

> So unexpected a prospect of the busy haunt of men and ships in this wild and romantic tract, afforded this agreeable reflection: that there is no part of our dominion so remote, so inhospitable, and so unprofitable, as to deny employ and livelihood to thousands; and that there are no parts so polished, so improved, and so fertile, but which must stoop to receive advantage from those dreary spots they so affectedly despise.

In Pennant's new utopia, cities and wilderness 'must be obliged to acknowledge the mutual dependency of part on part, howsoever remotely placed, and howsoever different in modes or manner of living'.

Six days later, *Lady Frederic Campbell* passed into the Sound of Jura, and after an excursion to see the great whirlpool of Corryvrekan,

Pennant landed on the eastern shore of Seil Sound, beneath the 'small, but elegant' house of Ardmaddie. Here, he took leave of his skipper, Archibald Thompson, acknowledging his attention to the expedition's aims, his 'obliging conduct throughout and skill in his profession'. At Ardmaddie, Pennant found his groom and horses waiting, ready for the onward journey through mainland Scotland, and eventually back to Chester. 'Thus ended,' he concludes, 'this voyage of amusement, successful and satisfactory in every part, unless where embittered with reflections on the sufferings of my fellow-creatures.'

That night, at Ardmaddie, Pennant had a dream; 'a waking of the soul'. In this dream, the explorer is confronted by a clan chieftain from two centuries earlier. Armed with a targe and huge claymore, the grizzled warrior explains to Pennant how the 'mighty chieftains' were transformed into 'rapacious landlords', exchanging the 'warm affections of their people for sordid trash'. The misery and idleness which now fill the glens can only be addressed if the 'famished clans' are instructed in 'the science of rural economy', in fishing and weaving, and given the opportunity to serve in Britain's army and navy. In the dream, the chieftain tells Pennant that he must inform the world of the poverty he has witnessed.

The book which Thomas Pennant came to write is all the more remarkable for its triple role, as the first thorough guide to the natural history of Scotland, as the literary 'key' which would unlock the mysteries of Scotland to outsiders, and as a humanitarian plea to address the suffering of those closest to home.

WILLIAM
COBBETT

1822–6

Champion of the countryside

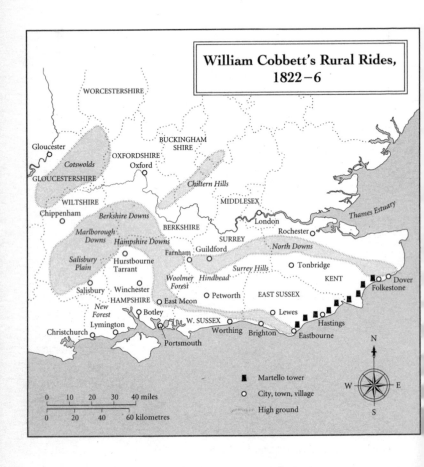

William Cobbett's Rural Rides, 1822–6

WORCESTERSHIRE

Gloucester

Cotswolds

GLOUCESTERSHIRE

BUCKINGHAM SHIRE

OXFORDSHIRE

Oxford

Chiltern Hills

WILTSHIRE

Chippenham

Berkshire Downs

BERKSHIRE

MIDDLESEX

London

Thames Estuary

Rochester

Marlborough Downs

Hampshire Downs

SURREY

Farnham Guildford

North Downs

Salisbury Plain

Hurstbourne Tarrant

Surrey Hills

Tonbridge

KENT

Dover

Salisbury

Winchester

Woolmer Forest *Hindhead*

Petworth

EAST SUSSEX

Folkestone

HAMPSHIRE East Meon

New Forest

Botley

W. SUSSEX

Lewes

Hastings

Christchurch

Lymington

Worthing Brighton

Eastbourne

Portsmouth

■ Martello tower

○ City, town, village

High ground

0 10 20 30 40 miles

0 20 40 60 kilometres

N

W E

S

When William Cobbett set out on horseback in the early 1820s, Britain was reeling from war, threatened by revolution, and struggling to adjust to runaway industrialisation and a population explosion. The countryside appeared traumatised by sudden change. Riding the back-country of south-east England, summer and winter for four years, this incendiary journalist brought the rural crisis to the doors of Westminster. Scribbled in inns and farmhouses, the account he kept of his tours to the agricultural front-line is an exhilarating mix of invective and rustic vignettes. Rural Rides is a snapshot of the countryside in mid-revolution, and the last glimpse we have of England as a truly rural land.

*

'This morning I set off, in rather drizzling rain, from Kensington, on horse-back, accompanied by my son James...' It was Wednesday, 25 September 1822. Aged fifty-nine, William Cobbett was leaving home on the first of his 'Rural Rides'. On the saddle of each horse was a thin leather roll containing spare clothing. They carried no map, but knew where they were going. Heading west along Kensington Road, the two riders passed through the turnpike gate, then turned left onto a rutted lane which kinked gently downhill through fields and smallholdings to Earl's Court and Walham Green. Passing several muddy junctions, they picked up another lane, lined with cottages, which led to Fulham and the bridge over the Thames.

For the next five days, father and son wove a zig-zag course through Middlesex, Surrey and Hampshire, to the little village of Hurstbourne Tarrant, where an old friend of Cobbett's kept a farm. As Cobbett observes, he could have covered the sixty-six miles from Kensington in about eight hours. But that wasn't the point. His object was 'not to see inns and turnpike-roads, but to see the *country*; to see the farmers at *home*, and to see the labourers *in the fields*'. On back-roads and field paths, the two Cobbetts could explore a Britain invisible from the turnpike.

Riding at walking pace, there was little that Cobbett could miss. With every mile, he noted the state of the countryside, the mood of the labourers, the soils and the crops. This autumn the rain had come, he decided, just in time for the wheat-sowing season. The turnips looked good, if a little '*backward* in some places'. And the fine summer had brought 'excellent' fruit: grapes were 'as good as those raised under glass', and apples 'much richer than in ordinary years'. The hop harvest had been 'not only large, but good in quality'. In fields and inns, he chatted with all classes of countryman, from destitute hop-pickers to opulent yeomen. Throughout the ride, there is a spirit of discovery; of travelling with a stranger's eye. At Chertsey, he'd come across a livestock fair and investigated the prices being paid for horses and cattle. In mid-Surrey, he found a bridleway which led down to a 'narrow and exquisitely beautiful vale', a vertiginous Garden of Eden, with fine soils, ample woodland and corn-fields 'nearly as steep as the roof of a tiled house'. A necklace of small lakes lined with meadows and hop-gardens completed the picture. In this vale of plenty, there were coppices for hop-poles, and charcoal for the powder-mills. By implication, this is a land which can look after its own.

On this introductory ride, Cobbett took James back to his roots. Avoiding the 'level road' to Guildford, they turned onto the open grassland of the North Downs and climbed to the crest of a hogs-back ridge. Behind and in front of them was a seemingly infinite pattern of heath, field and woodland. For one hundred miles, between his birthplace in Farnham and the white cliffs of Dover, the high, green wave of downland undulated across southern England like the time-worn wall of a lost generation of giants. Geology is seldom so emblematic. Chalk is the youngest of England's rocks, and there is nothing else in the geological record which has such a telling relationship with landscape and farming. It's given us billowing downs for sheep, and watered vales for cattle. Cobbett was born on chalk, and most at home on chalk. Midway between the city and the sea, these downs were known in Cobbett's day as 'the Surrey Hills', for this section of the North Downs neatly bisects the county. 'This county of Surrey,' muses Cobbett, 'presents to the eye of the traveller a greater contrast than any other county in England. It has some of the very best and some of the very worst lands, not only in England, but in the world.'

Two days later, on the county's western border, Cobbett walked his horse beneath a towering oak on a village green. He remembered the oak from his childhood, when it was 'but a very little tree, comparatively'. Now, he tells his son, it is 'by far the finest tree that I ever saw in my life'. With James pacing and counting, the oak was subjected to a full survey. Reckoning it to be 'full *thirty feet round*' its trunk, with 'fifteen or sixteen limbs, and many of them from five to ten feet round', Cobbett assessed its circumference at 'about three hundred feet'. The oak appeared to be free of decay, and it had 'made great shoots in all parts of it this last summer and spring'. There were 'no appearances of white upon the trunk, such as are regarded as the symptoms of full growth'. By the time he had finished, the Tilford Oak had been elevated to the status of a national monument.

On they rode, over the river and across sandy heathland to a deep, narrow valley known as 'the Bourne', an old Viking name given to places by springs and young streams. The soil here was too poor to attract landowners, and the valley was scattered with the cottages and pigsties of families who'd acquired the skills to live well from infertile ground. They were known locally as 'Bourners'. 'We went to this Bourne,' recalled Cobbett, 'in order that I might show my son the spot where I received the rudiments of my education.'

Standing before the stream, Cobbett remembered those days:

There is a little hop-garden in which I used to work when from eight to ten years old; from which I have scores of times run to follow the hounds, leaving the hoe to do the best that it could to destroy the weeds; but the most interesting thing was a *sand-hill*, which goes from a part of the heath down to the rivulet. As a due mixture of pleasure with toil, I, with two brothers, used occasionally to *desport* ourselves, as the lawyers call it, at this sand-hill. Our diversion was this: we used to go to the top of the hill, which was steeper than the roof of a house; one used to draw his arms out of the sleeves of his smock-frock, and lay himself down with his arms by his sides; and then the others, one at head and other at feet, sent him rolling down the hill like a barrel or a log of wood. By the time he got to the bottom, his hair, eyes, ears, nose and mouth, were all full of this loose sand; then the others took their turn, and at every roll, there was a monstrous spell of laughter.'

Only a mile away, in the centre of Farnham, stood the Jolly Farmer Inn. Cobbett's father, George, had been the landlord, and a farmer. William had grown up under an open sky and here in the Bourne, he recognised the origins of his own nature:

I am perfectly satisfied that if I had not received such an education, or something very much like it; that, if I had been brought up a milksop, with a nursery-maid everlastingly at my heels, I should have been at this day as great a fool, as inefficient a mortal, as any of those frivolous idiots that are turned out from Winchester and Westminster School or from any of those dens of dunces called Colleges and Universities. It is impossible to say how much I owe to that sand-hill; and I went to return it my thanks for the ability which it probably gave me to be one of the greatest terrors, to one of the greatest and most powerful bodies of knaves and fools, that ever were permitted to afflict this or any other country.

Cobbett's county has changed a little. The Jolly Farmer has been renamed the William Cobbett. The Bourne has become a manicured suburb puddled with swimming pools, and Surrey's tranquil byways are now an automotive Hades. Tilford's oak is still on the green, though, a treasured stump which breaks into leaf each spring.

*

There are two young Cobbetts. The William (or 'Bill') known to his brothers and sister was a mischievous, rebellious boy who revealed few signs of 'uncommon intelligence'. There was, apparently, 'nothing about him of the prodigy', although older brother Tom did remember William enjoying his father reading aloud from his newspaper. Parliamentary speeches were a favourite, and Cobbett later told his daughter that he used to wander on the common 'making speeches to the furze bushes'. Misdemeanours reported by his siblings included cutting from his father's map the head of a crocodile because it looked ugly, and absconding from pig-keeping because there was 'some business that better suited his taste'. To Tom, his younger brother was 'an ungovernable rather than a tractable youth'; a shirker of steady work, with 'an obstinate resolution for what he was bent on'.

For his own readership, however, Cobbett created a diligent boy of the soil who began working the land when he was so young that he was 'hardly able to climb the gates and stiles'. William raced through a rustic syllabus from bird-scaring and weeding to harrowing barley. After learning to hoe peas, he wrote, 'I arrived at the honour of joining the reapers in harvest, driving the team and holding the plough.' His principal ambition was, he recalled, 'surpassing my brothers in the different labours of the field'. His education was heath and furrow: 'No teachers of any sort,' he would later claim. 'Nobody to shelter me from the consequences of bad, and no one to counsel me to good behaviour.' Biographer Richard Ingrams takes the view that Cobbett was, from the beginning, exceptionally 'self-centred and self-sufficient'.

At least twice during the Farnham years, Cobbett walked away from farming. At the age of eleven, having learned of the botanic gardens at Kew, he set off on foot across the heaths, with thirteen and a half pence in his pocket. Passing through Richmond, he spotted in a shop-window a book called *Tale of a Tub*. Intrigued by the title, he bought it for three pence. In Cobbett's version of events, Swift's satirical assault on the church led to a conversion on the road to Kew. Ingrams thinks that it was less likely to have been Swift's sophisticated theological narrative which moved the boy than the exhilarating torrents of words; that Cobbett fell to a 'verbal intoxication'. The book remained with Cobbett until it was lost overboard in the Atlantic. A second breakout from Farnham, at the age of nineteen, saw Cobbett heading for Portsmouth and his first sight of the sea. From a long, high down called Portsdown, he gazed down stubbled fields to the naval dockyards and a silvery passage separating the mainland from the Isle of Wight. Like many a young labourer before and since, his impulse was to join a ship. He was ejected from the first vessel he boarded, and when he applied more formerly through the Port Admiral, he was again rejected.

The Portsmouth episode opened his eyes to further shores. 'I sighed for a sight of the world;' he recalled, 'the little island of Britain seemed too small a compass for me. The things in which I had taken the most delight were neglected; the singing of the birds grew insipid, and even the heart-cheering cry of the hounds … was heard with the most torpid indifference.' The final break came on 6 May 1783: 'I, like Don Quixote,' began the farm boy from Farnham, 'sallied forth to seek adventures. I was dressed in my holiday clothes…' Aged nineteen years and two months (although he actually thought he was seventeen at the time, since he mistakenly believed that he'd been born in 1766), he took the London turnpike and found a job with a Gray's Inn lawyer. He was trained to draft documents in a brisk, copperplate hand, in what was a tedious, if invaluable, apprenticeship for a man who would ultimately write something like thirty million words for publication.

The making of Cobbett, the Rural Rider, took another forty years, a couple of continents, and several reversals of fortune which included imprisonment and bankruptcy. He hadn't lasted at Gray's Inn, and after a few months, he enlisted with the recently formed 54th (West Norfolk) Regiment of Foot, and sailed – as Corporal Cobbett – to adventure. The regiment landed in Nova Scotia in 1785 and then moved on to the wilderness of New Brunswick, where Cobbett made the most of 'skaiting, fishing, shooting, and all the other sports of the country', including canoeing. While there, he was reading everything to hand, from Shakespeare and Milton, to more of Swift. Already an incorrigible improver, he compiled a handbook on mathematics and geometry for his fellow infantrymen. But the intemperate forests were also nurturing a rebel, and when Cobbett reached the rank of sergeant major, he collided with 'the epaulet gentry', most of whom, so it seemed, neglected their regimental duties so that they could 'swagger about and get roaring drunk'. Back in England, when Cobbett attempted to get four of his superior officers court martialled for profiteering from his men's food rations, he found himself stitched up by the accused, and in March 1792 he was forced to flee to revolutionary France, and then to recently independent America. 'The Thing', as Cobbett would come to call the establishment, had created a contemptuous patriot. Settled with his new wife in Philadelphia, America's political nerve-centre, Cobbett found work teaching English, but soon began writing political pamphlets attacking American republicans, and their frenzied enthusiasm for all things French and revolutionary. He was so successful that, in June 1800, a volley of libel suits forced him to flee back to England.

History is ill-equipped to record the privately held fears of nations, but there is every reason to suppose that these were extraordinarily anxious times for the 'ordinary' person. Revolution gripped the western world. The American Revolution had been followed in 1789 by the French Revolution. In Britain, radicals raised the spectre of a *coup d'état*. Absent for the best part of sixteen years, Cobbett returned to a country in crisis. Harvests had failed and food prices had soared. Britain was in the midst of the greatest, most expensive war it had ever fought, and Pitt had been forced to introduce a new tax – income tax – to pay for munitions and equipment. War weary and fearful of invasion by revolutionary France, the country was wide open to home-grown insurrection. The Navy had mutinied, twice. Food riots were hitting cities and market towns. In the countryside, ricks were burning. Common land was being enclosed by a new breed of acquisitive farmers and landlords, and rents were spiralling. On average, land rents rose by 80 per cent between 1790 and 1813. Back in Farnham, Cobbett found two of his brothers struggling for survival on their small farms. Labourers across the Home Counties had lost their livelihood:

The *clock* was gone; the *brass kettle* was gone; the *pewter dishes* were gone; the *warming pan* was gone... All was gone! How miserable,

how deplorable, how changed that Labourer's dwelling, which I,
only twenty years before, had seen so neat and happy!

Cobbett went back to the land, using money he'd earned in America,
to buy a house and eighty acres of land in Hampshire, on the sunny
side of the South Downs. The soil was nothing special, 'a deep
and stiff clay', Cobbett said, but it was good for oaks and for wheat.
Here, he experimented with species imported from America and
planted over 20,000 trees – mainly oaks, elms and ashes. He kept
Botley for twelve years, while his political life resumed its reckless
trajectory. Having attacked prime ministers Addington and then Pitt
for making peace with Napoleon, he launched his vitriolic period-
ical, the *Political Register*, which briskly matured from a Tory
organ to the mouthpiece of radical reform. The aim was not
revolution, but 'a pretty complete change of men' at the top, and a
roots-up reform which would allow the free election of politicians,
and the means of making 'change in the management of affairs'.
The price to pay for radical journalism was a two-year spell in
Newgate Prison, and then a second flight to America. When he
came back to England two years later, the reform movement was in
disarray, infiltrated by government spies, and shocked by the
massacre in Manchester of eleven reformers, and the wounding of
400. The government blamed the Press, and new measures crippled
the circulation of Cobbett's *Register*. Bankrupted, he had to sell his
beloved Botley and move to London.

By the beginning of 1821, Cobbett and his family had been back
in England for just over a year. In April, they moved into a small
cottage in Kensington, then a fashionable suburb draped over a hill
just to the west of Hyde Park. Gazing down from the heights was
Kensington Palace. On the north side of the village, the area known
as 'Gravel Pits' gave way to open country which ran down to Notting
Dale and Notting Barn, but the soul of the village lay to the south.
Here was London's most lively suburban strip. For a few hundred
yards along each side of the turnpike, a busy, transitory community
jostled for space amid workshops, houses and over a dozen inns. The
Cobbetts had managed to get hold of an undeveloped, four-acre

plot on the south side of the turnpike, between Tucker's candle factory and the Scarsdale House Boarding School (a site now occupied by Kensington High Street Underground Station). The walled smallholding already contained a pigeon house, and Cobbett quickly imported three cows, and laid plans to breed turkeys and to establish a seed farm and nursery garden.

For most people, a four-acre research station would have been an adequate challenge. But Cobbett was also busy publishing instructional guides on rural self-sufficiency, 'containing information relative to the brewing of beer, making of bread, keeping of cows, pigs, bees, ewes, goats, poultry, etc.' Writing the introduction to *Cottage Economy* in July 1821, he launched his campaign to fight rural poverty and to create '*abundant living* amongst the people at large'. Three months later, with winter drawing in, he rode out from Kensington to Hampshire on a mission to gather information from the agricultural front-line. His report appeared in the *Political Register*: 'The farmers here, as everywhere else, complain most bitterly,' he wrote, 'but they hang on, like sailors to the masts or hull of a wreck.' In only eight years, between 1814 and 1822, the wages of agricultural workers plummeted by one third.

Over the next ten years, Cobbett undertook many more rides, but the ones which he eventually packaged in 1830 as the *Rural Rides* took place in a four-year period, between 25 September 1822 and 26 October 1826.

*

A map describing Cobbett's *Rural Rides* would look like a tangle of noodles. Never has a documentary author created such an unchartable itinerary. His strenuous aversion to turnpikes, and the obscure locations he wanted to reach, meant that many a journey got from A to B by way of Z. In general, he roamed in an area which extended from Kent in the east to Wiltshire in the west, and as far north as Gloucestershire. More often than not, he headed west from London, through Surrey and Hampshire.

No matter how far Cobbett rode from Kensington, the capital maintained its presence. But this was not the London celebrated by

Defoe a hundred years earlier for its ability to permeate the provinces with trading wealth. To Cobbett, London is the 'Great Wen', the wart, the revolting sebaceous cyst on the face of Britain. And it wasn't just London. The Industrial Revolution was creating a multitude of mini-Wens, 'other Hell-Holes', as Cobbett put it, 'of 84 degrees of heat'. The problem was not the nature of cities themselves, but the people who ran them: 'the monopolizers and the tax-eaters and their purveyors and lackeys and harlots'. Cities waged war and bred corruptions like paper money and speculation. They harboured 'The Thing', and they were growing at a frightening rate. London's population in 1820 was just over one million. Only one century earlier, the population had been 300,000. And two centuries before *that*, when John Leland was walking to school across the yard of St Paul's, London had been – by modern standards – a small town of 40,000.

By Cobbett's day, London was perceived as two zones. The inner, metropolitan zone was an urban mesh of 9,000 streets and 180,000 houses crammed into an area measuring about four by seven miles. Outside this built-up zone was a broad suburban swathe of villages and market towns whose character could be seen as more urban than rural. When John Cary published his exquisite one-inch-to-the-mile pocket atlas of the metropolis in 1817, he extended his survey to 'the country fifteen miles round London'. Thomas Moule's map, 'The environs of London', understood the suburban radius to extend for about eight miles.

Cobbett loathed the suburbs. 'All Middlesex is *ugly*,' he memorably pronounced. London's satellite communities were fair game for abuse. The Middlesex villages of Twickenham, Hampton, Sunbury and Shepperton, writes Cobbett, 'consist generally of tax-eaters' showy tea-garden-like boxes, and of shabby dwellings of labouring people, who, in this part of the country, look to be about half *Saint Giles's*: dirty, and have every appearance of drinking gin'. When Cobbett has to return to London at the end of 'a most beautiful ride through the Weald', he ascends the steep flank of the North Downs, then suffers a collapse of spirit: 'When you get to Beckenham, which is the last parish in Kent,' he sighs, 'the country begins to assume a cockney-like appearance; all is artificial, and you know [sic] longer feel any interest in it.'

For Cobbett, rural England began where Middlesex ended, on Chertsey Bridge. His methods for engaging with the countryside were almost as stringent as William Gilpin's 'Picturesque rules'. Turnpikes and carriages were 'out'; field paths and horses were 'in': To see the country properly, he wrote, 'you must go either on foot or on horse-back. With a *gig* you cannot get about amongst *bye-lanes* and *across fields*, through bridle-ways and hunting-gates; and to *tramp it* is too *slow*, leaving the *labour* out of the question, and that is not a trifle.' Public transport was out of the question, too: 'In any sort of *carriage*,' he ruled, 'you cannot get into the *real country places*.' Cobbett's countryside was open and accessible. He wasn't limited to 'public footpaths' and 'public bridleways'; he doesn't come across barbed-wire blockades or 'Keep Out' signs. Flexibility was essential, for bad weather could close roads, or make progress too difficult. His rides were often wonderfully spontaneous, changeable affairs: 'On Monday,' he writes while overnighting in Dover, 'I was balancing in my own mind whether I should go to France or not. To-day I have decided in the negative, and shall set off this evening for the Isle of Thanet; that spot so famous for corn.'

Although Cobbett's routes appear whimsical and convoluted, some of them at least may have been quite carefully planned; on one occasion, he mentions that he 'must adhere to a certain *route* as strictly as a regiment on the march', in order to return to London 'by a certain day'. To this end, he had '*written* the route' in advance. Earlier, when setting off to explore Kent, a county he knew little, he writes that he 'got a list of places from a friend in Sussex, whom I asked to give me *a route to Dover*, and to send me through those parts of Kent which he thought would be interesting to me.' In the same passage, he admits that he 'had not looked at a map of Kent for years, and, perhaps, never.' Given that the great age of British mapping was in full swing, it's a fairly astonishing confession. The first Ordnance Survey map had just been published, in 1801, and it covered Kent. By the 1820s, the OS and various private publishers had printed maps of southern England in unprecedented detail and accuracy. During a ride in the far west, another new territory for Cobbett, he made a tracing from a 'fine map' belonging to Sir Thomas Winnington, of Stanford Park in Worcestershire, to help him find his way home through the unfamilar back-country of the Cotswolds. The result was infuriating: 'A *route*, when it lies through *villages*, is one thing on a *map*,' complains Cobbett, 'and quite another thing on the ground.' He wasn't the first to discover that a map could be a misleading simplification: 'Our line of villages, from Cheltenham to Fairford was very nearly straight upon the map; but, upon the ground, it took us round about a great many miles, besides now and then a *little going back*, to get into the right road; and, which was a great inconvenience, not a public-house was there on our road, until we got within eight miles of Fairford.' The suspicion that Cobbett could not read a map is supported by his own attempts at cartography. A couple of years after *Rural Rides* was published, he produced his hefty *Geographical Dictionary of England and Wales*, which included the most deformed county maps published in the nineteenth century.

In this age of GPS and market-induced phobias about 'getting lost' and 'losing time', there is something enormously liberating about Cobbett's attitude to navigation. He senses his way forward, using a combination of topographical nous, memory and local advice. Luckily for his readers, it doesn't always work. In Kent, he suddenly finds himself 'upon the sea-beach', apparently unaware that he has ridden all the way to the English Channel. 'Never,' he muses, 'was I so much surprised as when I saw *a sail*.' In deepest Surrey, having been warned not to try the direct route between the villages of Chiddingfold and Thursley because of thick woodland, Cobbett goes ahead anyway ('the great thing was to see the interior of these woods; see the stems of the trees, as well as the tops of them'). Inevitably, he gets lost, but the occupant of an isolated cottage agrees to act as his guide, and Cobbett is led through a sylvan paradise into an ash coppice, which produces an impassioned diatribe upon the economic and social benefits of planting the heaths of southern England with locust trees. A fast-growing deciduous hardwood, the locust is ideal, argues Cobbett, for fencing, hedge stakes, hurdle stakes, fold-shores and furniture. Not only that, but the stump of each locust could produce two eighteen-inch locust-pins for shipbuilding – sufficient, he reckons Cobbett (at 22,000 locust trees to the acre), to construct a seventy-four-gun ship. Unlike paper money, 'which only takes the dinner from one man and gives it to another', the locust tree 'would be a prodigious creation of real and solid wealth'. This is the tree which could put Britain back on its feet; it is, trumpets Cobbett, 'of the very first importance to the whole kingdom'. And he had put his money behind his pen by sowing a locust plantation in Kensington. The results had been mixed; trees he'd sold to an unnamed 'gentleman' the previous year had all died. Cobbett blamed hares.

Mud-spattered and curious, Cobbett had the knack of disarming those he met on the road. Rural England was his heart, soul and manner, and Cobbett had that travellers' gift of humility. In an age of metropolitan ostentation, he could pass for a ploughman: 'Never,' observed the journalist James Grant, 'were the looks of any man more completely at variance with his character. There was something so dull and heavy about his whole appearance, that any one who did not know him, would at once have set him down for some country clodpole ... who ... had never read a book, or had a single idea in his head.' Cobbett, however, was confidently in his element. To a man who had honed his survival skills in the forests and rapids behind the ragged shores of the Gulf of St Lawrence, southern England was unthreatening. The days of highwaymen on Hounslow Heath, and of August snowstorms, were gone. He could ride through England's softest shires as if they were a vast market garden. He was entirely at ease in the countryside.

★

Although there was no such thing as a typical day in the saddle for Cobbett, the style of his travelling invited the kinds of incidents and insights that made a man feel glad to be alive. He had one of his most fruitful days on the road late in November 1822. It was a Sunday, and he had set himself the goal of riding from Hambledon, a village in the South Downs not far from Portsmouth, to the village of

Thursley, about five miles south-west of Godalming. Unusually, he had a map. Unfortunately, the map described Hampshire, and Thursley was in Surrey. Undeterred, he simply plotted a straight line towards a village called Headley, on the edge of his map. From there, he reckoned it was 'about five miles' to his destination. Embarking on a straight line would have been a perfectly logical method of navigating at sea, but on land, it set Cobbett on a collision course with a precipice and a swamp. Relishing the prospect, he set out 'in spite of all the remonstrances of friends, who represented to me the danger of breaking my neck at *Hawkley* and of getting buried in the bogs of *Woolmer Forest*'.

It takes an intense engagement with the landscape to turn a one-day ride through Hampshire and Surrey into an epic which reads like a surveying expedition in the heart of a new continent. There was, of course, an easier route between Hambledon and Thursley. A mere twenty-seven miles, it involved following the London turnpike over the top of Hindhead. But Hindhead was a problem. The 800-foot hill was one of Cobbett's most loathed locations. Not only was it covered in barren heathland, but it had been disfigured by one of the government's Semaphore stations, and it lay within the 'sink-hole' borough of Haslemere. It was also said to be haunted. Hindhead had to be avoided at any effort.

It all started well enough. The opening miles from Hambledon are bathed in an expectant glow, as Cobbett and his servant ride north over the shoulder of Old Winchester Hill and onto the long, downland ramp descending to the Meon Valley: 'If I had not seen any thing further to-day,' sighs the Rural Rider, 'I should have dwelt long on the beauties of this place. Here is a very fine valley, in nearly an elliptical form, sheltered by high hills sloping gradually from it; and, not far from the middle of this valley there is a hill nearly in the form of a goblet-glass with the foot and stem broken off and turned upside down. And this is clapped down upon the level of the valley, just as you would put such goblet upon a table. The hill is lofty, partly covered with wood, and it gives an air of great singularity to the scene.'

What follows is characteristic of Cobbett's carrot-and-stick journalism. No sooner have we fallen for East Meon, than he beats us soundly with the truth: 'I am sure,' he continues without breaking-out a new paragraph, 'that East Meon has been a large place.'

A 'large place'? Readers of the *Political Register* knew this to be the opening rumble of the Depopulation Rant. Here was yet another village that had suffered the flight of its labourers: 'The church has a Saxon Tower pretty near equal, as far as I recollect, to that of the Cathedral at Winchester … and it shows that the church (which is still large) must, at first, have been a very large building.' And there was more amiss in East Meon. On the ride over from Hambledon, Cobbett had observed 'many square miles of downs near this village, *all bearing the marks of the plough*, and all out of tillage for many many years'. Then he raises his riding crop and begins thwacking those responsible for desecrating Hampshire's downs. There is 'not one single inch', he starts, 'but what is vastly superior in quality to any of those great "improvements" on the miserable heaths of Hounslow, Bagshot, and Windsor Forest. It is the destruct-ive, the murderous paper-system, that has transferred the fruit of labour, and the people along with it, from the different parts of the country to the neighbourhood of the all-devouring *Wen*.' And off he goes, accusing the government of inventing Census returns which show Britain's population to have increased by four million over the last twenty years. The rant is followed by an open letter to one of Cobbett's enemies in the 'Pitt-system', George Canning, in which he asks the head of Foreign Affairs 'what *sort of apology*' is going to be offered to the nation for allowing the 'French Bourbons' to intervene on behalf of the royalists in the Spanish Civil War. Within the space of a few lines, pretty East Meon has become a war zone. But then the carrot is proffered again, and Cobbett leads his readers away from the Meon and across the Petersfield turnpike into a disquisition upon soil-types and the benefits of spreading chalk on fields of difficult clay.

At a friend's house near the turnpike, Cobbett asked for advice about the hazards ahead. 'I got instructions to go to *Hawkley*,' relates Cobbett, 'but accompanied with most earnest advice *not to go that way*, for that it was *impossible to get along*.' The words 'not' and 'impossible' being terms of encouragement to Cobbett, he set off towards Hawkley, receiving further inducement from a woman in a wayside cottage who warned: 'Sir: you can't *ride* down: will your horses go *alone*?' Cobbett was most in his element when there was new land to explore: 'On we trotted up this pretty green lane; and indeed, we had been coming gently and generally *up hill* for a good while. The lane was between highish banks and ... out we came, all in a moment, at the very *edge of the hanger*! And, never, in all my life, was I so surprised and so delighted! I pulled up my horse, and sat and looked; and it was like looking from the top of a castle down into the sea.'

Although his horse was standing no more than ten miles from the sandy valley he'd rolled down as a boy, Cobbett realised that he was gazing upon a landscape that was utterly foreign: 'Those who had so strenuously dwelt on the dirt and dangers of this route, had said not a word about the beauties, the matchless beauties of the scenery. These hangers,' he explains, 'are *woods* on the sides of *very steep hills*. The trees and underwood *hang*, in some sort, to the ground, instead of *standing on* it. Hence these places are called *Hangers*.' Deciphering the folds in the slopes, Cobbett saw that he was on the edge of a convoluted, wooded cliff which had protruding spurs, 'like *piers* into the sea'. The ends of two of these promontories are, he writes 'nearly perpendicular, and their tops so high in the air, that you cannot look at the village below without something like a feeling of apprehension'. Despite the bare, winter trees, 'the spot', he concludes, 'is beautiful beyond description, even now.' In the distance, the two riders could make out the vast heaths of southern Surrey and the looming bulk of Hindhead: 'Men, however, are not to have such beautiful views as this without some *trouble*. We had the view, but we had to *go down the hanger*.'

Cobbett, a few months from his sixtieth birthday, stepped gingerly over the edge:

The horses took the lead, and crept down partly upon their feet and partly upon their *hocks*. It was extremely slippery too; for the soil is a sort of *marle*, or, as they call it here, *maume*, or *mame*, which is, when wet, very much like *grey soap*. In such a case it was likely that I should keep in the *rear*, which I did, and I descended by taking hold of the branches of the underwood, and so *letting myself down*.

Having survived the descent, and remounted, they crossed a field, then a farmyard, forded a river and then joined one of the strangest roads Cobbett had ever seen. Ahead of them was a deep, gleaming trench: 'The banks were quarries of *white stone*, like Portland-stone, and the bed of the road was of the *same stone*; and, the rains having been heavy for a day or two before, the whole was as clean and as white as the steps of a fund-holder or dead-weight door-way in one of the Squares of the *Wen*.' It was, Cobbett realised, bedrock: 'How many ages it must have taken the horses' feet, the wheels, and the water, to wear down this stone, so as to form a *hollow way*!' He was wrong about the Portland limestone, though. This was chalk.

At the village of Hawkley, they asked a farmer for the way to Thursley. Again, Cobbett was advised to abandon his projected route through the 'low countries' and to head instead for the turn-pike over Hindhead. Again he declined, but as he approached the bogs of Woolmer Forest (the name comes from 'Wolf Mere'), yet another passer-by warned him off his route. 'These people,' he complains, 'seemed to be posted at all these stages to turn me aside from my purpose.' A short while later, a more helpful local pointed out the little-used track they should follow through the dreaded mires. Following hoof prints in the spongy soil, Cobbett instructs his servant: 'Keep you *close to my heels*, and do not attempt to go aside, not even for a foot.' With some relief, they entered Headley: 'This road was not,' he admits, 'if we had been benighted, without its dangers, the forest being full of *quags* and *quick-sands*.'

Woolmer reminded Cobbett that Crown lands were being wasted with plantations of fir. Why fir, Cobbett wants to know, 'seeing that the country is already over-stocked with that rubbish?' There should be an investigation, he demands: 'Is there a man in Parliament that will call for it? *Not one*.' And, he continues, there never will be, 'until there be *reform*'.

Cobbett and his servant reached Headley at dusk, just as it began to rain. They must have been riding for the best part of eight hours. In the warmth of the Holly Bush ('a nice little public house'), they sat down to cold bacon, bread and milk, and Cobbett began to feel uncomfortable: 'I at first intended to stay the night,' he recalled, 'an intention that I afterwards very indiscreetly gave up. I had *laid my plan*, which included getting to Thursley that night… I began to feel ashamed of stopping short of my *plan*, especially after having so heroically persevered in the "stern path", and so disdainfully scorned to go over Hindhead.'

The servant, by now, has disappeared from the tale: 'There was a *moon*, but there was also a *hazy rain*. I had heaths to go over, and I might go into quags. Wishing to execute my plans, however, I, at last, brought myself to quit a very comfortable turf-fire, and to set off in the rain, having bargained to give a man three shillings to guide me out to the Northern *foot of Hindhead*.' There, he hoped to find the village of Thursley, and the house of his friends, the Knowles.

Well, to cut a very long story short, the man led Cobbett through darkness and driving rain for six miles in the wrong direction. Various misadventures ensued, which culminated in the sodden pair emerging from the trees onto the turnpike close to the summit of Hindhead; 'that very Hindhead,' curses Cobbett, 'on which I had so repeatedly vowed I would not go!' Maddeningly, they then had 'the whole of *three miles of hill to come down at not much better than a foot pace*, with a good pelting rain at our backs'. The guide was denied his three shillings for luring Cobbett onto the Hindhead turnpike after claiming that he knew the back-road to Thursley. With 'skin soaking' and 'teeth chattering', an exhausted, elated Cobbett changed into dry clothes and warmed up before his friend's fire: 'Thus ended,' he muses, 'the most interesting day, as far as I know, that I ever passed in all my life.'

*

While filming *Rural Rides* for the BBC, we hitched a lift across part of Hampshire, in a hot-air balloon. From the air, the extent to which the physical patterns of rural England had been reinvented during Cobbett's life are vividly apparent. At 500 feet, all you see is a vast plain of evenly coloured crops, ruled occasionally by fine, pencilled lines of tarmac. There are few hedgerows, and no humans. It's a landscape born of the revolution which obliterated the traditional 'open field' pattern of agriculture. Ever since they had been introduced to the landscape in the great farming revolution which had swept the island in the late Saxon/early medieval era, open fields had been as much a part of rural England as elms and fords. Most villages with tillable land were surrounded by hundreds of long, narrow strips of cultivation, which were rotated between crops and pasture, and managed communally. Any one farmer might cultivate several strips. Catch sight of an open field today, and it would be an extraordinary sight: a multi-textured, many-coloured blaze of stripes arranged in a chaotic patchwork of blocks, rather as if a child had practised hachures with every pen in the house. And at various times of the year, those stripes would have been covered with people, hoeing and ploughing, weeding and planting. At the peak of the open-field system, around the time of the Black Death, around one-third or one-quarter of England was farmed in strips. The abandonment of open-field farming began gradually, with farmers exchanging strips to create continuous blocks of land which they demarcated with hedges. In this piece-meal fashion, the process of 'enclosure' had been slowly altering the form of the English landscape for at least 500 years before Cobbett rode over the horizon. But from the 1720s through to the 1840s, a tidal wave of enclosure by private Act of parliament swept the land. Within a year or two of an Act being passed, a parish could see its multitude of strips being entirely replaced by a few large, enclosed fields, owned or managed by the few. In all, something like 3,000 English parishes were affected, and 4.5 million acres of open field wiped out by parliamentary enclosures. Around two million acres of heaths, commons, mountains, moors and 'barren' land were enclosed, too.

Peering over the edge of the balloon basket, with a copy of an open-field map from 1653 to hand, I watched as the village of Nutley slid towards us. The 300-year-old map showed the village at the hub of an intensely detailed pattern of strip cultivation. On the outskirts of the village, I was able to match a block of seventeenth-century open fields against the modern hedges and fences. In one place (later I found that it was called 'Burnham Field') no fewer than ninety-nine strips had been amalgamated into a single, modern field. Parliamentary enclosures had a disproportionate impact on chalk uplands.

In principle, Cobbett was not against a rationalisation of land-use, but Acts of Enclosure all too frequently drove labourers from the land and destroyed existing stands of valuable timber and common grazing. His comments on the transformation of Waltham Chase, an area of open country and woodland close to his old farm at Botley, in southern Hampshire, is typical. Hearing of a new Act to enclose the Chase, and knowing it as 'very green and fine', and populated by a great many families, Cobbett was appalled: 'Therefore, besides the sweeping away of two or three hundred cottages; besides the plunging into ruin and misery all these numerous families, here is one of the finest timber-lands in the whole kingdom, going to be cut up into miserable clay fields, for no earthly purpose but that of gratifying the stupid greediness of those who think that they must gain, if they add to the breadth of their private fields.' The Chase was enclosed.

Cobbett was convinced that the emptied villages he kept coming across had been sucked dry by parliamentary enclosure. *Rural Rides* is scattered with references to churches – such as All Saints at East Meon – which seem too large for the local population. On a ride in the summer of 1826 across Salisbury Plain, he borrowed from a friend 'a *very old* map of Wiltshire', from which he traced the location of every church, manor house and mansion in the Avon valley. Astonishingly, there were no fewer than thirty churches in as many miles. When he rode down the Avon, which had been described to him as 'one of the finest pieces of land in all England', he found a ghost valley. Cobbett assessed the agricultural output of the valley, and weighed it against the existing population of 9,116 persons. There should have been, he concluded, an enormous food surplus, but the people and the produce of the Avon were going 'from this valley towards the WEN'.

What Cobbett could see from his saddle, didn't accord with government figures:

> I do not believe one word of what is said of the *increase* of the population. All *observation* and all *reason* is against the fact; and, as to the *parliamentary returns*, what need we more than this: that *they* assert, that the population of Great Britain has *increased* from *ten* to *fourteen* millions in the last *twenty years*! That is enough! A man that can suck that in will believe, literally believe, that the *moon is made of green cheese*.

But it was Cobbett who believed in celestial dairy produce. Britain's population was exploding. By the first official census in 1801, Britain's population had increased by about 25 per cent since 1750, which was about 50 per cent above the European norm. Between the 1801 and the 1821 census – the twenty years Cobbett was referring to – the returns did indeed show a surge of four million Britons. In concert with the political cataclysms Cobbett had lived through, he was also in the grip of a demographic revolution.

For many at the time, Cobbett included, the figures were too incredible to believe. And in the underfilled churches, abandoned plough-land and relic villages, he genuinely believed that he could see the evidence of a tax-eaters' hoax to justify low wages and further enclosure. The very rural 'improvements' Cobbett despised had converted Britain into the most efficient food producer in Europe. Enclosures, turnpikes and canals had already helped to make English agriculture 2.5 times more productive than the continent's leading farmer, France. Along with improved hygiene, it was the staggering productivity of British farmland that was fuelling the population increase. While Cobbett's *Cottage Economy* was trying to woo labourers back to smallholdings, the number of Britons working in agriculture was in freefall, from 75 per cent in 1750, to a mere 21 per cent by 1851. Cobbett's eyes were not deceiving him. There *were* fewer people working on the land, and those who had survived, *were* often living in poverty, in a rural culture which had acclimatised to sudden dispossession. But he was wrong about population growth: in the fifty years leading up to the publication of *Rural Rides* in 1830, Britain's population had doubled in size. Lingering in England's agrarian past, and locked to his rural itineraries, Cobbett refused to accept that ports, towns and cities had replaced the cottage as the labourer's habitat. As for the enormous churches, their scale reflected the ambition and prosperity of their medieval builders. Building big had moved you closer to God.

*

It is at the outer limits of Cobbett's rides that he discovers the extremes of injury to man and landscape. A distant sixty miles from the Great Wen, the Cotswold Hills, the Channel coast and the New Forest extracted from Cobbett some of his most impassioned diatribes. The further from London he rides, so it seems, the less pleasing he finds the land. And the more evidence he uncovers of squandered taxes and rural injustice.

In the far west, where the Cotswolds peer across the Vale of Severn to Wales, the problem was partly geology. Cobbett just didn't like limestone: 'ugly country', with thin soils of *'stone brash'*, no trees, and fields divided by walls – an alien sight in chalk country. Without a surface 'smooth and green like the downs', Cobbett laments, 'this is a sort of country, having less to please the eye than any other that I have ever seen, always save and except the *heaths* like those of Bagshot and Hindhead'.

The limestone had another unfortunate characteristic. Unlike chalk, it's a good building stone. Where the clay-lump and timber cottages of the south-east crumbled and rotted once they'd lost their roofs, abandoned limestone buildings remained as eerie shells: 'But how melancholy is the sight of these decayed and still decaying villages in the dells of the Cotswold,' sighs the visitor, 'the ruins do not *totally disappear* for ages!' Withington, deep in the hills, displays '*all* the indubitable marks of most melancholy decay': a complex of intersecting lanes which he thinks were once streets; a large, open space where markets or fairs might have been held; a church 'like a small cathedral'; and two large, old houses with stone upping-blocks against their walls. These, he decides, 'were manifestly considerable *inns'*. A man he finds in a barn confirms that Withington once had three public houses. Here, concludes Cobbett, is yet another village whose fields have been grabbed by 'some tax-eater' or 'wicked loan-mongering robber'. Today, Withington's honey-coloured cottages and hideous acres of stone brash lie at the heart of an Area of Outstanding Natural Beauty.

Cobbett's horror at the permanence of stone is a bizarre reversal – in just a century – of the wonder expressed by Celia Fiennes and Daniel Defoe, for whom stone was the material of the future. But they had travelled in an age when industry was still a novelty, and when the countryside teemed with toiling folk who sold their surplus produce at thriving market towns. Cobbett's Britain was the laboratory of irreversible change; of revolutions in industry and agriculture; of explosions in population and urbanisation; of experiments in political reform. He was right to be fearful. Cobbett couldn't have known that this era of convulsion was also the dawn of the 'Anthropocene' – a recently identified geological era which began with the Industrial Revolution. In this new epoch, Man, say leading geologists, has become the principal driver, triggering a range of profound impacts which include rising global temperatures, a transformation of erosion and deposition patterns, acidification of the oceans and changes to the carbon cycle. These unprecedented changes are on such a scale that they are creating a 'significant stratigraphic signal', changing the physical, chemical and biological environment in such a way that it will appear in our geological record. The transformations Cobbett feared in Britain, spread around the world, and in the space of just 200 years, have disrupted the planet's natural systems.

There was little in capitalism to console Cobbett. Paper money and stock-jobbing were eroding self-reliance and turning Britain into a nation of spineless hypochondriacs. And nowhere was there a more repellent exhibition of urban excess than in the Cotswold town of Cheltenham, a 'watering place', splutters Cobbett, 'that is to say, a place, to which East India plunderers, West India floggers, English tax-gorgers, together with gluttons, drunkards, and debauchees of all descriptions, *female* as well as male, resort, at the suggestion of silently laughing quacks, in the hope of getting rid of the bodily consequences of their manifold sins and iniquities'. It's fair to say that you wouldn't have caught Cobbett in a jacuzzi: 'When I enter a place like this,' he finishes, 'I always feel disposed to squeeze up my nose with my fingers.'

Just as far from London, in the opposite direction, Kent hid even more horrors than Gloucestershire. In the south-east corner of England, where the chalk ran right to the sea, Cobbett found outstanding soils, yet poverty and waste. There was much to his liking in the orchards and hop-gardens, the stands of timber and the corn. But when he eventually reached the coast, he found a military frontline littered with extravagant relics. Hythe, he thunders, 'is half *barracks*; the hills are covered with barracks; and barracks most expensive, most squandering, fill up the side of the hill.' Nearby, he comes across an enormously costly, thirty-mile canal which had been constructed as an invasion barrier. And then he works himself into a whirlwind about Martello towers: 'I think I have counted along here upwards of thirty of these ridiculous things, which, I dare say, cost *five*, perhaps *ten*, thousand pounds each; and one of which was, I am told, *sold* on the coast of Sussex, the other day, for TWO HUNDRED POUNDS!' (Nowadays they sell for half a million quid.)

Here on the margins of Kent, he discovered where the taxes had gone; the taxes that had crippled rural labourers: 'All along the coast there are works of some sort or other; incessant sinks of money; walls of immense dimensions; masses of stone brought and put into piles … The whole thing, all taken together, looks as if a spell had been, all of a sudden, set upon the workmen; or, in the words of the Scripture, here is the *"desolation of abomination, standing in high places"*.'

One military edifice symbolised more than any other the futility and bungling which lay at the core of Britain's costliest war. Dover, 'ancient, most interesting, and beautiful', is chewed and gouged by caverns, tunnels and trenches. 'This is, perhaps,' rages the ex-sergeant-major, 'the only set of fortifications in the world ever framed for mere *hiding*. There is no appearance of any intention to annoy an enemy. It is a parcel of holes made in a hill, to hide Englishmen from Frenchmen.' All the French had to do, explains the old soldier, is to land on the adjacent, flat beaches of Romney Marsh or Pevensey Levels, and bypass Dover's 'honeycomb' defences: 'And for a purpose like this; for a purpose so stupid, so senseless, so mad as this, and withal, so scandalously disgraceful, more brick and stone have been buried in this hill than would go to build a neat new cottage for every labouring man in the counties of Kent and of Sussex!' Pitt's real fear, believed Cobbett, was not French beach-landings, but an invasion of ideas; Cobbett once referred to the titanic struggle with Napoleon, as 'the late wars against the liberties of the French people'. In dumping the old order, the 'spirited and sensible' French, reasoned Cobbett, had rid themselves of the burden 'of which our farmers so bitterly complain'.

Nowhere was the cause of that misery clearer than here in Kent, on the fertile Isle of Thanet. Alongside the vast barns, the huge crops of wheat and the enormous ricks, Cobbett found labourers' houses 'beggarly in the extreme', and the people 'dirty, poor-looking; ragged'. Compared to the impoverished gravels and sands of heathland further west, Thanet's level, chalky soils were 'a garden indeed'. But the people were in a wretched state: 'Invariably have I observed,' scrawled Cobbett, 'that the richer the soil, and the more destitute of woods; that is to say, the more purely a corn country, the more miserable the labourers… In this beautiful island every inch of land is appropriated by the rich. No hedges, no ditches, no commons, no grassy lanes: a country divided into great farms.'

In some counties, the number of small owner-occupiers fell by as much as 40 per cent between 1770 and 1825. This was the future of farming. For ordinary folk, Thanet was uninhabitable: 'All the rest is bare of trees; and the wretched labourer has not a stick of wood, and has no place for a pig or a cow to graze, or even to lie down upon. The rabbit countries are the countries for labouring men. There the ground is not so valuable.' England's threatened tribes of countrymen would have to look to the woods for survival.

Cobbett saw trees as the last resource of the cottage economy. Thousands of miles in the saddle had convinced him 'that people in woodland countries are best off, and that it is absolutely impossible to reduce them to that state of starvation in which they are in the corn-growing part of this kingdom. Here is that great blessing, abundance of fuel at all times of the year, and particularly in the winter.' Cobbett's enormous tree nurseries, and his endless column inches in the *Register* promoting their sale and distribution, was rooted in his belief that woodland would be the salvation of the cottager.

Cobbett delayed visiting the largest, best known forest in southern England until the end of his final Rural Ride. When he eventually took the long road south-west, late in October 1826, he mentions that his purpose was to investigate how much progress had been made in establishing locust-tree plantations, but it turned into an extended field trip which produced more words than any equivalent-sized tract of land in *Rural Rides*. Three days of zig-zagging, getting lost, and chance encounters, produced the material he needed to conclude his four-year quest.

In a sense, it did all have to come to an end in the New Forest. Here were the worst soils he had ever seen; soils so spectacularly bad 'that a poorer spot than this New Forest, there is not in all England; nor, I believe, in the whole world'. It was even 'more barren and miserable', he decided, 'than Bagshot Heath'.

In theory, such an 'intolerable heath' was, of course, ideal for subsistence families, who would find in the forest everything they needed: timber for building and fuel; common grazing for cattle and sheep; plentiful game to hunt, and beech cover for pigs. Cobbett claims to have seen in the forest, 'many, many thousands' of pigs in just one day. On one occasion, he counted 140 hogs and pigs within sixty yards of his horse. With elaborate calculations and historical research, he argued that the Forest had once supported a huge human population. So why not again? There was, as always, a problem. The New Forest was a Crown Estate and not available for colonies of labourers' cottages. Or for growing plantations of locust trees. Firing a closing broadside at 'the Thing', Cobbett demands that the Forest be handed back to the nation.

Cobbett wrote up his three-day exploration of the New Forest at Weston Grove, a grand house elegantly located on a promontory between the mouth of the River Itchen, and Southampton Water. The views, he concludes, are 'the most beautiful that can be imagined'. Like a conjuror pulling his best-kept trick out of his hat at the end of the show, Cobbett produces the owner of Weston Grove, Mr William Chamberlayne, MP for Southampton and beacon of political virtue. Chamberlayne, an old friend of Cobbett's from his Botley days, owned all the land between the Itchen and the Hamble, and was so generous to his day-labouring men that he had held their wages at thirteen shillings a week for twenty years, despite the national collapse in incomes. Here, at last, is the model land-owner:

> I know how much good he must do; and there is a great satisfaction in reflecting on the great happiness that he must feel, when, in laying his head upon his pillow of a cold and dreary winter night, he reflects that there are scores, aye, *scores upon scores*, of his country-people, of his poor neighbours, of those whom the Scripture denominates his brethren, who have been enabled, *through him*, to retire to a warm bed after spending a cheerful evening and taking a full meal by the side of their own fire. People may talk what they will about happiness; but I can figure to myself no *happiness* surpassing that of this man who falls to sleep with reflections like these on his mind.

*

For years, Cobbett had been predicting that the crisis in the country-side would come to a head in the early winter of 1830. Right on time, Kent and Sussex went up in flames, and then Hampshire, Berkshire and the western counties. Labourers turned on farmers, smashed threshing machines and demanded higher wages. Two thousand were arrested, and special commissions condemned to death nineteen rioters, imprisoned 600, and transported to Australia and Tasmania a further 500. In the months that followed, pressure for parliamentary reform intensified until – in 1832 – the Reform Act was passed 'to prevent', in the words of its chief architect, Earl Grey, 'the necessity for revolution'. Cobbett, an MP at last, spent his final years in a rented farm at the foot of the Hog's Back, the long, high ridge of chalk which provided the opening prospect of *Rural Rides*.

H.V. MORTON

1929–33

By Bullnose to Skye

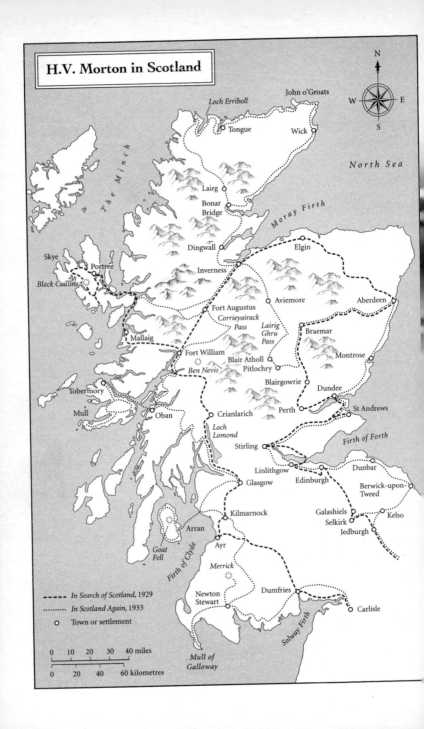

H.V. Morton in Scotland

Loch Eriboll

John o'Groats

Tongue

Wick

The Minch

Lairg

Bonar Bridge

Moray Firth

North Sea

Skye

Portree

Black Cuillins

Dingwall

Elgin

Inverness

Aberdeen

Mallaig

Fort Augustus

Corrieyairack Pass

Aviemore

Lairig Ghru Pass

Braemar

Fort William

Ben Nevis

Blair Atholl

Montrose

Pitlochry

Blairgowrie

Tobermory

Mull

Oban

Crianlarich

Perth

Dundee

St Andrews

Loch Lomond

Stirling

Firth of Forth

Linlithgow

Dunbar

Glasgow

Edinburgh

Berwick-upon-Tweed

Kilmarnock

Galashiels

Kelso

Arran

Selkirk

Jedburgh

Goat Fell

Ayr

Firth of Clyde

Merrick

Dumfries

Newton Stewart

Carlisle

Mull of Galloway

Solway Firth

- - - *In Search of Scotland, 1929*

········ *In Scotland Again, 1933*

○ Town or settlement

0 10 20 30 40 miles

0 20 40 60 kilometres

When mass-produced motor-cars began rolling off production lines in Cowley and Longbridge in the 1920s, the man who led the charge into the countryside was a journalist in a Bullnose Morris. The evangelist of recreational motoring would have been appalled by his success; the number of cars on British roads has exploded from a few hundred when Morton was a child, to 31 million today. But, to a generation seared by war and then the Great Depression, H.V. Morton's motoring odysseys promised romance, adventure and an archipelago of delights. In Search of England *was published in 1927, and it was quickly followed by* In Search of Scotland *(1929),* In Search of Ireland *(1931) and* In Search of Wales *(1932). With forty books to his name, Morton became the most successful travel-writer of his generation.*

*

The car Morton drove had three gears, a top speed of around forty and looked a bit like a highly polished bathtub bolted to pram wheels. He called it 'Maud'. Approach a Bullnose Morris today, and it is immediately apparent why motoring was so adventurous in the 1920s. There are no seat belts and no roof (although some kind of canvas awning can be stored in a cavity at the back). Entering the driver's seat is a bit like clambering into the cockpit of a biplane, stepping off the running board and then lifting and twisting each leg over the nickel-plated broom handle used for dipping the headlights. All the instruments and controls are at odds with a modern car. The pedal which influences the speed of the contraption nestles between the clutch and the brake, placed so that a moment of inattention from a modern driver will cause the car to accelerate into double-bends and garages. Where you would expect to find a speedometer, there is a large ticking clock. Should you ever suspect the vehicle of going fast, a pair of binoculars will be required to read a distantly located dial above the passenger's left knee. A quaint glass tube running up the centre of the dashboard turns out to be the petrol gauge. You can't actually *see* the petrol inside it, so the only way of finding out whether you're almost empty is by lowering a dipstick into the tank. And each time you park, you must remember to turn off the petrol using the big brass plumbing tap beneath the dashboard. Just in case she catches fire as you walk away.

Henry Canova Vollam Morton was born in Ashton-under-Lyne in the summer of 1892. His mother was a Lowland Scot and his father a newspaperman. The Mortons were disposed to mobility. Joseph Morton had been born in India, studied medicine in Edinburgh and then switched to journalism just as newspapers became the medium for the masses. Circulations were soaring, new titles were being launched, and old titles amalgamated. In the space of just seven years at the turn of the century, the *Daily Mail*, the *Daily Express*, the *Times Literary Supplement* and the *Daily Mirror* all appeared for the first time on newsstands. The *Mail's* circulation catapulted from zero to over a million in its first three years. Newspapers were glamorous and risky, and the workaholic editor of the *Ashton-under-Lyne Herald* had ambitions beyond Lancashire. Chasing up the editorial ladder, Joseph moved the family to Manchester and then Birmingham. Young 'Harry' saw more of his mother, who brought him up on tales from her homeland. 'Some stray old wind from Culloden blew,' remembered Morton, 'into my nursery when I was a child, for almost the first stories I heard were stories of Skye and of a brown-eyed prince hiding in a cave.' Bred on the folk heroics of Bonnie Prince Charlie, Rob Roy and William Wallace, for Morton Britain was a land of light and shade; of teeming metropolis and mythological wilderness.

This was also a Britain waking to hypermobility. The expanding rail network already stretched to over 20,000 miles, and roads were becoming busier by the year with all manner of vehicular inventions, many of them forged in the workshops of Birmingham and its industrial satellites. A new type of vehicle – the motor-car – could occasionally be spotted, but the device which gave flight to Harry Morton was the 'safety bicycle'. Multiplying cavalcades of pedal-propelled machines had been tearing along England's byways since the 1860s, and by the time Harry's parents moved to Birmingham (home, as it happened, of Britain's largest cycle manufacturer, Starley Brothers), cycling had become an Olympic sport, and John Foster Fraser and his two companions had cycled around the world in 774 days. Bicycles were exciting, simple, convenient and cheap. Railways had created a culture of efficient, mass-transportation, but bicycles offered a return to the long-distance freedoms that were once enjoyed by lone horsemen. Anyone with a few pounds to spare could buy a bicycle and take to the shires in the spirit of Fiennes and Defoe. In 1897, the Scottish Mountaineering Club could report that its members were using bicycles to reach peaks way beyond railheads. By then, there were around one million active cyclists in Britain, and H.G.Wells had given English fiction its first cycling hero, the gravitationally challenged Mr Hoopdriver in *The Wheels of Chance*.

Harry Morton, an H.G.Wells fan, got the bug in around 1909, escaping from Birmingham into the lanes of Warwickshire and pedalling as far as Coventry, Warwick and Stratford-upon-Avon, where he could indulge in his passion for the theatre and girls. 'It is not easy to explain to the young the layer of tranquility that appeared to be spread over England in 1909,' he would recall, 'and a modern generation would find it difficult to believe that one could cycle for miles along roads and lanes meeting only a farmer in his trap, a shepherd with his sheep, cows moving across from one pasture to another, and loaded wagons drawn by two or more huge shire horses. The roads of England were a cyclist's paradise; never again will there be anything to match it.'

Those last, long summers before the outbreak of the Great War imprinted upon Morton's memory the England he would later come back to find. 'I have come to the conclusion,' he would write, 'that the only completely magic age in life is between the ages of ten and fourteen, a time when the senses are vividly aware of beauty yet unawakened to evil.' In April 1909, three months before his seventeenth birthday, he left school and took a short-term teaching job, then joined his father's paper, the *Birmingham Gazette and Press*, as a junior reporter. He stayed with the *Gazette* for four years, and then, in 1913, he left his rustic playground for the capital. Packing three crates of books, he set off for London. He was twenty-one.

Morton's eventual return to the shires to search for the essence of England may not have occurred if his arrival in Fleet Street hadn't coincided with the most catastrophic war to strike the planet. Having cut his teeth on the *Evening Standard*, the young provincial had graduated to Northcliffe's mighty *Daily Mail*, early in 1915, just as world affairs intervened. Morton's war was peculiarly uneventful: he found himself serving as a cavalry officer in Essex, trained as he put it, as if he was 'going to fight Napoleon'. On being demobbed, he surprised himself by recovering an enthusiasm for journalism, but he had lost his pre-war momentum. He found himself back on the *Standard*, and it wasn't until he joined Beaverbrook's *Daily Express* at the end of 1921 that he won his day of fame on the front page. A year after joining the paper, he was despatched to Luxor to cover the opening of Tutankhamun's tomb. His story made the front-page headline.

In Morton's romanticised version of events, the emergence of Egypt's fabulous king from his lost vault in the Middle Eastern desert was also the moment which defined his own calling. After the tomb had been covered again, Morton decided to extend his Middle Eastern tour so that he could visit Jerusalem. Aptly, it was here that he had a revelation. Writing later, behind the guise of the amusingly feeble narrator he had created for his travel books, Morton relates that he had been feeling unwell. 'In the black depths of misery', he had climbed a hill overlooking the Holy City, and there he had succumbed – in the absence of a woman to convince him otherwise – to the conviction that the pain in his neck was 'the first sign of spinal meningitis'. What actually happened in 'the cold, unhappy mountains of Palestine' was known only to Morton, but it was unquestionably a clever place to suffer a personal crisis. Four years later, he was able to begin the book that would re-launch his career with the words: 'I believed that I was dying in Palestine'.

Jerusalem turned him towards a green and pleasant land: 'I took a vow,' wrote Morton, 'that if my pain in the neck did not end for ever on the windy hills of Palestine I would go home in search of England, I would go through the lanes of England and the little thatched villages of England, and I would lean over English bridges and lie on English grass, watching an English sky.' Thus did 'H.V. Morton' begin his progress from homesick hypochondriac to national treasure.

It took Harry Morton four years of Fleet Street graft to navigate his way through the dispiriting labyrinth separating journalism from authorship. It wasn't until the spring of 1925 that he got the break he needed, when the chairman of Methuen invited him to collate into a book a series of newspaper articles he'd written on London. *The Heart of London* was an immediate success, and in an incredible spate of productivity, Methuen published a further four of Morton's books about London by the end of 1926.

In the midst of this spate of book production, Morton rekindled the fevered vision he'd had on a hill above Jerusalem. He would take to the lanes of England again. Armed like Leland with a commission, he would strike out from London, as the *Express* announced, 'at random into England and discover people and places'. His conveyance would be 'a two-seater motor-car'. In post-war Britain, this was a fantastically liberating image.

The ex-cyclist and cavalryman in Morton saw the motor-car as the key to unlocking England's identity. At heart, Morton despised mass transportation. The train carriage and the motor-coach were an assault on a traveller's right to stray from the beaten track; in his books, the image of the 'charabanc' crammed with pitiable trippers lurches onto the page whenever Morton feels the need to reassert his vehicular supremacy. And he knew he was backing a winner: by the time Morton took to the road for his new *Express* series, the railways had lost their monopoly. The number of passenger journeys being taken by rail had been stagnant since before the war, but the number of cars on the roads raced from 77,000 in 1918 to 981,000 by 1929. Between 1920 and 1925, the number of motor buses on the road leapt 25 per cent. The bicycle, celebrated for a few short decades as the 'King of the Road', had been usurped. The car promised all the independence of bicycle travel, at three times the speed and none of the effort. And car prices were in freefall, dropping by a whopping one third between 1923 and 1929. 'More people than in any previous generation are seeing the real country for the first time,' enthused Morton. 'The roads of England, eclipsed for a century by the railway, have come to life again; the King's highway is once more a place for adventures and explorations.'

The vehicle which Morton adopted for his newsprint tours was not a racy Bentley Speed Six Tourer but the ubiquitous 'Bullnose' Morris Oxford. The £300 Bullnose was Britain's top-selling car, and accounted for 45 per cent of the British market. Favoured by district nurses and travelling salesmen, this was the people's car. You were more likely to get knocked down by a Bullnose than by any other model of motor vehicle. With the wind in his hair, Morton set off to rediscover pre-war England: 'For the first time in history,' he wrote, 'these panting and efficient little machines were beginning to take individuals and families all over England, inaugurating a new age of discovery, called, in the typically deceptive English way, "motoring". Probably nothing like it had occurred since the days of medieval pilgrimage.' The old cavalryman was not a convincing motorist: 'I have had a frightful time with "Maud",' he once confessed to his *Express* readers. 'She indulged in two entirely temperamental punctures the first day and developed a hysterical engine yesterday … An expert, however, has done things to her interior.'

The *Express* ran the pieces through the spring and summer of 1926. By June 1927, Morton had executed a skilful cut-and-paste job, and assembled his motoring excursions into a single, geographically coherent journey in a clockwise direction around England, from London to Land's End, then up the western side of the country to the Scottish border, then back down the east. Maud was removed from the story, which gave Harry's narrator more room to manoeuvre. He called his book *In Search of England*. The 'H.V. Morton' who sets off in search of 'people and places' is driven by nostalgia rather than an internal combustion engine. He is obliged to record his impressions of 'New England; an England of crowded towns, of tall chimneys, of mills and canals of slow, black water; an England of coal and chemicals; of cotton, glass and iron'. But the England of his choice – and quest – is 'the beautiful Old England', an England crossed with pilgrims' ways and dotted with musty pubs; an England populated by Chaucerian packmen, and calloused flint-knappers. On Morton's fantasy island, even the traffic jams are cultural adventures: 'In front of me was a heavy forty-five horse-power touring car containing a rigid old man in a young Stetson; in front of him was a dashing two-seater driven by a woman; in front of her was a closed limousine full of American tourists; in front of them was a family in a Ford; in front of that was a Rolls Royce, and leading the procession was a hatless young obstructionist lying full length in a fifteen horse-power scarlet bath with aluminium fittings and an exhaust pipe like a stove-pipe.'

Methuen had to reprint *In Search of England* twice in its first six months. 'I have made a name for myself,' Morton confided in his diary, 'and I am 36.' Two years later, Morton exported his quest to Scotland.

*

In Search of Scotland took motoring to the end of the road, and beyond. At one level, it was a loose memoir of a petrolhead's adventures in the Highlands and Lowlands. At another, it was a deeply personalised quest for a lost cultural ideal. The book appeared in 1929 and was followed in 1933 by a sequel, *In Scotland Again*. Both books had an edge to them which had been absent in Morton's English jaunt. The middle-class Londoner was at his most displaced in the wind-blown mountains, and in the interval between the two Scottish books, Britain had been devastated by economic disaster. Just three months after the publication of *In Search of Scotland*, the Wall Street stock market had crashed and triggered the Great Depression. Overseas demand for British products collapsed and, by the end of 1930, unemployment had more than doubled to 2.5 million.

The narrator had changed, too. The traveller who heads for the glens in 1929 is a lot more adventurous than the motorist who managed to traverse the Lake District two years earlier without getting out of his car. In Scotland, he leaves the road to climb mountains, hike over misty bealachs and visit remote islands. On one occasion he even takes to the sea on board a working trawler. The car is less visible. Indeed, some of the episodes he writes about in Scotland – such as the visit to Skye and his journey through the Grampians – may not have involved the use of a motor-car at all. 'It hurt me,' he writes of the misted Don one autumn morning, 'to go over roads so quickly in a machine when I would have been walking with wet boots on grass and through the browning bracken of the woods. I stopped…'

His Scottish excursions are also populated by a different species of hero and heroine. Up here, Morton can draw on the cast of his mother's land. Bonnie Prince Charlie strides the heather of Culloden and the shores of Skye, Rob Roy lurks in the Trossachs and Robert the Bruce stalks the hills of Galloway. Covenanters, Jacobites and dispossessed crofters drift into chapters like armies of wraiths. As Morton's England subsided into the Great Depression, and national socialism began to exert its grip on listless Europeans, the clans were upheld by many of Morton's ilk as the last thread connecting Britons with a more ordered, feudal past – 'a genuine link', as Morton put it, 'with the Golden Age'. He viewed Highlanders as 'the lineal descendants of the Homeric heroes'. Up here, too, Morton can associate himself with the last generation of British travellers who could legitimately call themselves 'explorers'. 'Most Englishmen,' avers Morton, 'who know little about the history of Scotland and nothing at all about that of Ireland, do not realize that, with the exception of the North and South Poles, the Highlands of Scotland were the last portion of the earth's surface to be explored. This sounds inconceivable, but it is true!'

Among the doughty trailblazers Morton turns to are men like Thomas Pennant, Johnson and Boswell, and dubious Sir John Carr, whose *Caledonian Sketches* of 1807 were lapped up by travellers who'd turned to the Highlands because war prohibited continental tours (*The Quarterly Review* had been unsympathetic to Sir John, panning his book as derivative, and recommending that its author be punished by 'tight flagellation'). Although he'd read widely on Scotland, and been brought up by a Scot, Morton gives the impression that he is setting off into the great unknown in the manner of his illustrious heroes: 'There is,' he suggests in his introduction, 'something to be said for books written by an explorer who admits frankly, as I do, that he knew nothing about Scotland when he set out, because then commonplace knowledge comes freshly with an air of discovery...'

Scotland was even better suited to exploration by car than England. There were far fewer rail lines north of the border, and in Morton's view, the 'easy and comfortable escape' offered by rail travel had created a generation of idlers who'd left 'no record of a circuit of Scotland since the day of the horse and coach'. Now, announced Morton, 'with the motor-car we have returned to road travel, so that once more books will be written from the standpoint of Pennant, Boswell and Carr, by men able to move freely about the country in touch with the inhabitants'. There was only one snag: Morton wasn't facing storms at sea in sailing ships or riding a locally procured horse over unmapped terrain, but tearing along tarmac in a modern motor-car. His trials were more humdrum: the losing of underwear in hotel rooms, the occasional blister. And rain. Somewhere between the era of horse and the car, adversity had been replaced by absurdity.

I wondered, before I set off in Morton's tracks, which maps he had used. Only once does he give any real clues. Right at the start of *In Search of Scotland*, as he leaves England on the long road north, he stops his car in the Cheviot Hills, picks up his map, and strikes off over a field to a heathery summit so that he can take his bearings: 'What names men have given to these hills! How snugly they fit! To my left is Corby Pike and Windy Crag, Dour Hill and Hungry Law; six miles away is Bloodybush Edge and Beefstand Hill. Six names as tight and racy as a ballad! On my right looms the bulk of Blackman's Law and beyond it the height of Oh Me Edge. It is almost too good to be true!'

In the British Library Map Room, I found each of these place-names on *"The Times" Contour Motoring Map of Scotland in 6 Sheets*, published in 1921 by Geographia in Fleet Street, just a few doors from the *Express* office. The maps had been carefully engraved at a scale of three miles to the inch, under the direction of Alexander Gross, a Fellow of the Royal Geographical Society. Three categories of motorable road were marked, together with distances, steep hills and golf courses. A rich palette of greens and browns gave an immediate sense of the lie of the land, and every square inch was crammed with minutely italicised place-names, of villages and streams, hills and peaks, forts and churches. Major footpaths, such as the Lairig Ghru through the heart of the Cairngorms, were shown. The motorists using these maps were expected to leave their machines and strike out for the hills.

Following Morton through the Southern Uplands, I felt mildly embarrassed that I'd ignored such a wonderful region for so long. Glen Trool, with its secret loch, is like a less-trodden version of the English Lake District. By Loch Trool, where Robert the Bruce had bloodied the English in a warm-up for Bannockburn, Morton had paused by the memorial and re-enacted the fourteenth-century independence campaign across several pages. 'Bruce in Galloway and Prince Charlie in the Highlands,' he sighs, 'the two most romantic men in the history of Scotland.' Above the loch, he climbed Merrick, the highest peak in southern Scotland. The view was sensational. To the west, he could see the island of Ailsa Craig, and eastwards, a chain of lochs lying in 'utter solitude'. Merrick is now on my wish-list of future peaks. 'Here,' concludes Morton, 'far south of Glasgow, is a wilderness deeper than that of the better known Highlands.'

I did follow Morton up Goat Fell, the highest mountain on the island of Arran. It's a thrilling hill to climb, though a little less Himalayan than Morton implies. It was up here that he revealed doubts about the suitability of his chosen transport: 'Give me sunlight,' he sighs, 'a blue sea, the dry smell of heather, and the hill streams brown with peat, and you can have all the motor-cars in the world.' Goat Fell was a tiddler of a hill, but it soundly beat Ben Nevis as a viewpoint. 'From the Ben,' explains Morton, 'you look over miles of mountain-tops; from Goatfell you see land and water.'

Eventually he would come across the perfect mountain view, and here too, water would be essential to the composition.

Leaving Arran, Morton was confronted by some rather inconvenient geography. The ferry which had transported him back to the mainland, put him ashore at Ardrossan. From here, the spirit of enquiry should have led him northward, along the coast and then up the Clyde to Glasgow. But on the pretext of having run out of socks, he took a more direct route to the 'black city', thus avoiding the Clyde altogether. Morton had his reasons for dodging Scotland's greatest river. The Scottish economy had been in a bad way long before the crash of 1929, but by the time Morton came north for his second Scottish book, three years into the Great Depression, the situation in Scotland's manufacturing belt was absolutely desperate. At the height of the Depression in 1932, nearly one third of the Scottish workforce was out of a job. Unemployment among shipworkers on the Clyde was running at over 50 per cent, and newspapers were carrying stories about Glaswegian razor gangs. None of this was particularly suitable material for a feel-good travelogue. Later in the chapter, Morton does insert a brief, sepulchral description of a visit that he made to the offices of a Clyde shipyard – 'a solid, polished mahogany room from which all knowledge of world chaos had been carefully concealed'. It's a bleak passage, in which he recalls the 'bright prosperity of the Edwardian Age ... the age before the War', when men in silk hats and frock coats took orders for ocean liners and Britannia's warships. On a great polished table surrounded by gigantic padded chairs, stand pots 'that hold about half a pint of ink'. When Morton's friend shows up, he takes him by the arm and leads him out 'into the silent place where the empty slipways go down to the Clyde, in order that the magnificent room might hear nothing of our troubles, and go on dreaming of the old ships and the old times and – the old cheques'.

The Mortonian palliative for economic distress is romance. Myths and heroes give body to a nation's self-belief, and each 'Great Age' reminds us that more will follow. But behind Morton's mask of authorship, there was a troubled man who knew that the Britain he described was a lie. His 'word pictures' were as selective as Gilpin's picturesque views. Behind the chummy, middle-class mixer known as 'H.V. Morton' was a man who wondered in his diaries whether Britain wouldn't be better off with Adolf Hitler; behind the family man whose pages are decorated with pretty girls in frocks, was a serial philanderer who treated his numerous mistresses like so many motorway service stations. He did, however, come to address the poverty he'd shied from on the Clyde. Shortly after the publication of *In Scotland Again*, the Labour Party published a 48-page booklet by Morton, called *What I Saw in the Slums*.

*

Morton's Lowlands are a prelude to his Highlands. Then, as now, the most striking gateway to the Highlands was the water-filled, glacial trough which slices south from the Grampians to the Clyde. To Victorian tourists, there were four Scottish lochs worthy of appreciation; Loch Katrine in the Trossachs was admired for its delicate colouring; Loch Coruisk on Skye for its 'wild grandeur', Loch Maree for its 'dignity'. But Loch Lomond had them all: 'a greater variety', as Baddeley put it in his guide of 1895, 'of the elements which we admire in lake scenery than any other Scottish loch'. Above all else, Lomond was 'the most beautifully "islanded" lake of the kingdom'. In Baddeley's day, the loch and its surroundings were largely unspoiled; tourists heading out of Glasgow would take the steam train to Balloch, at the southern foot of the loch, and then transfer to a steamer for the twenty-five-mile voyage into the mountains. Adventurous passengers could disembark at Ardlui and join the new West Highland railway, which would take them on to Fort William. Then came H.V. Morton, puttering along the western shore in his personalised transportation. Travelling at his own speed, past crag and promontory, he was able to gaze upon the mists 'stealing from the hills', and look upon the loch-side rowans and rowing boats. He could stop and take a photograph. From the stitched leather seat of his open-top tourer he could smell the woodsmoke as he motored through Luss. To accommodate the millions of Mortons who followed him, the A82 has now been widened, straightened, and supplied with motoring amenities – from car-parks and lay-bys to lavatories and viewpoints. It is a hellish coupling between tarmac and the picturesque; between the realised worlds of Morton and Gilpin.

Less distressing is the road over Rannoch Moor. This was one of the sections of Morton's itinerary that I was able to repeat in a Bullnose, and it was up here at dusk that I sensed for a moment the spirit of twenties motoring. For eight miles the road snakes through a dun tundra of lochans, rocks and bog. It was a clear evening, at the end of winter, and the mountains beyond the moor were creamed with snow. The slipstream was freezing, and every time I nudged the old beast into third, the revs faded until I could hear the wind rushing over the ornamented bodywork of the eighty-year-old Morris. Eventually the road tipped into the throat of Glencoe and there was the prow of Buachaille Etive Mor, and the crest of Aonach Eagach. Grinning on the car's open-air bench seat, I felt as if I was viewing my favourite peaks from a slow-moving sofa.

The indolent Mr Toad who searched for England in the *Express* is a distant memory by the time the Grampians fill H.V. Morton's windscreen. 'I decided to walk the Lairig Ghru,' he announces. To remind his readers that he is undertaking the most extreme trek in Britain, Morton calls on his guidebooks:

> There is no pass to compare with it in all Scotland,' says Mr. Seton Gordon. 'One of the wildest and grandest passes of the lofty Cairngorm Range,' says Mr. Muirhead, who adds, 'There is no inn or house of shelter on the route.' 'This is about the longest day's march in the Highlands,' says Mr. Baddeley. Forty miles! It was a rash and impetuous adventure for one who had 'done no walking since the War.

Morton's 'War' had been spent in Essex, rather than Flanders, and in truth he'd done quite a bit of walking since 1918. In the pages of *In Scotland Again*, he'd already climbed two mountains (Merrick and Goat Fell), and had hiked the length of the Corrieyairick Pass. So he wasn't quite as catatonic as he implies. And it seems that his Cairngorm epic was not as solitary as he suggests. Morton seems to have been in company; his biographer Michael Bartholomew has published diary entries recording that Morton drove with two companions from Edinburgh to Aviemore on 12 September 1929, then walked through the Lairig Ghru the following day. Not only was he not apparently solo, but the Lairig Ghru episode had not been part of the single, continuous journey described in the book.

But Lairig Ghru would be good for sales. Among those who had popularised Britain's ultimate pedestrian adventure was Baddeley, who'd opened his guide with a first-hand account of a narrow escape he'd had when trying to walk over the Cairngorms from Braemar to Aviemore, in April 1876. On the way, Baddeley and his friend had planned to climb Ben Macdui, the 3,900-foot mountain which dominates the mid-section of the Lairig Ghru. Equipped with sandwiches and 'a fair quantity of whiskey', the pair had set off up the wrong glen, climbed the mountain in Arctic conditions, failed to descend into Lairig Ghru due to sheer ice and snow, then got lost for the night in Rothiemurchus Forest. After twenty-one hours, they found the road to Aviemore.

So this was the nature of the challenge that Morton had set himself. It didn't help that Baddeley's misadventure had been thrilling readers of the *Thorough Guide* for more than thirty years. Morton's account of his own traverse of Lairig Ghru is correspondingly melodramatic: 'In certain lights,' he begins, 'the Larig Ghru, seen from Aviemore, looks like an early Italian painter's idea of hell. It is seven and a half miles away: a great cleft in the Cairngorms: steep, dark, cruel, with something about it that suggests to you that there, if anywhere, a man might find the last dragon.'

Sensibly, Morton and his friends approach Lairig Ghru from the north, so that they would avoid blundering for hours through Rothiemurchus Forest at the end of the day. Instead, they tackled the trees first thing in the morning. Morton's Cairngorm experience could not measure up to Baddeley's, but he manages to make it sound tough enough. After six miles, his pack 'felt like a piece of granite' and it rained incessantly. As he climbs into the cleft of the pass, with water squirting through the eyelet holes of his boots and 'every unused muscle' aching, he confesses that he'd seldom been happier in his life.

Climbing through Lairig Ghru today, it's possible to tick off the various features Morton mentioned: in clear weather, the 'few white dots which were houses', six miles away over the forest in Strathspey, are clearly visible as the suburban sprawl of Aviemore; the 'gaunt mouth' of the pass is just that, for the path curves around the mountainside just above the tree line, and is suddenly swallowed by an ominous defile. The 'avalanches of stones' can be identified as vast heaps of glacial rubble, and when he writes of there being 'no more melancholy sight than the Larig', it's easy to understand how depressing it must have been in the rain and mist. The crest of the pass, the 'crazy wilderness of red granite boulders', is all too recognisable. 'Here,' writes Morton, 'the track ends and you have to climb and slide over the rocks.' The Pools of Dee, 'three tarns of icy water', still sit like glacial puddles at the southern exit of the pass. Down by the cataract known as the Linn of Dee, a 'small white building' continues to gaze at Victoria Bridge. Unable to use the bridge because the Royal Family were at Balmoral, Morton had waded the river, then staggered up to the cottage in a state of advanced exhaustion. Inside, he had succumbed to 'the joyful warmth of a peat fire'.

Morton's description of his Cairngorm traverse rings true at every step. He suffered for his words. But he was treading a very old path. This shortcut through the mountains must have been in use since the Mezolithic Age, when hunter-gatherers would have favoured it as the fastest, least dangerous route through the heart of the Cairngorms. The pass was known to cattle thieves in the 1700s, and just sixty years before Morton undertook his 'solo' trek, Lairig Ghru had been a droving route for cattle heading from the Spey to Braemar and the south. Apparently, it was used as a cattle route until about 1873. Men from Speyside were sent up into the Lairig Ghru every spring, to clear the track of boulders which had tumbled down during winter frosts.

*

A little bit of jeopardy can go a long way in a travel book. But motoring is not the most exciting activity in the world, and Morton didn't make it easier for himself by skipping both the Outer Hebrides and the fjords of the west coast. Only once did his itinerary give him the chance to take on Pennant.

'I came to a mighty resolution...' he announces in Inverness. 'I decided to go north and see what John o'Groats is like.' Nowadays, a three-hour spin up the A9 is not going to make a bestseller (unless you're Bill Bryson). But in 1933, the road to John o'Groats was quite a drive. The distance was around 150 miles, with a tight coil of hairpins above the tiny coastal village of Berriedale. As Morton cues his adventure, one can detect echoes of Camden and Pont: long-gone geographers warning of wolves and wilderness in the land of Calgacus. Morton had a decent map, but this would be the furthest he had ever strayed from London in his motor-car. (Having cycled to John o'Groats – from Land's End, naturally – I'd sooner tackle the Braes of Berriedale by bicycle than Bullnose.) This, then, was as courageous as British motoring could get, and Morton makes the most of the geography:

> The three most northerly counties – Ross and Cromarty, Caithness, and Sutherland – are the least known in all Scotland. If you look at a railway map you will see that, with the exception of one line running along the east coast from Inverness to Wick and Thurso, these enormous counties are without the railway... So here in the extreme north of Scotland is an area of nearly 6,000 square miles which is right off the main line of communication. If any part of Scotland can in these days be called 'unknown', when one of the most efficient systems of motor coaches explores the Highlands, I think these three northern counties deserve the name.

So off he putters, into the unknown. And true to his predecessors, he writes about wolves and wild country. Morton seems to have driven from Inverness to John o'Groats in a single day. After many hours of gear-changing and wrestling with bends, he left Wick for the final 'seventeen long, awful miles' to John o'Groats, 'miles at that time of night and after such a long day, when each mile seems like ten'. He was nodding off at the wheel: 'Every shadow on the road became a grotesque flying demon and the blanched walls seemed to beckon me to destruction.' Morton was disappointed that John o'Groats hadn't 'the finality' of Land's End or Scotland's southern tip, the Mull of Galloway, so he hiked the two miles to Duncansby Head for a view he would 'never forget': the Stacks of Duncansby and the prospect north across the blue Pentland Firth and its treacherous skerries. The cliff path is still as Morton saw it, unsullied by modernity and rising by degrees to the gigantic splinters of Duncansby's photogenic sea-stacks. Dashed by tides which collide between the North Sea and the Atlantic, this is one of the most spectacular turning points on the British coast.

From Duncansby Head, Morton headed west towards Cape Wrath, and like Pennant, he found himself drawn inexorably towards a bleak confrontation with his own vulnerability. Initially, the road was stupendously exciting: 'In no part of Britain,' he gasps, 'is the cliff scenery so consistently fine.'

Then, as his car chugged around the mountainside beyond the crofts of Coldbackie, he suddenly saw the Kyle of Tongue and found himself 'in another world: the world of loch and yellow weed, of high, impregnable hill and dark gorge, of brown moor and wild forest'. Down at the waterside, there was, he relates, a little ferry which conveyed foot passengers across the mouth of the sea loch to rejoin the coast road on the far side. But motorists had to take the long route, a twelve-mile drive all the way around the shore of the loch. For Morton, this was one of the most memorable roads in Scotland. At first, the road twists and turns through a patchwork of hard-won fields, heading all the while towards the castellated peaks of Ben Loyal; 'the Coolin of Sutherland', thrills Morton, 'rising in a series of precipices to a height of 2,505 feet … a hill on which Norse gods might have sharpened their swords'. At the head of the loch, the narrow, single-track road turns tightly and follows the western shore back towards the coast. The views are wonderful: a foreground of tidal shallows set against stands of birch and the luminescent slopes of Ben Loyal. 'What a wilderness it is,' writes Morton, 'this northern coast of Sutherland! I felt, as I invaded it, more remote from civilisation than when I crossed the Sierra Nevada… Every mile plunged me more deeply into the wilds. It is the very workshop of God.'

Today, motorists career across the mouth of the Kyle on a modern concrete causeway, but the old road is still there, tempting the inquisitive into a by-passed paradise. Morton was right: a motor-car is an invasion of this place, and the only ways to absorb its beauty are to leave the village of Tongue wearing boots or riding a bike.

Beyond the Kyle of Tongue, it all went horribly wrong for Morton. The road ascends a bleak, heathery moor, then plummets to the grey waters of a desolate sea loch. 'And as it grew dark,' he recalls, 'and the long northern twilight fell over Loch Eriboll, all sense of adventure deserted me. I wanted to hear some one speak. I wanted to see a fire. I wanted to get away from the threat of the hills and their implication that I, and all men, were intruders on the surface of the earth.' In Durness, he could find nowhere to stay, and ended up in a fisherman's hotel down on the shore of the nearby Kyle. In the morning, he bolted for Inverness. His escape route, down the road that has become the A838, was dramatic.

Leaving Durness, Morton found himself hemmed in by 'another Glencoe, and with Glencoe's air of dark brooding'. To his left loomed the crags of Beinn Spionnaidh and Cranstackie; to his right, the ramps of moorland rising to Ghlas-bheinn and Farrmheall. Behind these two hills lay one hundred square miles of wild country, terminating in Cape Wrath. This was the district Timothy Pont had labelled 'Extreem Wilderness' during his sixteenth-century reconnaissance of Scotland, identifying between his little pictogram of Farrmheall and Cape Wrath, a mountain pass called 'Bhellach maddy or Woolfs way'. Thomas Pennant had been heading here in 1772, when he was defeated by the terrain at Ledbeg. Since then, a surveyor called Peter Lawson had tamed the wilderness by connecting Durness to Ledbeg. On the roadside beneath Farrmheall, Morton came across a memorial erected by Lawson as 'a mark of gratitude and respect to the inhabitants of Durness and Eddrachillis for their hospitality while projecting this road'. The memorial is still there, cast in iron, painted yellow and set behind a drinking trough of fresh water. I've paused here several times, always in mist. It's dated 1883, when horses and feet were the only means of reaching the most remote corner of Britain by land.

★

With devastating speed, cars reconfigured Britain's landscapes. In the ten years following the publication of *In Search of Scotland*, the number of cars on British roads nearly doubled, from 981,000 to just under two million. Today, the total is 31 million. And rising. The race to make wider, straighter, faster roads has left Scotland littered with single-track relics. If you know where to look, you can find them scattered across Ordnance Survey maps, where they survive as wriggles of faint, pecked lines bypassed by clean, blood-red slashes. Some of the relics are just a few hundred metres long; others run for miles. East of Skye, the road Morton drove so excitedly 'over the roof of the Highlands' has been superseded by the A87. 'If you wish to penetrate,' begins Morton, 'a country as wild and desolate as anything in the British Isles, take the road from Fort Augustus that branches right at Invergarry…' Follow this road today, and it disappears into the waters of a vast reservoir which has flooded Glen Loyne. Amazingly, eight glorious miles of this broken, pot-holed road can still be traced from the north, clawing upward to 1,400 feet above sea-level. The views are as rewarding as they were in Morton's day. Even better, the road is closed to traffic.

Bridges have had a far greater impact than the piecemeal removal of old roads. Throughout the Highlands, from Ballachulish to Tongue, Dornoch to Kessock, serpentine loops of loch-side roads have been restored to tranquillity by brief spans of concrete and steel. But the bridge over Kyle Akin is different. Of all the modern structures in Scotland, the one most likely to make Morton spin like a broken camshaft in his grave, is the Skye Bridge.

'I feel,' Morton had thought as he approached Mallaig and the ferry to Skye, 'that I am on the way to wreck a dream.' Harry had grown up with this place, and it had to deliver a lifetime's worth of expectation. 'Skye, for me,' he reminded himself, 'has always been shrouded in the splendour of a lost cause. The sound of it is like a sword going home to its scabbard … It cannot be compared with anything.' The readers of the *Daily Express* wouldn't have appreciated wrecked dreams over breakfast, and so Morton's Skye doesn't disappoint. The small ship which is to convey him up the Sound of Sleat to Kyle of Localsh is satisfactorily horrendous:

'drenched' in the smell of 'pea soup, mutton fat, batter pudding', and packed with a carnival of sheep dogs, a black horse and shaggy islanders in plus fours and unpolished boots. Typically, there is also 'a beautiful, long-legged girl in Harris tweed ... perhaps, the daughter of some clan chieftain going home to a castle on a rock'.

At Kyle of Localsh, Morton transfers to the Skye boat, a paddle steamer which will take three hours to sail west past the island of Scalpay and Raasay, to the capital of Skye, Portree. In choosing to leave the mainland at Mallaig, Morton had created a sea voyage which would consume an entire day; sufficient to provide four pages of material, and to create the illusion that Skye was a remote, Atlantic outpost.

Skye was uniquely lit in the English imagination, set-dressed in literature and art to create a wildly romantic, fantasy island. The sketchy sixteenth-century printed descriptions of the island by Donald Monro, George Buchanan and William Camden had been overtaken by the more methodical enquiries of visitors such as Martin Martin and Pennant. But with the arrival of Johnson and Boswell the year after Pennant, the process of mythologising began. It is on Skye that Pennant is dismissed by Dr Johnson ('the dog is a Whig'), while the canny Boswell pulls off the Scottish scoop of the century by tracking down and interviewing the woman who had famously aided the escape of Bonnie Prince Charlie, 'the celebrated Miss Flora MacDonald'. Skye forms the core of Johnson and Boswell's convivial excursion of 1773, providing them with a wonderful catalogue of encounters, and a wealth of information on Hebridean culture and economics. Once embedded in Sir Walter Scott's *Lord of the Isles*, Skye became an essential way-station for poets, painters and then mountaineers. Turner came here, and so did Robert Louis Stevenson, George Fennel Robson, Horatio MacCulloch, Alfred Williams and John MacWhirter. By the 1830s, the first climbers were pushing into the deeper recesses of the Cuillins.

Four centuries of media attention preceded Morton's voyage 'over the sea to Skye'. There was a huge back catalogue of books and articles describing the island. Much of this popularity was due to the fact that it was relatively accessible; ever since the opening of the

'Skye Railway' to Stromeferry in 1870 (and then to Kyle of Localsh in 1897), and the opening of the West Highland Railway to Mallaig in 1901, city-dwellers could take a train all the way to the ferry slip. Baddeley's description was typical: 'The scenery of the Island of Skye differs more than any other in Britain from that which mankind are familiar in the ordinary walks of life, and for this reason it is popularly called "savage".'

'Skye…' muses Morton as the ferry approaches the island. 'To me it is pure romance … I cannot hope that anyone who has not felt the shadow of Skye for the first time will understand it. It would not have surprised me to see a galley put out from the dark shores and to come face to face with Ulysses or Jason…'

Morton's search for Highland Scotland is concluded on Skye. Here, he provides his readers with the quintessential mountain, castle and town. He heads first to Sligachan in the centre of the island. This is the most important road junction on Skye; the point at which travellers head east and south, or north or west. Beside the junction is the Sligachan Inn, warmly recommended by Baddeley for being 'a capital house' on the grounds that it enjoyed 'less of the "la-di-da" flavour than the majority of such places in Scotland'. The present inn was built in about 1830, and it is still the island's Base Camp for the many-hued pilgrims who wash to Skye's shores. 'Here,' observes Morton, 'are salmon-fishers, deer-slayers, artists in oil and water-colour, mountaineers, and the clipped voice of that which was once the English ruling class.'

Morton arrived in the dark, so it wasn't until morning, when he stepped outside, that he saw the Cuillins close up. Initially 'mesmerised' by the Vesuvian cone of Glamaig ('He looks as though he might at any moment give a terrible explosion and belch flame'), he takes a few steps forward, clears the boundary wall of the inn, and instantly becomes aware of 'something tremendous' to his right. The sight, he recalls, 'of the "Black" Coolins hits you like a blow in the face!'

I have spent nights in the Sinai Desert, I have slept in the Valley of the Dead in Egypt, I have seen the sun rise from the summit of the

Silvrettahorn in Switzerland, I have stood all night on a ship in a great storm off the coast of Crete, I have been impressed by a number of other experiences, but I have never in all my life seen anything like the 'Black' Coolins standing, grape-blue and still, in morning sunshine.

Many have stood on that spot and gaped. Stretching skyward is a fang of riven stone, and what appears to be the beginnings of an impossibly sheer ridge. The fang is Sgurr nan Gillean, the 'peak of the young men', first climbed by a forester and a scientist, back in 1836.

'I gasped,' continues Morton, 'I lost my breath…' And so he goes on, asking his readers to imagine Wagner's *Ride of the Valkyries* 'frozen in stone and hung up like a colossal screen in the sky'. The Highland section of *In Search of Scotland* is about to reach its literal high-point.

'I sling a haversack full of rations over my shoulders,' he announces, 'make sure I have plenty of matches, take a map, a strong ash-stick and strike off over the hummocky moorland into the Valhalla of Glen Sligachan.' Morton planned to hike the four miles or so up the glen and then climb the pass which opened the way to Loch Coruisk, on the southern side of Skye. It was a well-tramped route, used for the best part of a century by mountaineers, and described in some detail by Baddeley. In his day (thirty years or so before Morton's visit), a pony and guide could be hired at Sligachan for the round trip to Loch Coruisk, for the sum of eleven shillings. (It doesn't seem entirely improbable that Morton availed himself of a similar service, but decided that a 'solo hike' might appear more adventurous for the book.)

Morton never reached Loch Coruisk. There was no need. He was searching for the perfect view, and Baddeley had told him precisely where to find it. Having tramped down the glen and climbed up to the col, he turned right and followed the ridge of Druim Hain a little way north-westwards. Here, Baddeley had promised, he would find a 'fine view' into Harta Corrie, 'the wildest recess among the Coolins'. Behind the corrie, continued Baddeley, Morton could expect to see 'the deep-scored precipices and jagged pinnacles' of the entire Black Cuillin range.

Until Morton led me to this spot, I wouldn't have believed such a view existed in Britain. I have been there twice now, and will go back. It was Baddeley who pointed out that 'the most truly beautiful views of British scenery are obtained from minor elevations, of from 500 to 1,500 feet above the valleys from which they rise'. He is right. Drum Hain stands at about 1,000 feet above sea level, about three miles from the ridge, and forms a rocky viewing gallery at a mid-point in the arc of the Black Cuillins. Facing you is a single ridge almost six miles long. Only here, on Druim Hain, is it possible to absorb the ridge in its entirety. It is a spectacle of unrelenting ferocity. 'This,' announces Morton, 'is surely the grandest and most gloomy view in the British Isles.'

From the Cuillins, Morton headed northward to Dunvegan Castle. No other castle in Britain can compete with the seat of Macleod of Macleod: 'Everything you have read about enchanted castles, captured princesses, wizards distilling the Water of Life, victims dying of thirst in dungeons, mermaids swimming up in moonlight to lure a man to his death, men beaten back to a whistle of swords and a hail of arrows, comes true as you see the turrets of Dunvegan lifted in the dusk above the trees on a spur of rock that leans over an arm of the sea in Skye.'

Morton knew that he had no chance of outclassing Johnson and Boswell, whose long stay at Dunvegan Castle a century and a half earlier is an unsurpassed insight into the life, views and domestic style of an eighteenth-century clan chieftain. By the time Morton reached Dunvegan, the castle was being opened twice a week to tourists. Morton found Dunvegan occupied by a middle-aged Englishwoman who acted as a guide and caretaker for the twenty-third clan chief, who was now over eighty and living – according to Morton – in England. In a glass case, Morton was shown the famous Fairy Flag, 'a tissue-frail bundle of fabric, brown with age, which looks like a yard of tussore silk'. According to Macleod lore, the flag could be waved to save the clan from disaster, but only three times. Waved for a trivial reason, it would invite catastrophe. The first occasion it had been waved, it helped the Macleods defeat the Macdonalds in battle. The second time, it brought a cattle plague to an end. But the third time, it had been waved by Macleod's factor, a man called Buchanan, who had decided in 1799 to test the curse. A series of terrible disasters befell the clan.

Morton's final call on Skye was the island's capital, Portree, where he sat 'in candlelight in the inn … waiting for a ghost'. That ghost was, of course, his boyhood hero, Prince Charles Edward Stuart. 'The rain beats up in sudden fury against the window. It is just such a night as that, many years ago, on which Prince Charlie said good-bye to Flora MacDonald in this room…' And off Morton goes, into the tale of brave Flora and the prince in disguise. 'Is there a more operatic farewell in history?' wonders Morton. 'Think of him standing there in the candle-light, hunted, beaten, bedraggled, in borrowed clothes, £30,000 on his head and all England after him…' In the event, it isn't Bonnie Prince Charlie who appears for Morton, but 'a vision of my own making: Flora MacDonald standing there, holding the miniature, still warm from his hands…'

Portree itself is the perfect haven for a wistful Englishman: 'A handful of houses stands among trees above the bay. Below is the wooden jetty to which the paddle steamer ties up each night with a ruby-red lamp on her masthead – our only reminder of the world. Life is quieter than in any capital I have known. The sound of Portree is not the roar of wheels, but the blowing of kine in the morning and the bleating of sheep at night. There are about nine hundred inhabitants, a few lamps which are lit on the coming of winter-time; one street of those satisfying shops full of sweets, aniseed balls, humbugs, boots, groceries, post-cards, jumpers, tobacco, and every-thing you can possibly want in this life; a tremendous square with its war memorial; a police force consisting of an inspector, a sergeant, a constable; and a jail which would certainly collapse if they found a prisoner for it!'

The next morning at dawn, Morton walks down to the quayside, and a paddle steamer called *Glencoe*. 'I hate to leave Skye,' he mourns. 'I place it with Lindisfarne, Tintagel, and Connemara among the magic regions of this world.'

The paddle steamer fills up with sheep, shepherds and dogs. A soldier in the Cameron Highlanders gets a boisterous send-off. Down the coast at Broadford they berth to take on the mail and bulging sacks of whelks labelled for London. As the steamer approaches the mainland, Morton spots the smoke of a railway train: 'We are indeed,' he concludes, 'back in the world.'

↠ *Further reading* ↞

GERALD OF WALES

Gerald of Wales, The Journey Through Wales and The Description of Wales,
    translated with an introduction by Lewis Thorpe, Penguin Classics, 2004
A History of Wales, John Davies, London, 1994
The Matter of Wales, Jan Morris, London, 1986

JOHN LELAND

John Leland's Itinerary: Travels in Tudor England, John Chandler,
    Gloucestershire, 1998
The Itinerary of John Leland in or about the years 1535–1543, Lucy Toulmin-Smith
    (Ed.), foreword by Thomas Kendrick, London, 1964 (5 vols)
Maps in Tudor England, P.D.A.Harvey, London, 1993

CELIA FIENNES

The Illustrated Journeys of Celia Fiennes, Christopher Morris (Ed.), Gloucestershire
*Through England on a Side Saddle in the Time of William and Mary, Being the
    Diary of Celia Fiennes*, introduction by The Hon. Mrs Griffiths, London, 1888
England's Thousand Best Houses, Simon Jenkins, London, 2003

DANIEL DEFOE

Daniel Defoe, A Tour Through the Whole Island of Great Britain, abridged and
    edited with introduction and notes by Pat Rogers, London, 1986
The Storm, Daniel Defoe, London, 2003
The Life of Daniel Defoe, John Richetti, Oxford, 2006

WILLIAM GILPIN

Observations on the River Wye, William Gilpin, London, 2005
The Romantics and the British Landscape, Stephen Hebron, London, 2006
This Other Eden, Seven Great Gardens and 300 Years of English History,
    Andrea Wulf and Emma Gieben-Gamal, London, 2005

THOMAS PENNANT

A Tour in Scotland and Voyage to the Hebrides, 1772, Thomas Pennant, Andrew Simmons (Ed.), introduction by Charles W.J.Withers, Edinburgh, 1998

Peoples and Settlement in North-West Ross, John R. Baldwin (Ed.), Edinburgh, 1994

The Highland Clearances, Eric Richards, Edinburgh, 2002

WILLIAM COBBETT

William Cobbett, Rural Rides, introduction and notes by Ian Dyck (Ed.), London, 2001

The Life and Adventures of William Cobbett, Richard Ingrams, London, 2006

The History of the Countryside, Oliver Rackham, London, 1995

H.V. MORTON

In Search of Scotland, H.V. Morton, London, 2000

In Scotland Again, H.V. Morton, London, 1933

In Search of H.V. Morton, Michael Bartholomew, London, 2006

GENERAL READING: THE PAST

The Discovery of Britain, The English Tourists, 1540–1840, Esther Moir, London, 1964

The Englishman's England: Taste, travel and the rise of tourism, Ian Ousby, Cambridge, 1990

Geography, Science and National Identity, Scotland since 1520, Charles W.J. Withers, Cambridge, 2001

The Little Ice Age: How Climate Made History 1300–1850, Brian Fagan, 2002

GENERAL READING: THE FUTURE

Sea Change, Britain's Coastal Catastrophe, Richard Girling, London, 2007

Six Degrees: Our Future on a Hotter Planet, Mark Lynas, London, 2007

The Final Call: In Search of the True Cost of Our Holidays, Leo Hickman, London, 2007

Intergovernmental Panel on Climate Change: www.ipcc.ch

⤙ *Acknowledgments* ⤚

Great British Journeys has been a rucksack of joy: this book, eight one-hour films for the BBC, a DVD and various related articles and speaking events. Many people have been involved in what for me has been a wonderful couple of years.

The first I would like to thank is Annabel, for more patience and understanding than I deserve, and our children for putting up with the absenteeism.

At AP Watt, Derek Johns, Rob Kraitt and Yasmine McDonald put (and kept) the show on the road, and at Weidenfeld & Nicolson, Robin Douglas-Withers, Michael Dover, David Rowley, Justin Hunt, Tony Chung, Elizabeth Allen and Mark Rusher were responsible for producing this glorious book and getting it on to the shelves. The eight films were produced by Tern TV's outstanding team in Glasgow: Will Aspinall, Ian Ballantyne, Harry Bell, Emily Brunt, Jamie Gillespie, Ishbel Hall, Dan Lyth, Julie Maclaren, Neil Mackay, Helen Margerison, Angela Smith, David Strachan, Ian Stroud, Michael Waterhouse and Paul Wilson. At the BBC, I'd like to thank Neil McDonald, Richard Klein and Roly Keating. And finally, I would like to thank the crew who – along with Michael, Will, Ishbel, Emily and Helen – shared months of storms, snows and blistering heat to turn these stories into films. They are: Steve Robinson, Peter Eason, Mike Robinson, Barney Carmichael, Edmund Wright, Mark Littlewood and Lyndon Bruce.

⇢ Index ⇠